RETURN

RETURN

A Journey Back to
LIVING WILD

LYNX VILDEN

HarperOne
An Imprint of HarperCollinsPublishers

Arrow artwork © Shutterstock

A version of the story "Color of Being" was published in *Women in Nature: An Anthology* in 2014.

The names and identifying characteristics of some of the individuals featured throughout this book have been changed to protect their privacy.

HarperCollins books may be purchased for educational, business, or sales promotional use. For information, please email the Special Markets Department at SPsales@harpercollins.com.

FIRST EDITION

Designed by Bonni Leon-Berman

Library of Congress Cataloging-in-Publication Data has been applied for.

ISBN 978-0-06-321510-8

23 24 25 26 27 LBC 5 4 3 2 1

To my mother, who gave me life to reason,

to my daughter, who gives me reason to live,

and to the wild within us all—

don't leave us, we need you

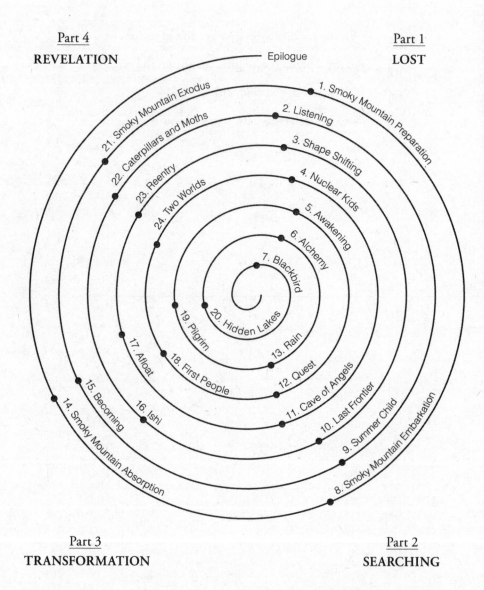

Part 4
REVELATION

Part 1
LOST

Part 3
TRANSFORMATION

Part 2
SEARCHING

Epilogue

21. Smoky Mountain Exodus
22. Caterpillars and Moths
23. Reentry
24. Two Worlds

1. Smoky Mountain Preparation
2. Listening
3. Shape Shifting
4. Nuclear Kids
5. Awakening
6. Alchemy
7. Blackbird

19. Pilgrim
20. Hidden Lakes
13. Rain
17. Afloat
18. First People
12. Quest
15. Becoming
16. Ishi
11. Cave of Angels
14. Smoky Mountain Absorption
10. Last Frontier
9. Summer Child
8. Smoky Mountain Embarkation

CONTENTS

Preface ix

PREFACE

Circle Up

The oak logs glow orange in the fire, casting shadows against the faces circling it. The clan members sit on rough-hewn benches and skins. They are silent after their meal. A sheep carcass hangs from a pole leaned against the rock wall just outside the circle. No predator will dare come close since the people sleep side by side under the limestone overhang that shields them from all but the fiercest storms. The trees beyond the edge of the sheltering rock are silhouetted against the night sky. Between the leaves of hazel, beech, and oak one can glimpse emerging stars. An owl calls and something scuttles in the dry leaves beyond the circle of firelight.

Someone quietly starts to hum a tone that throbs and pulses as the volume rises and falls and ebbs away only to rise again. Another takes up a stick beside the fire and taps out an even rhythm enhancing the singer's note. Several more add their voices to become a choir, layering upon one another, a harmony developing, a melody, no words but it feels like a conversation. Still more take up sticks or rocks and bring a new cadence to the song. The percussionist rises and punctuates with staccato intermittent raps against the wall behind them, and the figure's shadow starts to leap and dance as someone else adds wood to the fire that bursts into a golden blaze. A few remain silent, eyes fixed on the flames, a head leans against another's knee, but as the spontaneous music gains momentum, all are seized by the energy; they rise and move in a circle, dipping, spinning, wood clacking, stone tapping, voices clambering and descending with reckless nonconformity. They become transfixed in a kind of trance and time seems to take on a new dimension. The song eventually finds its natural end without any signals; there is no conductor, just a group of beings tied together by forest, fire, and camaraderie. They melt back down into the circle and still no one speaks.

I look at my clan; we have only known each other for a week and it seems incongruous that we could feel so connected in such a short time. They came to me to participate in a class, to learn Stone Age skills and get away from the modern world in which we all live to varying degrees. There is a boy from the village; his grandfather owns the land and this kid is having his first experience away from his family. There is a doctor, a writer, a girl just out of high school, some young travelers not fixed to place who are roaming and experiencing whatever calls them, a plumber, a couple of computer programmers, and a military man. We are in France but we speak five or six languages between us; some struggle to express themselves in English but our common language is as old as humanity itself.

There is a story and a journey I would like to share. It's not a straight path, it's more of a circle or a spiral so vast that at times its arc may appear to have a beginning and an end but do not be fooled by this illusion.

This journey is my return, a return to the ways of our ancestors, a return to a simpler life, perhaps to what came before our world was so heavily dictated by our modern conveniences, a return to listening deeply to Earth, and what she has to say. For me, this journey is pivotal because we humans face an immediate peril, the degradation of the environment, which is foundational to our existence, and without which we have no mother to return to.

The story is about us . . . and Earth.

The earth gives us the opportunity to physically exist—without her we cannot live. We are of Earth, we shape her, she shapes us. We, all too often, seem to have forgotten this.

I want us to remember where we come from. It has never been more important.

Even though I was born in London, one of the largest cities in the world, I have spent most of my adult life living outside, striving for a connection to nature that few of us modern humans achieve. While I am subject to the whims of modernity and will sometimes pass some days or nights in the confines of four walls, hurtle through the sky in an airplane, or trundle across continents in trains, cars, and buses, I have built a life based on entirely different principles. Sometimes described as a primitivist, the last modern hunter-gatherer, or a woman outside of time, I have spent the last twenty years teaching groups of students how to live with the land in a respectful and conscientious manner, and I have also spent this time reducing my own impact and material needs. Even though I have yet to spend more than a month or two each year directly sustained by nature, this curiosity has driven me and given me a life purpose that is all part of my own return.

Return is an invitation to this remembering, an exploration of what a closer relationship with the natural world can offer us and a timely reminder—and even a warning—of what we stand to lose through our forgetting. I'd like to invite you on my journey, from my childhood in London and rural Sweden, to my teenage years in Amsterdam, from my Stone Age experiences with my students in the mountainous western United States, to my personal pilgrimages in the Himalaya, the Middle East, and Namibia.

More than thirty years ago, I crawled out of a sweat lodge escaping the moist oppressive heat and sank fully onto the damp ground. I'd grown up in London, spent my teens in punk bands and on its city streets, far from this untouched natural world. Covered in mud, my face streaked with sweat and tears, I whispered to Earth my promise. "I will love you and cherish you, I will learn how to live and share what you teach me." This was the moment I discovered my life purpose, setting me on the path to who I am today.

I was twenty-four years old, more than half my lifetime ago, and I'm still learning and still teaching. After that morning outside the sweat lodge, I dedicated myself to soaking up as much knowledge as possible about ancestral living skills. Soon I was teaching at various gatherings around the US and landed myself a summer guiding job at an outdoor survival school in the canyonlands of Utah. I realized that the hard-core survival approach was not what I wanted to do. Instead I was interested in helping people discover how to thrive in the wilderness, not just "survive" it and then head back to civilization for a hot shower and a cheeseburger. At the time, I didn't know if this was possible. I wondered if we modern people would even be able to stay alive on an all-wild food diet. I wasn't sure if we had lost the ability to live as hunter-gatherers but I knew one thing: I was willing to die if I found out that my body and mind were no longer functional under such circumstances.

A decade ago, I founded Living Wild, a small school in north-central Washington State. I was intrigued by the idea of learning to live as a hunter-gatherer, bringing people into a closer connection with nature in a way that couldn't be done in just a day or two. As a modern human, born into a culture of resource exploitation, I wanted to see if it was still possible to live sustained by nature in its purest form. My goal was to offer high-quality instruction in Stone Age living skills to give people the tools and confidence to live in the wilderness simply yet comfortably.

We have found over the years that the Stone Age skills that we teach are just a little piece of the puzzle that represents what I believe is our true humanity. A renewed focus on community building, gratitude and grief tending, and connecting with our ancestors all play a part in addition to the hands-on skills required to live in closer harmony with the land. I believe that on some fundamental level, we recognize that we've lost an essential intimacy with the natural world and with Earth and she is calling us back. There is a hunger to reconnect with—to return to—this profound part of ourselves.

Around the fire, we, who were mostly strangers to one another just a week ago, arrange ourselves in order of age. Usually I find myself completing the circle as the oldest member of the group but tonight the wise and serene herbalist is my senior by more than ten years.

I ask them to quietly consider what is most important to them at this phase of their lives. Some murmured translations occur and we sit again in silence as we contemplate who it is we are just now.

I look to the young boy and pass him the talking stick that everyone now knows is the method for designating the speaker. He speaks softly in French and says his family is important to him. The seventeen-year-old girl takes the stick in her hands and shares her need to distance herself from her parents' expectations, unsure whether her desire to strike out into the world and not continue her studies is just rebellion or if it is indeed her deepest desire. The next couple of young adults express similar life concerns about the state of the world and how to navigate within a society that attempts to press people into a mold as functional citizens. Some hold college degrees but they have no life experience and want to keep absorbing knowledge before having to make seemingly irrevocable life decisions. A young mother who has come alone, leaving her toddler with his father after a recent separation, is in an agony of blended guilt and relief. The freckled fellow who takes the stick next has just been discharged from his term in the army. As we continue through the group—the osteopathic doctor who came with the herbalist, the woman who left her husband to be with a woman much younger than herself, the witty water engineer—I start to realize an exchange is occurring. The younger people in the circle remind the older members of our own dreams, joys, and challenges. Do we still hold the ideals of our youth or have we dulled and become cynical? We elders in turn now offer them the advice of our life experiences, encouraging them to follow their hearts, have patience, and be honest with themselves. The woman to my right is close to my age. I don't remember what her life's journey had been but she has grown children and she says so very poignantly that in spite of all our successes, mistakes, fears, and concerns, slowly peace comes. Whatever it was that I said myself afterward I do not recall.

Slowly, peace comes.

In *Return*, I want to take readers inside the peace, stillness, and silence we've left behind. We will reenter a world where we live with the seasons and from the land. The light we see is from the stars overhead, the rise and fall of the sun and moon or the flickering of the fire, we are heated by that sun and that fire, we drink the water that pours from the earth, or the sky. I will share my own experiences of connection with Earth through the skills I have acquired and taught, using the alchemy of earth, water, air, and fire to create tools and make fire. Our stone tools cut and shape the wood that becomes the bow with which we hunt for nourishment. Earth sustains us, circling the sun as we cycle through life, death, and rebirth. Without her we are lost. It's a truth we all fundamentally know but one that recedes in the rush and madness of modern life, the prioritization of convenience and money over time, community, and connection. I hope this book will help us remember.

When I am an old woman I shall live in a cave
A thousand wrinkles will cover my face
And the children will call me Shuwa Awah
And the children will sing Shuwa Awah

When I am an old woman I shall play the violin,
Gather Juniper berries and make my own gin
And my people will call me Shuwa Awah
And my people will sing Shuwa Awah

When I am an old woman I shall ride a gray mare
With wings on her hooves we shall fly everywhere
And the wind it will whisper Shuwa Awah
And the wind it will sing Shuwa Awah

When I am an old woman I'll be friends with the trees
Climb high in their branches of needles and leaves
And together so softly Shuwa Awah
They will tell me their tales of their power

When I am an old woman I shall rise with the dawn
In the heat of the summer I'll grow colored corn
In the heart of the winter Shuwa Awah
On the long shadowed snow Shuwa Awah

When I am an old woman I shall heal with my hands
And stories will travel to faraway lands
And the stars they will sparkle Shuwa Awah
And the stars they will sing Shuwa Awah

When I am an old woman I shall run with the deer
I'll talk with the eagle, the fish and the bear
And the animals call me Shuwa Awah
And the grasshoppers sing Shuwa Awah

When I am an old woman I shall speak many tongues
I'll sing from the hills at the top of my lungs
And the mountains will call me Shuwa Awah
And the valleys will croon Shuwa Awah

When I am an old woman my hair shall turn white
At a hundred and thirteen my steps remain light
And the next world will beckon me, Shuwa Awah
And I'll dance from this Earth in my power.

PART 1

Lost

1

SMOKY MOUNTAIN PREPARATION

It's the beginning of April, springtime in the Cascade Mountains. Fourteen students now all gather on my land on the Twisp River for the official introduction to the Stone Age Project, this year's five-month Stone Age immersion program. The excited, expectant faces beam from under woolly hats and scarves in the cool morning air, steaming mugs of hot herbal teas clasped gratefully in chilly fingers. The snow is still visible on the shady north-facing slopes and here by the river there are still a few receding patches. The students will be living here off the grid on my land learning ancestral skills and, it is my sincere desire, new ways to connect with nature. Gradually reducing our dependency on modern tools, plastic tents will be replaced by natural structures; trips to town, twelve miles away, become less frequent. Even the steel knives we use will be replaced by those of bone and stone as time goes by. Each person comes to the Stone Age immersion program for different reasons and with different aims. Some are here to challenge themselves in this hybrid environment that still maintains connection to contemporary living, while others are here for something more: in late August, those of us who are ready and able will embark on a four-week Stone Age excursion into the wilderness, entirely independent from modern society.

I have been running these extended programs for many years and have taught in various locations around the world: the Arctic tundra in northern Sweden, the forested mountains in eastern Italy, the limestone caves of southern France, the painted deserts of the American Southwest and the Namibian Kalahari Desert to name but a few. But it is here in the Pacific Northwest at the edge of a vast and largely untrammeled wilderness I have chosen to call my home. As the years go by, the land has taken me and shown me many of its hidden secrets and its familiarity makes it perfect for the courses that have been adapted to this stunning and wild terrain.

———————

The central fire is crackling and we first pass the talking stick and express our gratitude briefly in whatever way we feel moved: safe passage to arrive in this place after a long trip, thankfulness for the warmth of the fire, the breakfast eggs, the sunshine on a dewy spider's web, or the chasing, chattering squirrels.

There are logistics to address for a group this size coming to camp together for months on a small piece of land where the running water is the river and irrigation ditch. There is no cell service and the power system at my cabin is off-grid, a modest solar setup by anyone's standards. The light is returning rapidly, though, as the sun races north again toward summer so I have little need for electricity.

The new clan members come from near and far, a mixture of Americans, Canadians, and Europeans. One Canadian family has come with a seven-year-old boy, but the rest of the group range in age from twenty to early thirties.

Some of them I have met before when they attended a shorter class in prior years. Gareth and Polly are an American couple in their late twenties who have been living here all winter in their Mongolian yurt.

I met them at a gathering last summer and we have formed a deep friendship. Gareth is a bearded, muscular man, raised in New Jersey. He received a recent inheritance enabling him and Polly to explore options for leaving the city and treading a path that feels more natural and connected. Polly, a feisty, brilliant being with a clever tongue, is albino. With her white hair and unpigmented skin she must be extremely careful to avoid sun exposure. She is a word shaper and she and Gareth write songs that we all sing together. Rapturous, sensual, evocative music.

Marcus and Ben have also been here through the winter. Marcus put up a canvas wall tent on the land. He's one of the oldest of this group at thirty-three. A Berkeley graduate in engineering, intelligent, strong, good-looking, this man was living the American dream, with a high-paid job in California and everything going for him, but he felt that something huge, something important was missing. He was where he had always heard he should be and had become exactly what he had been groomed to be: a success. Now he was supposed to marry a beautiful woman, buy a big house, sire a couple of well-mannered kids, and play golf on the weekends while working all week for the next thirty years. Of course, they could take their expensive vacations every year then go home and continue the program while prepping their own children for exactly the same fate. Why didn't he feel this was enough? What was missing? He had done an online nature awareness course and had a premonition that in the stillness of nature he would find something precious, so he put his shiny future on hold and left for the forests and the mountains and the bright night sky to contemplate the other options that existed. After the winter in our little community, he decided to continue this path and participate in the whole summer immersion and the monthlong Stone Age excursion that follows. It's interesting to note that the students who come to learn these skills are largely from the same socioeconomic group:

urban middle-class young adults who have the time and resources to take four to six months off from their work or studies. I have often speculated whether this could be different, if these programs could appeal to a wider audience? It does happen that older people, countryside dwellers, ethnic minorities, and disillusioned corporate executives occasionally join us but they are the exceptions. It requires privilege to participate in these lengthy immersion courses. It's ironic that those wealthy enough to achieve a life full of comforts realize, with its attainment, that their lives still feel hollow and empty. Thus they continue their search for fulfillment outside of the conventional norms that value money and materialism as the gauge of success.

Ben, a California pot farmer, is one of the sweetest, gentlest souls I have ever met and his calmness makes him such an attribute when social disharmony erupts. He always seems to say exactly the right thing to help people recognize that there is a way through and none of us need to continue our suffering if we don't choose to. I call him this year's bodhisattva. I feel lucky to be blessed with such beings in nearly every group. They are the calm, equanimous ones that exude loving-kindness like a balm upon all within their presence.

Rick and James have taken this immersion course before and are here as my assistants. Rick, from Alabama, was raised on a farm. After leaving high school he sought an alternative existence by joining a death metal band. With his long dreadlocks, impish smile, and tattoos that cover much of his body, it's hard to imagine his conservative Baptist upbringing. He started practicing traditional skills several years ago and has the most experience of anyone in the group. He has already tanned several buffalo hides and made his own buckskin clothes and the others look to him in admiration. I'm happy to have him come and participate as an assistant in exchange for the class tuition.

This is James's third year here as an assistant. Twenty-six, with long black hair in two neat braids that drape his dark tanned shoulders, he looks like he just stepped off the movie set from *Last of the Mohicans*. He doesn't actually know his heritage because his mother was adopted but wherever he goes, Native Americans ask him his tribe and he has to admit that he only knows the Irish side.

That leaves eight newcomers. I'm confident that we will form a cohesive group, but it is never without effort. As an orientation, I talk through the general group chores that consist largely of gathering camp firewood, of which there is plenty in this forest dominated by ponderosa pine and Douglas fir, hauling water by bucket, and caring for our shared spaces.

I divide the group according to their preferences and skills.

Horse Clan, which includes myself, Gareth, and Polly, are responsible for the care and well-being of my three horses, Christy, Chaco, and Karma, who will become an integral part of our journey. We scoop up the manure in the paddocks in the morning and add it to the compost pile, ride them down to the pasture each day, and ride them back again in the evening when we give them their ration of hay.

Wolf Clan, led by James, maintains the fire, starting it in the mornings if necessary and banking it at night. They keep the woodpile stocked, chopped, and orderly.

Rick is the leader of the Otter Clan. In charge of providing the camp with a steady supply of water, they bring drinking water from the well and utility water from the irrigation flow. They keep the outhouse, hand washing, and dishwashing stations clean and organized.

Raven Clan are the timekeepers, led by Marie, a competent woman who runs her own wilderness programs in Germany. Ravens will clang the metal gong to alert the others when it is time to rise, eat, or start class. They keep the kitchen—a simple affair, a pole structure with a roof and open sides—clean and functional.

Every evening a cooking team of two are responsible for making a meal for the rest of the group. It's an efficient system and with fifteen adults means that no one needs to cook dinner more than once a week. There are plenty of roadkill deer in this valley and the neighbors will often call us to let us know where one is. The nightly chefs plan the menu around a meat dish, purchase and/or harvest the ingredients, cook the meal, serve it, and then wash the dish pans afterward. Everyone is responsible for washing their own bowl and utensils.

The meals are generally delicious, gourmet even, nourishing and healthy. Jenny, a British cook, has also been delegated to the Raven Clan. She lends her expertise and artistic expression to all her culinary pursuits. Our menu works well for nearly every diet preference except for vegans. Most of the initial vegetarians, including Jenny, are happily chewing down the good, clean meat after a few weeks and we can stop separating the meat from the vegetables. At the onset of camp, we sort through what everyone can and cannot eat. By the time we have excluded all the common allergens, we are left with animal protein, nuts and seeds, fruits, fats, and most plants and vegetables except the nightshade family. Together we relinquish the habit-forming substances of caffeine, sugar, and refined carbohydrates at the beginning of every immersion. It's wonderful to sit down together around the fire in the evenings and share these tasty meals that are not so very different from what we will be eating as we transition into the hunter-gatherers we will become on our Stone Age excursion.

I have found over the years that this diet adaptation is far easier to do as a group than attempting it alone. It can be daunting to give up a food such as chocolate, but we didn't have chocolate in the Stone Age. We remove our addictions and comfort foods during our immersion training sessions so as to already be free of our cravings in the wild.

We also need to set personal boundaries. I love to be in community but, like most people, I need some alone time for balance. Although I have a small cabin, I generally sleep outside at night, preferring the connectedness I feel under the sky. When I sleep enclosed by insulating roof and walls, I lose awareness of the night. I want to know if the wind picks up or a sprinkle of rain has brought out the scent of wet pine needles. I want to hear the footsteps of the animals, to discern if it is mouse, or deer, or bear. I want to see the changing colors as night shifts to dawn and cracks to day. To lie naked on a deerskin on a warm summer night is one of the most animalistic feelings one can experience. It sharpens the senses even passively while sleeping, making me a participant of the wild night. Mornings are when I feel most active and creative, and I have learned over the years how important it is to instill an understanding among my students of my personal time and space. I couldn't teach like this otherwise, and I couldn't be available for all the hours in the day that I am with them. So I tell them to not ask me questions while I am eating, don't disturb me when I am in my personal space unless they are invited or there is an emergency, keep class-related questions to designated class times and consider whether questions are relevant and necessary.

Learning to live together as a clan works best when boundaries are clear and consistent. When peace is disrupted, sometimes a good long talking session is necessary to clear the air but I have found that it doesn't work for everyone, that making music and singing together is often the analgesic we need to come together again. This is a particularly musical group.

We work with a week-on, week-off schedule. The "off" weeks are for finishing up projects and practicing new skills, reflecting on the teachings and generally giving time for absorption and integration. When setting up these monthslong immersive programs I like to build on the skills gradually, adding context so they make sense in a broader picture.

Although I've been teaching for many years, I am still and have always been a curious student. I share the skills I've learned from various native groups around the world, the Sami reindeer herders of Arctic Sweden, to whom I owe my greatest respect, being some of the first Indigenous peoples that I became acquainted with and, additionally, the peoples who inhabit the region of the earth in which I feel most at home. There have been many humans who have taught me throughout my life, mentors within the wilderness skills movement to which I still belong plus an array of Indigenous peoples across the earth: San hunter-gatherers of Namibia, Africa, Native American tribal members all over North America, even Buddhist monks on my wandering pilgrimage across the Himalaya, but Earth herself has been my greatest teacher.

During my classes, immersions, and Stone Age excursions I provide space for my students' experiences in nature that gradually build, gaining depth, breadth, and context so that when the clan walks out into the wilderness at the end of summer the change has been constant but gentle, and the shift into an entirely different mindset appears almost seamless.

The first class starts with our origins, our natural beginnings as a species as we evolved into upright beings. We explore the qualities of stone, wood, plant fiber, skin, and bone, and then in a magnificent alchemical mixing and rearranging of these elemental substances we modify and create the tools of our prehistoric ancestors' material culture.

2

LISTENING

We learn to listen to the stones.

Everything on this living planet has something to tell us if we find a way to listen. The stones are no exception and we head down to the rivers' rock-strewn banks where we sit in a circle again, always a circle that includes everyone and has no hierarchy. I ask the clan members to pick up a couple of stones beside them and we start to tap them together. Our musical group is instantly jamming. I often improvise a spontaneous session like this with whatever is at hand and call it "rock, stick, and bone band." We develop a complicated rhythm and the rocks speak to us in their tones; their shapes, sizes, colors, and textures; and the ways that they might break or endure. So many possibilities are expressed by this simple interaction with them. Just like us they have their own unique qualities and that is why it interests me less to name the things on the planet. Knowing the name of something can sometimes mislead one into thinking one knows the named. "Knowing" something comes with understanding its qualities, interacting or communicating with it in obvious or subtle ways. When I was a child, I had a special interest in rocks and semiprecious stones. Dazzled not only by the shining, polished amethyst and tiger's eye, I was intrigued by the facets of quartz that sparkled and shone within the common granite of Scandinavia. Because minerals feel less personal, except to geologists or child rock collectors, than, say, animals or plants, people are often amazed when they start to see the various qualities of stone. What does the stone sound like that will make a sharp knifelike edge? Which stones contain the hidden mystery of a spark that can be coaxed to a flame? Which stone can be shaped into a container or pounded into powder for paint? Who can grind hard seeds or be shaped into a tree-chopping axe? As knowledge grows, the relationships grow, and "things" become "beings."

Stone is the beginning of all possibilities, and this is no different today than it was a hundred thousand years ago, although our modern methods for extraction have become so sophisticated and aggressive that the connection seems to have become lost along the way.

Prehistoric lithic culture leaves us clues in the artifacts we find and analyze, but not a full picture because wood and bone rots away and disintegrates, as do the skin and fiber technologies that made up the rest of our material culture. Our remarkable opposing thumbs, nimble hands, and upright posture enable all sorts of dexterous maneuvers not available to other animals, but the capabilities of our teeth and claws are marginal. And that's where tools come in. There is a sense of liberation in realizing that the tools one needs are everywhere, often within a hand's reach. One can simply grasp a stick or a stone to address a task with these rudimentary tools, be it digging up roots, pounding a bone to access the precious inner marrow, or striking a flake to cut a piece of meat or skin.

We bind our world together.

Today this is done with an assortment of nuts and bolts, nails, screws, and chemical adhesives but when we return to our elemental resources we make cord.

The dry, bronze-colored dogbane stalks were harvested early last winter after their leaves had fallen. Today, scraping away the thin flaky outer layer with a bone knife exposes the fluffy, precious fibers. Marcus sits with meticulous concentration as he removes the long strands of fibers from the woody core, twisting then reverse wrapping them to produce a fine continuous cord. At first his fingers seem thick and clumsy as they grapple with this new skill but they soon find their dexterity. During the focused silence we produce strong cords for fishing line, nets, and countless other applications.

We tie and twist and wrap and spin and weave and knit all manner of fibers together, sourced from both plants and animals. The fibers standing alone are weak, but together, like ourselves, become strong.

Then there is fire.

It is fire that makes us human. We are the only animals that consciously and deliberately have this capacity to make fire. There are other toolmakers and users in the animal world for sure, but we are the only fire makers and that sets us apart.

Very often, when I share my knowledge of fire making, I am transported back to the first friction fire I achieved myself as a cocky youth of twenty-four at my first wilderness skills course and how I was duly humbled as I struggled for weeks afterward to create the second one on my own. After spending a week at the course in New Jersey, I returned to Sweden during a cold and damp December only to realize that the forest did not even contain the same type of wood I had been given in class for my bow drill kit. So I made kits from all the trees available to me: birch, beech, aspen, alder, rowan, oak. Failure at the end of each smoky drill. Exhaustion my companion, I traipsed back to my warm room and slung the latest fire kit into a box by the woodstove. I gave up. Then one night I dreamed of fire making and stirred myself to give it another try. Armed with my now dried birch drill and hearth I headed back to the woods. After the numerous failures, I didn't really expect anything else but went through the motions and wonder of wonders, there glowed my second bow drill coal, nestled in the carved notch. This was the fire I earned, this was the fire that taught me.

A thousand fires later, with my own novices around me, we blend the elements of stone and wood, cut and shape dry dead sticks with stone blades and coarse flat abrasive rock surfaces to create a wooden drill and hearth, an arm-length bow, and a palm-size socket with which to keep the drill from burning the hand that holds it. A strip of deer hide is cut with the sharpest of blades and tied to the bow enabling the fire conjurer to spin the drill upon the hearth. With this mechanical advantage—the speed and friction exerted on the drill, coupled with determination, dexterity, and intent—the fire maker spins and twirls the drill with such force and precision that gradually a whorl of smoke emerges from these conjoined surfaces. It is erotic, there is no doubt. Maintaining speed and pressure, the phallic drill erupts in its fertilizing climax, the ember. Smoking and glowing within the char dust nestled within the notched womb of the feminine hearth, the baby fire is then birthed and delivered into its grassy nest where the fibers feed and the long, slow breath of the fire parent nurtures the smoky baby into lively flame.

Polly leaps to her feet with a jubilant howl as her very first unaided bow drill fire bursts to life. She drops the blazing nest to the ground and does a little dance around it as the rest of us clap and cheer.

Welcome, fire, and thank you.

With this new tool of fire we feel suddenly akin to the gods. Fire as an ally is a marvelous shaper of wood. Bowls appear in dry sections of log that are burned and charred and scraped and burned again. With careful heating, rocks can boil the water in our wooden vessels and cook the roots dug with our digging sticks. The interaction of earth, air, fire, and water is made manifest as our minds envision and our hands enable.

The process of creating fire by ancient humans undoubtedly differed from region to region. I imagine the early hominids in Africa making fire by friction in a similar way that the contemporary San peoples have done until very recently, an unbroken methodology for hundreds of thousands of years, unnecessary to change by virtue of its simplicity and effectiveness. Theirs is the hand drill method whereby a stick is literally spun upon another stick to create the ember.

As people migrated northward into new cooler, wetter climatic zones, the plants also changed, and the mechanical advantage of the bow drill method was probably devised. The technology producing percussion fire, by which a flake of flint strikes a cobble of pyrite to create a spark, would have evolved with the availability of these resources. As we move, we adapt to our new environments, dropping and picking up new techniques along the way.

I have sat beneath the great baobab tree with a group of European students who came to the Kalahari to learn the vanishing ways of a displaced hunter-gatherer people who call themselves Ju/'hoansi. There we took turns, big pale Europeans and small dark Africans, stick upon stick, palms rapidly moving together twirling the soft wood shoots, which we'd been shown how to harvest and dry and straighten, carefully over a flame. This is always a community endeavor in this land. I have never seen a Ju/'hoansi make fire alone. They encourage each other with a repeated, "Ko, ko, ko, ko." A thin curl of smoke emits from the charred dust that our efforts have invoked. Then the coal is gently laid upon a nest of fine pale grass. Our breath mingles with the breath of the wind, coaxing the red glow until it bursts into yellow flame and a new fire is born. How many times might this ancient tree have witnessed such an event in its thousand or more years of patient being? How many times have black and white hands twirled the fire sticks together? Maybe not so many.

The great baobab tree is spread in a multitude of chaotic limbs, many thicker than the broad backs of elephants, rising up, curving horizontally then sweeping back down and into the earth as if searching for the reason that it lifted its succulent sweet shoots originally out into this arid and thorny desert. Other great arms lift and branch and reach beyond the height of the ivory tusks that have shredded and torn the knobby bark, carving pachydermal messages that healed over time into scarred stories of long ago. I nibble on the tender new leaves that sprout in little groups of fives, and high above, the swollen flower buds, green, the size of golf balls, pendulously swing in the light afternoon breeze.

Years into my Stone Age programs, I find myself on a huge and distant continent. I am in Africa. Namibia. I was invited to this desert land to participate in a cultural exchange as both teacher and student. Although this is my third time here in the village, it is an environment that is still new to me in almost every way. My desire to explore and learn from this place and these people has overcome my reticence to fly across the globe. Each visit reminds me of how little I will ever know of this land, the people, and their language, and yet how much I stand to learn.

Our group of twelve visitors are mostly from Europe, with a couple of white South Africans. The program's leaders have been working dedicatedly with the Ju/'hoansi, members of the San people, named Bushmen by their European colonizers. The San are an Indigenous tribe who have been displaced from their traditional hunting grounds and their hunter-gatherer way of life. The organizers are helping the San to find a business model in the form of a "Living Museum" to enable them to make some income showing Westerners like us their traditional skills while allowing them to continue practicing their lifestyle at least in theory. They are now sedentary, tied to the boreholes that the government drilled after the northern Namibia Khaudum

National Park was founded in the late 1980s, forcing them to move to the conservancy where they now live. Merely demonstrating their old ways is far from perfect but better than the drifting that has been the fate of so many of these beautiful, gentle people in their search for new ways to sustain themselves.

The old village healer's legs are so thin. They are black but also shaded with the colors of the land, shaded with the years and choices that he has made. The Kalahari sands and winds and sun are etched in him deeper than his skin. Perhaps even his bones are brittle and sun bleached beneath the taut, dusky skin? His thirst has been quenched by the water root and the blood of the kudu who accepts at last the coming spear with a steady, knowing gaze. This man is the rugged land incarnate set loose to express its being in human form. He is as far from my own expression of being, of snow-covered northern forests, as it is possible to be.

He wears a baseball cap that is worn through everywhere except the seams, and his short gray hair, patterned on his scalp, fills in the missing segments of cloth. Tattered trousers are covered at his waist by the shell-adorned traditional loincloth made from steenbok skin. He sits quietly on the periphery smoking, rarely speaking. What are his thoughts behind those seeing eyes? It is such a mystery to me in my own sphere of comprehension.

On the smooth gray bark of the baobab, stories have also been etched by human hands with names and dates carved more than a hundred years ago. White Boer hands marking the progress of the "Dorsland Trek." Other stories of grief mark the trunks, peppered by machine-gun shots and the memory of human destruction wrought here. The colonial history and exploitation of this land, as well as the war of independence between Namibia and South Africa in 1990, has scarred the earth and the people, but the baobab has outlived all of this and calmly keeps giving her shade, her fruits, her leaves and bark to both those who respect and those who pillage.

As dusk deepens and the heat subsides, we gather. Casting ourselves upon the ground at the great tree's feet like so many strewn leaves, we sit around a fire, the firelight playing on our faces. We watch the old man and his wife, brown and wrinkled, settle themselves slowly and deliberately before us. They have been invited from a nearby village to come and speak with us Westerners; they will tell us stories at the base of the baobab, tell us about the healing dances that have served their people since the beginning of time. He is the last giraffe dancer of this region—his dance will die with him. Earth will bury his secrets and scatter his bones. Beside him our translator stands ready. The old dancer begins, his voice rich and melodious, punctuated by his clicking tongue. How many stories have enthralled their listeners here beneath this canopy? How many times have these ancient people gathered in the protection of flickering firelight and shared soft staccato language under a spring moon? We look to our translator, who says nothing. The story goes on and on; the Bushmen hunters lain out beside us laugh and whisper as the animated voice and gesticulating hands of the old man rise and fall, but still our translator stays silent. I fall under this spoken spell and am lulled by its cadence and rhythm even though I cannot begin to comprehend the words.

We share a fire watch through the night; the African bush is still a place where predators roam and roar. I wake early to take my turn, and with the first rays of sunlight glittering into a fresh morning I see the baobab blossoms have burst exquisitely into flower.

The western US is now in the midst of the consequences of over a hundred years of fire-suppression policy. As the climate warms, accumulated forest litter ignites and blazes, ferociously destroying all that stands in its path. In the intensity of fire unleashed, even the rocks change color and fracture. The ancients and the world's Indigenous tribes today still know and understand the duty of fire in the environment to renew growth through the practice of controlled burns, cleansing the forest of sickness and imbalance. May the very element that makes us human not be our own undoing. Let us listen to the wisdom of those who still know and understand.

What is it that compels me to embrace this Indigenous wisdom? I was always intrigued by the tools and crafts of native cultures, poring over the artifacts in museums as a child and youth. The beauty of form with the simplicity, yet ingenuity of function made me yearn for a tribe that still recognized and valued such things. My respect for traditional material culture became entwined with my need for spiritual guidance that was not met by my urban British upbringing, which was the antithesis to the sense of connectedness that I sought. The way we behaved and treated Earth and one another was incongruent with how I felt on a deeper level. As a child growing up beside the river Thames in London, my parents warned me and my siblings not to touch the water with our bare skin, slathered us in sun cream to protect us from the sun's harmful rays, scared us into silence so we would not converse with humans we didn't know. We were not taught to develop our intuition to keep us safe. The cultural stories we were offered for human conduct were steeped in fear, mistrust, and Victorian morality. I wanted to run a thousand miles away. When I came of age to travel independently, I did just that. It was no strike of chance that led me to the periphery: the wild places and people who still held the secrets, myths, and ancient knowledge.

3

SHAPE SHIFTING

After the completion of the first week of class, the clans start to settle into their daily routines. A trip to town is organized to replenish food supplies and connect with the outside world. Exploratory walks are taken along the river and into the surrounding forest as the newcomers get a feeling for their environment. The skills of the first class are practiced and refined. Matches and lighters are hidden away when the firepit becomes a friction-fire-only zone so there is often the sound of a squeaky bow drill in the mornings. All the clan members are eager to do their share, care for one another, and develop new friendships. It is like watching a love affair unfold. I call it the honeymoon phase.

Shelter building is the subject of the second class. The vision for this camp is to have four lodges on the land representing the four elements. We built the Fire Lodge a year ago with another group. We come together there to hold ceremonies, sing, and make music as well as circle for conflict resolution, intention setting, and prayer.

The next lodge is the Earth Lodge, which will be reminiscent of the traditional pit houses used by the natives of this region. There are several ancient dwelling sites along the river that bear witness to the first inhabitants of this valley; now they are barely more than shallow depressions in the forest, forgotten relics of the past. Ben has already been digging the rocky ground for a week with a pick and shovel as part of his work trade for the class tuition. The Water Lodge will be situated beside the stream and be the women's Moon Lodge, and the Sky Lodge will be the men's lodge, a platform in the trees.

We make personal sleeping shelters, too. I send Marcus and Rick off to bring back a sturdy ridgepole for the shelter that we are about to make, the others gathering straight branches for the ribs. We measure out the tallest person in the group, Gareth, and tie the ridgepole to a tree using a fresh cord of spruce root. The ridgepole lies at an angle with the thicker end touching the ground. The ribs are placed side by side in declining size toward the bottom of the ridgepole.

This is ponderosa forest; the pine's long needles, grouped in threes, form a thick carpet beneath the mature trees and it is easy to rake and gather large quantities in a short time. We pile the needles onto the bones of the hut and soon have what looks like a giant triangular squirrel's nest. Stuffing more needles inside the hut, one of the new students disappears and is reluctant to come out again since it is so comfortable.

As the Earth Lodge pit reaches a depth of about three feet, we spend much of the week building the frame. Four posts support the central smoke hole exit, and pole rafters are peeled and burned to size then laid to the outside edge of the earthen wall.

It is a great community-building project and enables us to see how we work together. Marcus, our didactic engineer, wants to lay out plans that he scratches out on the bare earth. Rick, competitive and creative, is already one step ahead with another idea and I watch how they work it out, together with the input of my own vision. Listening to each other, finding compromise and agreement, is part of the challenge of community. I see how people's styles differ and await the inevitable clashes with attention and curiosity.

Building a spontaneous community like this each year is a formidable yet rewarding endeavor. During my first Stone Age Project I was unaware how vital it was to do the preliminary group building. It was consequently a bit of a social disaster. Within the first two weeks of the project, half the participants left because their expectations didn't match and we didn't have the time to negotiate our differences or the tools to mitigate them, being so consumed as we were with the difficulty of meeting our immediate physical needs for food, fire, and shelter. One can't expect a group of strangers to bond immediately when suddenly taken from their usual environments and thrust together to do something unfamiliar and ambitious. It takes time.

New groups spend the first couple of weeks on their best behavior, patient, tolerant, and forgiving of one another's shortcomings. Between weeks two and four, however, the cracks start to appear. The little habits that we all exhibit can turn quickly from endearing or quirky to irritating. Especially when tired, hungry, or cold, small criticisms or snappy comments can sting. This is when things actually start to get really interesting. How will we communicate together? How will we solve issues that arise when the dynamics become uncomfortable? I have often remarked that we do not have to be friends with everyone; we don't have to like everyone, and we will naturally be more drawn to some than to others. It's a matter of resonance. It is important, however, to be respectful of each other and find ways of communicating that can express and soothe our frustrations before they become irreversible obstacles. We try to manage this with daily "check-ins." It's important to know if someone slept badly, is worried or anxious about something, or is in pain or discomfort. It helps to find the compassion and empathy needed to recognize ourselves in others. We work, cook, play, sing, and sleep in close proximity, so learning about every individual's natural tendencies or behaviors is vital before we embark on our Stone Age excursion at the end of the immersion period.

One of our clan is Falcon, who has become part of my family. I met her a year earlier while teaching a class in England. When she arrived here this spring she expressed the resolve she had for a name change. Many of my students mark the onset of these nature immersions and Stone Age experiences with a new name. It gives us a discernible reminder to modify our behaviors, develop self-confidence, and drop old, dysfunctional habits. We get to grow into the new person that we aspire to become. Falcon suits her and is quickly and effortlessly adopted by her new clan as her hunger to see the world and the truth with the keen eyes of the bird that she has chosen as a namesake proclaims itself. I have started calling her my forest daughter. She is truly a creature of the forest, comfortable sleeping under any bush or tree in whatever British weather could throw at her. She tells me that her doctor parents can't understand her need to live so intimately with the wild. She spent her childhood in the woodlands and along the stream banks observing and cohabiting with England's rural wildlife. Both she and her friend Jenny, who has come for this immersion with Falcon, have until recently been vegetarians. They still cannot in good conscience eat the bodies of the industry-raised animals that our society offers them. Luckily here, they don't have to.

Alison is from Canada. Skateboarding on Vancouver's city streets, she became cynical of the suburban life that bored her. Her youth was spent partying, experimenting with soft drugs and alcohol together with her friends and brother. That was what made Ali's life seem tolerable. Then one day a couple of years ago she came home to find police cars lining her street and her house blocked off by emergency tape. She tells us the story and her eyes brim and spill a salty track down each cheek as she relives that horrific afternoon that sent her whole world into chaos. She recounts her brother's suicide in the basement of their family house, how she wanted to see him and help her parents clean up the blood that stained the floor. She felt she never got closure with him and it has left her empty and longing, so she turned to nature and is sitting here with her tear-streaked face. Many of us are also crying in sympathy but maybe also with the sadness of our own feelings of loss and separation.

Louis is the youngest adult in the group at nineteen. He timidly reveals that he cannot subscribe to a binary gender designation but doesn't know yet exactly how to describe himself on this spectrum. He's decided to take some time off before continuing his formal, academic education. He has long, curly blond hair and like most of our clansmen, his chin has not seen a razor for quite some time. Maybe never. Raised in New Mexico with his brothers and their single mom, this tall, skinny youth is on a quest to find himself. He went to a drum-making workshop and has also tanned a few hides already. Mature beyond his years, he frankly admits that he has no idea who he is yet and is sure that an immersion into nature is what his soul, his whole being, yearns for.

When I was Louis's age I was living in the squat houses in Amsterdam, hanging out at the gay bars and coffee shops, earning money cutting people's hair and working as a dishwasher in a restaurant. I was so relieved to be away from London and my parents. Despite the excitement and thrills of those times, I still knew I was lost and drifting.

All through my teenage years I sporadically kept journals. In one of them, I recorded a dream I had because it was so bizarre. Apocalyptic. It felt almost like a prophecy. I was at an outdoor music festival at night, and the music was playing on the stage. Thousands of people were dancing in the meadows, lying around, getting high and basically having a good time. I was with my childhood friend, Sasha. We were lying in the grass and staring up at the stars when all of a sudden a great comet ripped across the sky with a long, blazing tail. The whole sky turned red. It got insanely hot and as we jumped up, I grabbed Sasha's hand and started pulling her toward the forest that flanked the meadows. I was scared but I yelled to her: "We gotta run to the forest to watch it end," and we ran and ran. I woke up breathless and sweating.

Not long after this dream, something unexplainable occurred one day at a laundromat in Amsterdam. I was afraid to tell anyone about it, for fear it would somehow lose its magic and become ordinary, because at the time it was the most extraordinary thing that I'd ever experienced. I was sitting in front of a washing machine, watching my clothes go round and round through the glass door. I remember turning and looking out the window and across the street, and there was a man up on the third floor washing his windows. His hand was going round and round and round, too, same direction, same motion. That's when something happened, I wrote: "It's hard to explain. Somehow 'I' didn't exist anymore, there was no more sense or feeling of being me or sensation of a body or mind or being separate from anything else." I had an awareness of the perfection of the Universe. When I came back into being "me" again, I was no longer in the laundromat but walking down the street. I didn't understand what had happened, but I felt elated and I wanted to be able to feel that magic again.

It was more than a decade later that I gradually started to perceive this universal "oneness" as I spent longer and deeper periods immersed in nature, moving with her rhythm, unleashing the wildness buried deep within.

Louis and the other students are all here on their own personal quests, searching for something to fill the void, guided by their intuition that answers lie between the rocks and boulders, faint whisperings of truth rustling among the trees and honest reflection in the crystal clear waters of the alpine lakes.

———————◂——————

When I was a child back in England, our family lived in a brick row house. It was too small for my wild and active pursuits. When we had visitors I performed all kinds of gymnastic maneuvers to impress them. While I was somersaulting and standing on my head my mild and reticent mother would gently tell me to stop showing off. If our amused guests asked me what I wanted to do when I grew up, I said I wanted to save the world. Fortunately my father would often take my big brother and me to the common to play soccer to use up some of my excess energy. I loved to climb trees. I sometimes climbed so high I got stuck and my father would have to help me by telling me where to put my feet as I worked my way back down into his waiting arms. My mother, caring and protective, perplexed by this wild daughter she had spawned, was always worrying that I would fall and hurt myself. I had taken several falls from the metal climbing frame in the park and was known by name at the local hospital where they would stitch up my latest laceration. But it was different with the living trees. I felt that they held me and kept me safe. I never fell out of a tree. Ever.

The native trees along the Twisp River in Washington State are as diverse as the rocks and ourselves. The conifers, though dominated by pines and firs, include other species such as spruce, cedar, and larch. The riverbanks are lined with willows, alders, and cottonwoods. Aspen leaves rustle in the softest breeze, and the land is graced by the fruit-bearing saskatoons, elderberries, and chokecherries. The dry land willows have their own personalities from their river cousins, but during our immersion period, it is the dense, straight maples we approach for our digging sticks.

Spring in these mountainous foothills and valleys has been the season for the Methow tribal peoples to rejoice in the nourishing and starchy root crops. A lonely echo seems to haunt the gathering grounds since the natives of this land were relocated to the confederated tribal reservations to the east together with the remnants of eleven other decimated tribes. They still practice the ceremony of First Foods that ended the cold season of hunger and uncertainty. We join a handful of native traditionalists and about sixty local white supporters in the town for a spring feast of bitterroot, salmon, and deer. The elder who leads the ceremony seems to do so without judgment or anger toward the race that usurped his people from their native valley and pressed them together with a dozen other tribes on land less resourced and bountiful. I cannot escape the stamp of colonialism even though I'm a first-generation immigrant to this continent from a people of Scandinavian heritage, ex-Vikings who have largely stayed at home for the last couple of centuries. The fact that my skin is pale when the warmth of the sun has waned and winter strips me of my summer tan and my fair hair and blue eyes casts me without doubt among the perpetrators of global injustice. But today, armed with our durable digging sticks, our little clan of lost misfits and blended blood wander up into the hills to dig roots for our sustenance.

I see Rick standing impatiently, throwing his digging stick spinning into the air while Ali runs back to look for her gathering basket that she forgot by the river. I sense tension and cast Rick a questioning glance. He smiles but there is a hint of irritation as he mutters, "Waiting, always waiting for somebody." The first crack in our utopian group love affair; it's right on time about three weeks into our experience of living together. I welcome it and at the same time wonder how it will play out. I have had my own moments with Polly over the months she and Gareth have lived with me. She and I are both fiery spirits with strong personalities and opinions. Yet our abrasive moments gave rise to the necessity of digging in and uncovering the hurt and sensitive places that caused the friction in the first place.

As a result we are closer than before, the love is stronger, and our understanding of each other has taken on another dimension.

———————————◄

Over the years in this valley I've come to call home, I've had the fortune to harvest at the gathering grounds of the First Peoples who inhabited this place. I watch the changes through the cycling seasons and although I've absorbed knowledge through my mentors, students, and largely the land itself how to give as well as take, I know I still have much to learn.

We humans are not designed to be inert observers of nature. We impact, we interact with the planet's other beings. When we become conscious of the lure of greed and keep it in check, we can be again a valuable mechanism of regeneration as we perform our practices of harvesting from the wild in symbiotic relationship with the planet.

So it is with the roots. Some have designed themselves to spread their bulblets, helped by the coursing of tunneling rodents and our own digging, prying hands. Others find their niche in the dry and rocky hilltops, where the conditions are so harsh that their claim and right to exist is only made possible by their adaptive resilience. It is here that we unearth the bitterroots, peel them of their orange coats and plant back their little orange hearts with blessings. In return our sticks leave depressions where the rains can pool and the disturbed earth is loosened. But here also, we must be cautious of which roots and how many to take. Let the babies grow and thrive. Let the flowers of the strong bloom and seed. Let us come again with gratitude and participate in this exchange. Thus, life becomes a prayer merely by living it.

We head back to camp with our treasure, harvesting other roots and bulbs along the way. I make a point to focus on the poisonous plants thoroughly. I would hate for someone to confuse the mariposa lily for death camas, throw it in the pot, and poison us all.

Down by the river the nettles are shooting up, their little stings a reasonable exchange for their rich mineral and protein content.

For five days we clamber to the hilltops, crawl the streamside thickets, and peruse the meadows with our digging sticks and bags to collect and store roots and greens.

In the evening we finally sit down to meals augmented by blue-bells, yellow bells, fireweed, spring beauties, nodding onion, balsam shoots, and cattail rhizomes. Strings of drying wild foods now hang from the rafters of the outdoor kitchen, and the fire has become the scene for various cooking techniques that don't require a metal pot or pan.

Ali is sitting, staring into the fire, not her usual ebullient self as James and Marie, tonight's cooking team, bustle about stirring pots and adding ingredients. I sit down beside Ali and wrap my arm around her shoulder. A tear glistens golden on her lower lashes but she does not look up or speak. Just leans into me and we sit in silence, sharing the warmth of closeness that needs no explanation. She knows that when she is ready, there will be someone here to meet her, to hold her and step into the darkness together.

Between classes life goes on in camp. We're all becoming more familiar with each other and liaisons start to develop between the clan members. Usually once a week there is a trek into town to check the internet at the local library. My groups have become a colorful addition to the small rural community and they're easily singled out as they wander the main street smelling of woodsmoke and relishing a forbidden ice cream bar. As summer progresses the earth-toned pants and T-shirts are replaced with buckskins. Bare feet pad the pavement with the lively steps of a motley crew of twentysomethings.

The rewilding is a sure but gradual process.

4

Nuclear Kids

When I was twenty I was living in a small rural village in southwest Sweden with a couple, Bjorn and Gullan, who, though not related by blood, are like a family to me, theater people, easygoing creatives who were the opposite of my blood family. I'd been staying at their rambling countryside house (all white with red windowsills instead of the other way around as is traditional in Sweden) and helping them with their kids: five-year-old Emma and the new baby boy, Hugo. I'll never forget that morning when we heard an alert on the radio warning of mysterious very high radiation levels being recorded. It was later in the day that the Soviets acknowledged publicly that a reactor at the Chernobyl nuclear power plant was in meltdown. A wave of radiation was blowing northwest with the winds into northern Europe and Scandinavia.

I was in school again that spring, studying theater. After the Chernobyl accident my friends and I started talking about how insane it was that we have this nuclear power that produces such dangerous waste that nobody knows what to do with, and that will last for thousands of years. I mean, come on, what about the future? we said. What about us kids?

Early that summer, three baby jackdaws fell down from their nest in the chimney. I became their surrogate mother. I fed them at first with scrambled eggs and droppers full of water. Boy, did they make a racket! I wasn't sure how to be a corvid mother, but I assumed that after their feathers started developing, it was time to teach them to fly. I lined them up on a branch in the apple tree in the garden then climbed up there myself. They looked at me, all curious and a bit cheeky, and I jumped off the branch flapping my arms wildly. They hopped off and did the same, only they actually started to flutter a little bit, which was a good deal better than my effort. My menagerie and I were quite a sight walking through the village down to the store. I'd be pushing the baby in his pram, the birds sitting on the handrail, a big black dog, a striped cat, and a little blond Emma in tow.

A couple of my friends and I created a performance art group after the Chernobyl disaster because we felt like we needed to do something, say something about our frustrations. We called ourselves the Nuclear Kids. We shaved our heads and wore black overalls that we printed an atom sign on the back of. We wrote songs and started performing on the streets as a rebellion against the politics that drove—and still drive—the global system. Even then I was appalled that comfort and convenience seemed more important to most people than protecting the environment. They'd rather numb themselves in front of a TV screen than take any action to preserve the planet. Our street performances were well-received, and we were even making a little money, not getting rich exactly but we made a plan to do some kind of European tour that autumn. I wrote in my journal: "It's not easy growing up in a world that doesn't hold a lot of hope for the future. When the radiation has settled and the baby birds can manage on their own I reckon it will be time to head south ourselves and take to the streets with our show and see if it will make any difference. Ha, I remember when I was a little kid, I wanted to save the world. Guess I still care enough to try."

It is time to make bows and arrows.

With my students gathered around me I string my bow and flex it several times before letting loose an arrow at the straw bale target. It hits the mark with a satisfying thwack. I think back to one of my early bows that I made years ago in Montana where I lived a semisubsistence lifestyle with my second husband. We were fairly dependent on bringing meat to the table, and I remember stalking turkeys late one summer with that bow. I had heard a little group of them gobbling as they scratched and pecked at whatever they could find as they slowly wandered down to the creek away from our garden, which they regularly pillaged. One can get pretty close to a turkey even if they know you are there and I closed the gap, raised up, and pulled my bow to full draw . . . Overdraw, loud *CRACK*, and my bow splintered into three pieces. Yes, three. The tiller was perfectly balanced and both limbs failed simultaneously, leaving me with just the handle in my hand. I threw it half-heartedly, missing the alarmed and retreating turkeys.

Everyone has become well acquainted with the maple tree that we have made our digging sticks from, and now I show them what we are looking for to harvest a green wood stave for our bows. A branch in the middle of a clear stretch is okay. That can be the handle. A bend in one side is fine, it will add reflex. That little bug hole there is no good, it will weaken the bow. Generally we seek out clear, straight, long, branchless staves, about the thickness of a flexed bicep. The roughing out and shaping of the bow is done with metal tools to speed the process, though I usually illustrate how it would be managed using Stone Age techniques only. Sometimes the Stone Age technology is even superior to its metal counterparts. When using the ancient tools of stone and bone, it's important to remember that they don't behave the same as the ones we're used to. One has to adapt to find the best ways to use them so it's a kind of mental letting go of the preconception of how things work. One rarely chops or cuts as one would with a metal blade because the stone is different. The techniques used have to be modified to protect the tools and find their greatest efficiency. I always love the impressions made on people when a piece of wet rawhide is sliced by an obsidian blade like butter. The utterances of surprise make me smile. These stones are not scissors; for the right purpose they are better. Don't try to make a digging stick behave exactly like a shovel or a stone axe or a bone awl like their metal counterparts. Learn their qualities, relax, and be patient.

Since we only have five months together, not our whole lifetimes to practice and perfect the art of prehistoric tool use, we use metal axes, knives, and saws to save time. Over the following days, staves become bows, light and graceful with an even bend between the limbs. They need time to dry, so we take a break to make arrows, harvesting the shoots of rose or ocean spray, dogwood, or syringa. To prepare a set of matched primitive arrows is a feat of genius. The first ones are trials. We fletch them with the feathers of wild turkey and glue rawhide strips on the blunt tips for practice. The arrowheads themselves are fashioned from bone or stone. The irony of a lethal blade made from the leg bone of a deer to shoot his brother does not escape me.

Falcon is making a bow even though she can't imagine ever aiming it at an animal with the intent to take its life. It has been a difficult transition for both her and Jenny to reevaluate their relationship with meat as a source of sustenance. They see how their choices for being vegetarian made sense in an urban environment where they had no access to wild meat, but they are starting to think about the impacts of eating anything that is not grown or produced on the land that they inhabit. The absurdity, the madness of monoculture and packaging and transport across the globe has become glaring with the contrast of how we eat here, and a slow change of ethics is dawning.

Those whose bows are finished by the end of class have the satisfaction of watching their first arrow fly. The others will continue during the coming days to finish up their project while I prepare for our next class.

To draw a bow and let loose an arrow for fun at the target has little consequence other than perhaps losing one's arrow that took half a day to make. To aim at a living creature is altogether a different matter. To hunt with a high-power rifle or fish with modern equipment is also completely different than with ancient weapons. I don't consider myself a particularly experienced or accomplished hunter, but I am aware of my level of skill and I know at what distance and with what bow strength I might hope and expect a shot to be lethal. I probably err more on the side of caution and many times I have denied the shot simply because the circumstances were not ideal.

During morning check-in after breakfast in between class, Ali had asked if we could hold a talking circle in the Fire Lodge. Now as the daylight wanes we sit together around the small ceremonial fire and pass first a bundle of smoking sagebrush with which to cleanse our minds. The heady incense lends importance to the nature of our meeting. I take the talking stick and hand it directly to Ali without speaking; it is her circle, after all.

"I just want to know how everyone is really feeling." It's a simple request, but guarded. I have the impression that she has placed a tightly corked bottle in the middle of the circle. Who will open it? It was a brave start to acknowledge it and place it there for all to see.

She hands the talking stick to her right where Polly is sitting. Polly thanks her and sings a haunting ballad of love and loss then eloquently expresses her grief for the destruction of the planet. Jenny tells of her sadness to be separated from her partner who is not on this immersion, worried that, when she returns home, he might not understand who she is gradually becoming. The stick passes from hand to hand; some speak, some sing, some remain silent. Rick admits to his impatience; he wants people to be accountable and show up when we have a planned time to start class or go somewhere. Falcon sings a song of love for her homelands. Marie releases her deep insecurities around being good enough, capable in the eyes of others. Marcus tells us that his parents never talked openly and honestly with each other and how hard it is for him to do that as well, but he wants to break that mold and not repeat it when he has his own children. James laments his ungroundedness and anger at a civilization that values individuality over cooperation. I sing a song without words that contains a melancholy both soothing and despairing. I just let it come as it will. Louis cries silently but says nothing at all. Gareth makes a joke that makes us all laugh then adds seriously that he has been feeling really strong and connected and is so grateful for a brief but bright period of illumination. Ben channels a song from the wisdom and trust of river waters and then hands the talking stick, having made its full round, back to Ali. She holds it, caressing the feathers tied with a sinew cord that dangle from its knobby head. She doesn't speak for a long time and we wait, silent. Finally in a quiet voice Ali tells us in a matter-of-fact way, as though removed from the significance of its enormity, how she was abused as a child by a family friend. The confession is received without comment or exclamation while Ali continues to hold the stick. She says she has never told anyone this before and sits staring into the fire; finally, looking up, she hands the stick back to me. Words as a response seem wholly inadequate so instead I start to sing a tone.

The others bring their voices and we create a blanket of sound that wraps around the hurt, the pain, the shared and inconceivable burdens that affect us all. I rise and the others rise too. We step away from the fire so we can hold one another and Ali is guided into the middle, our arms encircling, forming a net of safety and love. Our voices mesh and the whole new amorphic being that is the sum of its human parts sways and throbs in unity. When we disentangle, we reembody our individuality once again taking our seats around the firepit. The bottle has been cracked open, the honesty and openness have poured out; it was inevitable. When one dares to share their vulnerability, then all are given permission to express their own. Authenticity. Honesty. Truth. We are held by the fire, the night, the trees, the stars, and one another.

The weeks drift by, the days grow longer, the conflicts build and release, the bonds deepen.

The bowhunting class is followed with animal processing. For many years I have sought out buffalo ranches and bought an entire buffalo to keep us fed for the months to come. A ranch in Idaho is willing to sell us an animal even in the springtime, so most of us rise the next morning in the dawning light and pile into vehicles. The Canadian family—Annabelle, Michel, and young Etienne—stays behind to prepare for our return later. The pickup's bed is half full with containers and tarps. We are quiet mostly, a combination of the shortened night's sleep and the anticipation of what we are about to witness. Falcon and Jenny ride with me. I can feel their nervousness. It will be their first time to be part of a large animal kill. Arriving at the ranch just a few hours later, it's still a cool morning. We're met by the foreman who asks us how we would like to kill the animal.

I tell him I would like to have him shot with an arrow. I was kind of joking; in the past we have sometimes had the ranchers shoot them on sight and sometimes we've brought them back alive to our camp and dispatched them ourselves, but always with a rifle. The guy is not fazed by my request and asks who wants to take the bow shot. I look at my stunned students and reply that none of us have the experience necessary to take such a large animal with a bow yet. But if he would be willing to do it, we would be grateful. It is agreed.

We drive out into the pastures in a large open ATV where the herd is grazing. They don't pay us much attention. The animal that we have purchased is a two-year-old bull and he wanders away a little from the rest of the herd. The foreman has a powerful modern compound bow, barely recognizable as the same weapon that we have been making and shooting in the last week, but I'm glad. No one wants to see the animal suffer. What happens in the next thirty minutes is quite extraordinary and I hope that it may convince some people of the humanity of bowhunting versus rifle hunting. "Our" buffalo is grazing peacefully and turns his body broadside to the archer who takes careful aim and releases the arrow with a quick twang. The arrow hits the bull and he startles, jumps, and runs a few paces. Then a bit unsteadily he returns to the bulk of the herd who have not behaved in any way abnormally. No great explosion has shattered the peace. They did not even look up with the shot. The young bull mingles among them for a minute or two, snatching a mouthful of grass here and there, then he lies down encircled by his family. This is the first time that the rest of the herd notices that something is not right. A couple of them nudge the young bull on the ground and he gets up on shaky legs. A few more steps and he's down again. We wait, almost holding our own breath. These things must never be rushed, especially with a bow shot. The great beast takes his last breath while the rest of the herd, still grazing, are nearby. Soon the tractor arrives and lifts the fallen buffalo with a chain to carry it out of the fenced pasture where we can gut it in safety. As the tractor driver returns to his seat, the two largest bulls in the herd approach the hanging carcass, and it's almost as though they are saying goodbye. We slowly drive our open vehicle back to the gate with the tractor following, the dead buffalo lifted high and swinging slightly. Behind him follows the entire herd in a slow progression. It is moving to watch this funeral procession. There never appears to be any fright or alarm. The whole thing was in fact peaceful.

The animal is lain upon the ground in a shady grassy area where I have told them that we want to do field butchering without hanging. They leave us alone and we circle the slain animal that will become so much to us and even a part of us. We sing to him. The song comes from our hearts; we saw him live, we watched him die, and now we will honor him in death by using as much of his physical body as we are capable of. The glaze of his eyes reveals the lack of the spirit that has departed. Now the work begins.

We unwrap our blades of flint and make the first cut low at the groin but not yet through the tight thin muscle wall into the abdominal chamber. First we slice just the skin all the way to the throat. Then with the aid of our tools we peel back the skin on the belly a hand's width to aid in the process of skinning after the guts are removed. This done, I carefully puncture the swollen belly and with a groan the intestines start to push out. We must not rupture the abdominal organs as we continue to cut, taking turns up to the point where the ribs meet the breastbone. I instruct Louis to slice the throat and if the blood were not already congealed, this is where we would catch the hot spurting liquid and whisk it in a bucket to make blood sausage or pancakes as we do when we slaughter domestic animals. Louis separates the trachea and esophagus from the muscle membranes surrounding it with a sureness and adeptness that surprises me. I am immensely impressed by Falcon, shoulder deep, practically inside the rib cage of the warm, steaming, and sticky carcass cutting through the diaphragm. With a gurgle of air the upper body cavity is penetrated. Reaching up from the rib cage one can feel the plump, firm heart nestled within the massive lungs. Carefully cutting by feel, for he cannot see, Louis is covered in blood as his hands at the throat reach toward the fingers of Falcon, who is loosening and cutting upward from below the ribs. The enormous innards are eventually wrestled out in one intact mass all the way down to the rectum. The heart does not beat anymore, but the life, so recently passed, still seems to vibrate or hover around us energetically as we work. The glistening liver is separated from the rest and I cut off small chunks of it with my stone knife and offer a piece to each member of our clan. We all eat it, bloody, juicy, and succulent. I catch Jenny's eye. Buffalo, you are part of us.

The somber mood of the kill has lifted and we're in the frenzy of work and joy knowing that we will have food that will last us for months. We empty three of the stomachs, the intestines, and bladder and seal them separately in buckets. Then the food organs in another: heart, liver, spleen, lungs, testicles. The tractor helps lift the empty carcass into the pickup, we settle up our accounts with the ranch manager after a hasty hand and arm washing, then dash off to the nearest gas station where we purchase a dozen bags of ice to stuff inside the warm open body to the bewilderment of a few wary drivers.

The sun is high in the sky now and we need to cool things off quickly. Class does not end on this day until 11:00 p.m. when we literally drag our blood-caked limbs to bed. Buffalo has been dismembered and separated. In piles lay the skin, head, and lower legs. Cooling in the stream in buckets are the food and utility organs. The front quarters, hindquarters, rib cage, and pelvis are all hanging in the trees awaiting further processing in the morning. We have several long days ahead of us.

A week later the buffalo is all taken care of. Half the meat has been dried into jerky for our trip into the wild, and half is canned in glass jars for the rest of the preparation time in camp.

The hide does not have its thick, luscious winter coat on account of its springtime slaughter, but we will use it for making rawhide containers. Some of the group, including the Canadian family, have ordered dry salted winter hides to make the thick warm robes for our coming journey.

Etienne is a quiet little boy with a gentle smile. He and his family live in a cob house that they built themselves in Quebec. Annabelle is a tiny woman with pale skin and dark hair. She and her son remind me of fairy folk, appearing and disappearing silently, listening and engaging in their whimsical, unobtrusive manner.

I would have been jealous of Etienne, who is homeschooled, when I was his age. I can still hear my quavering little girl's voice crying, *I don't want to go to school.* My parents were separating. I wanted to join the boys' clubs like my brother did. The boys went camping and made fires, but the girls got badges for cooking and cleaning and sewing. *Why can't I join the Boy Scouts, Daddy? Because you're a girl.*

I was good at soccer and played with the boys in the playground but when it came to being on the school team . . . *You can't because you're a girl.* So I pretended. I abhorred the dresses that showed my underwear when I stood on my head and did cartwheels. I pulled on my favorite jeans and T-shirt and dashed away before anyone could suggest that I dress in something more ladylike. I stood before the mirror and combed my hair back to make myself look as boyish as possible.

After my parents' divorce, my mother, siblings, and I moved into a council flat in a rough South London neighborhood. It was a difficult transition for all of us and I sought comfort in the small glimmers of nature that I could find.

Luckily, at the edge of our concrete council estate was Richmond Park. My little sister and our best friend, Sasha, had built a "camp" near the golf course. Watching the older girls wobbling around on high heels and covering their faces with makeup filled me with horror. I didn't ever want to grow up. I loved being eleven. Our harried mother, trying to raise three kids on her own, worked during the days while we were at school and took evening classes in teacher training to enhance her chances of finding more lucrative employment. This meant that we had little or no supervision after school, so we would jump on our bikes and go down to our camp by the park. There was a daunting iron fence that surrounded the park; the gates would be locked at sundown but we knew where the bars on the fence had been bent and we could squeeze through the gap and then there we were in our own magnificent wilderness. Nobody else there, just the deer, rabbits, squirrels, and foxes. There were sweet chestnut trees in the park, grand old beings that shed their prickly treasure each fall. We would yelp as we stamped on them and teased them out of their weaponed coats, then take our bounty home to roast them.

We have eaten the buffalo's organ meats that we ground and made into sausage, stuffing the mixture into cleaned intestines. The massive rib cage has been segmented and roasted on the coals, and we all enjoy this fresh meat that we eat with our hands. There is something so delightfully sensual in feeling the textures of food as they travel from hand to mouth without the disconnecting utensils of knife, fork, and spoon. I watch Etienne eat with relish, juices dripping down his little arms, his face smeared with glossy fat, and I am cast back to my own childhood dinner table. My father didn't like it when I played with my food. I can still hear my child-self thinking:

He says if I eat like a pig I will get treated like a pig and eat from a trough in the garden. I wouldn't mind eating in the garden with my bluebells that come back every spring.

Etienne's stepfather is so different from my father, who dressed in a suit and tie to go off to work selling insurance. Michel is an artist and expresses his creativity in every medium you can imagine but largely with the products of nature: mud, natural pigments, sticks and stones. Etienne is lucky there, too.

My clan and I prepare the precious buffalo fat that we have rendered and clarified to prevent it from going rancid and we will add it back to some of the pounded jerky together with dried berries to make the highly nutritious pemmican. This is the ideal traveling food, as its calorie-to-weight ratio is substantial. The protein of the meat feeds our own muscles, the berries give that quick energy boost, and the fat supplies the sustained energy and keeps the inner furnace burning helping to maintain body temperature. It feels good to see our dried food stores growing.

One day, with dark, stormy clouds rapidly approaching, I drove to town to source a pig for us to process from the feed store but instead came back with two fluffy kittens. I called Etienne to show him my spontaneous adoption and asked if he would like to name one of them. My question was immediately followed by a monstrous peal of thunder that tore open the heavens and the boy looked at me with wide eyes and whispered, "Thunder Dragon." "That sounds like two names to me," I replied and so Thunder and Dragon joined our little community too.

5

Awakening

I found myself in the Middle East at age twenty after a change of plans that made me start doubting my modern life and endlessly asking myself, *Who and what are we? Where did we come from? Where are we going?* The Nuclear Kids street show that my friends and I had performed as a social and political commentary in Sweden had been going great until one of the members of the group got sick so we had to cancel our proposed tour. I didn't know what to do instead so I started hitchhiking south with another friend and we made our way through Europe looking for work as we went. It seemed like we were always too early or too late for the seasonal farm work we were hoping to come across. I was entirely without direction during this period, and I knew it. I was just going with the flow. In southern Italy we hopped on a boat that took us to Israel where we finally found employment in the Negev Desert on a moshav farm growing tomatoes. There I met a handsome South African mathematician who was disillusioned by abstract life and had started traveling the world and studying farming methods as an alternative. We were a strange match; I was still struggling as a vegetarian while he liked nothing more than a barbecue full of sausage, steak, and bacon. He drank a couple of beers nightly and I was a teetotaler. We both liked sports and athletic pursuits, but we went about it in entirely different ways. He was strong and clever, though, so when he invited me to come to the US and spend the summer with him I said yes. I had just turned twenty-one. He worked in the apple orchards in Washington State and for the next four years we spent summers together in the US, and I would go back to Sweden and live with my surrogate family each winter. It was in Washington State that I had my first revelation about how I truly wanted to be in the world.

In the end, my frustrated, lost self found the key to the rest of my life in the wake of aimlessly traversing several continents.

My boyfriend and I often hiked the mountains of the North Cascades. He liked the military style of "hike until you drop" and "try to cover as many miles as possible in a day." It made me feel like I was in boot camp. Not my style at all. The resort town of Chelan offered all kinds of seductive outdoor activities such as waterskiing, sailing, biking, and hiking. I loved the warm climate and the dry hills dotted with sweet-scented ponderosa and spent many days roaming and exploring our vast back "yard." This was a big step from my childhood backyard in South London, camping in my tent with my survival book, or my grandparents' house in Sweden on the edge of a small but managed forest. Here, there was huge wilderness with wild bears and cougars. It gave me my first taste of being on a lower rung, below top predator. This awareness filled me with a wondrous excitement and an edge of wariness. I saw the great dark sky in all its magnificence for the first time, not faded and reduced by city lights or obscured by low-slung clouds and hemmed by the ubiquitous boreal forest. When the infrequent rains did come, they came as brief torrents with flashy electrical storms, and the dry land, suddenly soaked, released heady scents of unfamiliar plants and bushes. I was in awe.

As I gained confidence being outside in this new place, my forays into the wilderness steadily grew longer. I'd taken to trying to reduce the size and weight of my backpack and going slowly to look at everything along the way. Especially the plants. There was so much to learn. My thinking began to shift: The animals don't have to carry a bunch of food around with them, they know what to eat, they're equipped to live out there. It's all instinctual. What happened to us humans? The burden of bearing a heavy backpack reduced the joy and freedom of being light and unfettered. I figured that the best way to take less gear with me was to learn what I could eat in the wild so I could reduce the quota of weighty food in my pack. In my youth, I had picked berries and mushrooms with my grandparents in Sweden and had gathered sweet chestnuts in the park in London, but I didn't really know much about wild edibles. I started to carry plant identification books around with me. I found a book called *Tom Brown's Field Guide to Wild Edible and Medicinal Plants.*

Tom Brown's guide was different from others. It spoke of plants as if they were beings, not just botanical analyses of their component parts that can be categorized and filed away neatly. I was intrigued. After reading it from cover to cover, I discovered on the back page that the author ran a school in New Jersey where you could learn not only about plants but about other wilderness skills that I'd been wondering *Well, how did we do that before?* I'd already tried rubbing two sticks together to start a fire and I could feel the warmth from the friction they created, but I had doubted that anyone else was interested or still knew how to do such things. And here was a place where these skills were actually being taught. Without hesitation I enrolled at Tom Brown Jr.'s Tracker School.

Just a few weeks later, in a frenzy of excitement, I boarded a Greyhound bus and traveled across the United States to the Pine Barrens of New Jersey. My first night, though frazzled by the three-day journey, I instinctively felt that I had made the right decision as I bunked down to sleep in the rudimentary hayloft of an old barn with a group of other interesting and eager acolytes. There were thirty-five students, mostly young adults like myself but also some older people. To be with others who had similar values and interests was monumental. For a whole week! How had I not found them before? The class days seemed like a blur of the best things I'd ever done in my life, full of firsts, learning about both practical skills and the wisdom of native philosophy. There was a lot of talking and note-taking, a slide show to demonstrate the technique of dry scrape hide tanning, twining cordage from plant fibers, and hours listening enthralled to the charismatic Tom Brown telling stories about a life that would have seemed inconceivable to me before. As he mesmerized us I imagined him leaping out of a tree onto the back of a deer and killing it with a knife. Compare that with the prewrapped and packaged tidy little chunks of flesh that we are offered in the supermarkets.

My eight-year flirtation with vegetarianism had been waning as I became conscious that my food choices were unnatural in a rural environment. Hunting wild game constituted a large part of my rural neighbors' diets. This week at Tom Brown's school catalyzed my changing beliefs about what we eat. What might it be like to hunt for one's meat instead of supporting the domestic meat industry? Could I do that someday? Would I? I was plagued by the irresponsibility of eating meat without killing it oneself and pledged to learn how to kill something quickly and humanely.

Another slumbering awareness was slowly bubbling to the surface like trapped gases released at the bottom of the ocean. These small bubbles of consciousness around the big question of "Why life at all?" had been reactivated, and the spiritual entity that was awoken in Amsterdam a few years earlier—as I sat in the laundromat on a seemingly innocuous washing day—was percolating, patiently awaiting contemplation.

Making fire with sticks, by friction, was undoubtedly one of the most profound moments of my young life. We were several days into the class and I was loving every minute of it. Instructors handed out coarse pieces of dry cedar wood with which to make our fire kits.

I am fairly deft and capable with my hands and was one of the first students to produce my bow drill kit and embark on the steep learning curve that requires coordination and stamina in equal measure to coax a glowing ember from the rapid spinning of the drill. I was so self-confident in my achievement that I threw my kit into the flames at the end of the week, convinced that I didn't need to carry any more extra baggage on the airplane to Sweden, where I was headed afterward. I thought I'd go straight to the forest near the village and build a new kit when I got there.

On the last day of the class we held a sweat lodge ceremony. We dedicated hours of preparation gathering an enormous pile of firewood, placing the lava rocks in a precise pattern and then lighting a fire to heat them. The ceremony was to be held following a Lakota tradition.

Being inspired by material or spiritual culture other than one's own brings up the relevant question of cultural appropriation. What's okay, and what's not? A sweat lodge ceremony in the Lakota tradition held by non-Lakotas seems inappropriate to me today and I encourage my students to examine their intentions. My view is that if we have rejected our own cultural practices we would do well to create new ones rather than adopting those of someone else. But, if I am invited to participate in a ceremony with the people whose culture created it, I feel honored.

Like many other Europeans, my upbringing was so empty of spirituality with its holidays that were mere excuses to indulge in consumer and gastronomic excess that as a twenty-four-year-old I was keen to experience something Earth based instead of church based.

So I crept into the dark lodge stripped down to my underclothes, whispering a prayer at the entrance and moving clockwise around the pit in the center that was to receive the heated rocks. When all were seated, a rock was delivered, glowing red and placed carefully in the central pit with a pair of deer antlers. Then another and another. Each rock was greeted with gratitude and a small sprinkle of sage that filled the confined space with fragrant smoke. When the last rock had found its place, the cloth door was dropped and we were consumed by the darkness, the moist heat, and the songs and prayers that followed.

When I crawled out of that sweat lodge, hours, though it felt like eons, later, I had been stripped bare of my preconceptions. I knew I had found the thing that I'd been looking for. Everything made sense and I could feel the dreadful hole inside of me was going to be filled. After all those years of searching, searching for how to be a whole human, feeling lost and fragmented, searching among the arts—poetry, painting, music, singing, theater, and dance—for my most true form of self-expression, I had known there was something missing, something that would tie it all together. Now here it was, what I discovered embraced all my passions. I found the love of my life. Earth.

Back in Sweden that winter I changed all my plans. I broke up with my boyfriend, canceled the volunteer work I had lined up in an orphanage in Bangladesh, and set about earning money to take more wilderness courses in America while diving deeply into these new skills in my ancestral wintry environment.

I felt as though I had been viewing the world in black and white and suddenly was able to perceive color. I was still riding the wave of spontaneity. Every time I came back to the lands of my Nordic blood I moved back in with my surrogate family, Bjorn and Gullan, and their children—Emma and Hugo—and they welcomed me as one of their own. Having been back and forth between America and Sweden for the last few years my backpack was always ready; I couldn't stay still for long. Now I felt drawn to the north, to the land of my maternal lineage. I didn't question my impulse. In America, I had been exploring the edges of the wilderness with a growing compulsion. In Sweden, I lived near the forest and worked jobs in the theater, but I felt myself stretching toward something wilder, something I couldn't quite put my finger on. I asked now-nine-year-old Emma if she wanted to come north with me to see the Arctic, wild, snowclad lands that appealed to my sense of adventure. I could hardly believe it when Emma's parents let me take their daughter. That they trusted me meant so much.

We flew to a little town called Gällivare. It took three flights on flimsy little planes and I was not, and I admit I'm still not, the most courageous of flyers. It was stormy and bumpy and visibility seemed to be about nil. By the time we touched down on the icy runway I was already pretty sure that I wasn't going to fly back south again, we would just have to take a bus or hitchhike.

We booked ourselves into a tiny hostel in Gällivare, an iron-mining town founded on the lands of the Sami, the Indigenous peoples of the north, of whom a large number still make a living by reindeer herding in this region. Their land, Sapmi, stretches across the northern borders of Norway, Sweden, Finland, and Russia but is not recognized officially by any country.

Emma and I visited the Gällivare museum. I had become deeply interested in how traditional peoples of the earth adapted to their environments. Their methods make sense; they have purpose as well as beautiful form. The Sami belong to this land and their crafts reminded me of some of the North American native peoples' crafts. I saw a pattern of their reindeer skin boots in an exhibit, with turned-up toes as a method for binding on their skis, not dissimilar to the Apache rawhide-soled moccasins, though for them I'd heard it was to protect the toes from kicking cactus spines. I meticulously copied the pattern of the Sami winter boots onto a scrap of paper so that I could try to make a pair for myself later. There were drums there, too, painted with alder bark dye usually with a sun depicted at the center. Many figures and symbols graced the ancient skin surfaces telling stories or offering some form of divination. The Sami have long since been Christianized, but the mysterious and magical ways of the old faiths connected to nature carry through in their culture. Emma and I hitchhiked to another little town called Jokkmokk a bit farther south. Wherever we went, people asked if we had come for the Sami market that has been happening annually for nearly four hundred years. The market originated as a way for the government to extort taxes from the native peoples for using their own land. They were required to pay in meat and skins for trading purposes since they didn't use a monetary system. I didn't know anything about it at the time, but I figured we should check it out.

———————◆———

We sat on wooden benches in the big barn in Jokkmokk, watching the fiddlers spilling out of the corners. Each musician was driven by unseen forces as fiddlers can be, present and attentive, yet somehow absent, too, caught in a place otherworldly. Their fingers danced wildly, rosined bows leaping from string to string in unspoken accord with each other. The dancers, in soft reindeer moccasins or thick woolen socks, spun around the wooden walled room, hot faces shining.

The man sitting beside me watched the dancers. He had broad

cheekbones, an aquiline nose, cropped fair hair, and several weeks of beard growth. He looked intermittently at his watch and then his gaze drifted back to the timeless scene of the folk dance.

He was from Germany; his name was Thorsten, which means "The Stone of Thor." A Norse god's name. I was not that versed with Nordic mythology but I knew the names of the week in many of the Germanic languages derive from the Norse names including Thursday (Thor's day). Thor was the god of thunder; he carried a stone hammer and was not afraid to wield it. I glanced at the handsome young man close to me. The name suited him; he seemed to be full of power.

Emma and I had met Thorsten and his brother at the hostel a couple of days earlier in Gällivare. He and I had talked long into the polar night about dreams and the rich fascination we both had for the northern lands. I'd seen a fierce light burning in him then and was drawn to him. I'd gone to bed filled with thoughts and dreams inspired by this strange man. They had left the next morning and we hadn't exchanged any contact information so I did not expect to bump into them again. But there we all were in Jokkmokk, in a sweaty room full of dancers twirling around to a lively polka. The attraction held me spellbound. He looked at his watch again like it was too late and he really should be going.

"Why do you look at your watch so often?" I had asked. The music was swelling and vibrating.

"I'm seeing how long I have to live." The dancers' soft feet whispered faster across the floor.

"And how long do you have?" I had said, wondering if this was a game but cautiously uncertain.

"Maybe two months," he answered, looking at me, serious. This was no game.

"What's wrong with you?" The dancing, frenzied, seemed far away like a TV set with the sound turned down.

"I have cancer," he said. "And in two months I shall have an operation that will either kill me or save me." I was silent. The scene around us went on unchanged, but inside I quietly assembled my impressions. So that is why he burned with the fierce light, he saw everything in a different perspective, the perspective of the man whose time is running out. Different from the healthy young man who tumbles on recklessly with an eternity of assumed experiences ahead of him.

"Don't worry about it. It's not so bad." His eyes were soft and wise. I wanted to touch him, to comfort myself in my own sorrow but I didn't dare. He told me his story that night after we all left the dance and lay on our sleeping bags on the floor of the school building that had opened its doors to the hundreds of young market visitors like ourselves who had arrived without planning a place to stay.

He'd learned of the disease a year ago. *Leukemia*, they'd told him. *You're dying.* He said that he fell into a very deep black hole at first, very frightening, very dark, but it had only lasted a brief moment. He'd spent that year learning, learning how to see and sort right from wrong, good from bad, and suddenly the things he'd thought previously important became unimportant and he immediately changed his life.

He talked of his discovery of the love that he had for his friends and family, the love of the earth and of life itself. He told me how he spent last summer walking the length of the Kungsleden, a trail that stretches for 270 miles from the north of Sweden along the mountainous backbone that separates Sweden from Norway. He did it alone. He said he'd wanted to think about his disease but he didn't. He met people on the trail, he walked, he was happy. He told me that if he had to die so soon he would be a little sad but it would be okay because he'd had a good life and he was satisfied with it.

He'd spent much time, as he was doing now in the north of Scandinavia, living with the earth, not just on it, aware and respectful of its power.

Such beautiful, shining wisdom one does not often encounter, sometimes in the old but rarely in the young. Such a gift he'd offered me. Such beautiful lessons. The Northern Man, as I thought of him, had touched me. Nature had sent me a friend. *Please, Nature*, I asked, *don't take him away again.*

Thorsten and his brother left on the train after the market was over and this time we made a plan to stay in touch and meet again. A few weeks later, on my way back to America, I stopped in Hamburg, his hometown, to see him. We spent a couple of days talking and talking and holding each other. He said to me as the train pulled away from the station, "This is not the last time we meet." Next time, Thorsten, next time. I had hoped that it would be in this lifetime, but it was not to be. We had our last conversation while he was in hospital awaiting his bone marrow transplant after I had returned to America that summer. Then the silence.

Ah, Thorsten, Northern Man, small son of Thor. Perhaps I've never met anyone who has changed my thinking so much in such a short time. What a special man he was. He was dying but I fell in love with him anyway. I carry him with me.

If I ever have a son, I promised myself, *I will name him Thorsten Sky.*

6

ALCHEMY

In preparation for the hide-tanning class, the Living Wild students and I accumulate dozens of deer hides during hunting season that we preserve in salt. Before the beginning of class, we soak the hides for a few days in trash cans and add ashes from the fire. The ash reduces the bacterial buildup and aids in the scraping and softening process.

Marcus looks at the cuts on his hands from the stone blades we used to process the buffalo. He opts to wear rubber gloves while handling the ripe-smelling deer hide that he is about to scrape. He finds it hard to imagine that this wet, slippery, and stinky thing will ever be something that he will want to wear, but he takes the scraper that has been made from one of the buffalo rib bones and leans firmly against the wooden beam that the hide is draped over and starts to push the hair and grain off in a quick, sharp, rhythmic pattern. It is labor intensive and takes several hours even for a strong man like Marcus, then the whole process is repeated on the membrane side of the skin. Everyone else is doing the same with their own hides; some have already tanned before and know what it means to tan a minimum of eight to ten deerskins to make a complete set of clothing: weeks of backbreaking labor. I also introduce them to the method of bark tanning, another process using tannic acid extracted from the fresh inner bark of various trees. We tan salmon skins because they can be completed in a relatively short time. For added insulation we also tan the furs of fox, rabbit, and coyote for hats and vests that will be greatly appreciated in the high country during early fall on the cold and frosty mornings that I know will be coming.

Several enormous rectangular racks made from poles have been assembled and half a dozen winter buffalo skins are stretched out tight on them. Scraping these dried hides is a totally different process from the deerskins that are scraped wet. A sharp tool is required to thin the buffalo hides and the steady rasping sound of the scraper permeates the camp as layer upon layer, hour after hour, day after day, the skin is thinned in preparation for the softening process.

Ali has scraped a number of holes in her buffalo hide—it's hard not to when it's your first one—and an occasional half-shouted expletive informs us all that the scraper just busted through again. Every hole made is a hole to sew up during the softening process where a mixture of brains, fat, and warm water is blended into a light creamy soup with which to soak and work into the hide repeatedly for many more hours of intensive labor.

It's hot out and the exertion makes the sweat run into Ali's eyes. It's time for a break. We run down to the river and cool off and wash away the sweaty grime and the weary frustration that accompanies these long days of toil. I watch her as she dips her bare body below the surface and explodes back up with a gasp, noting how shy she was in the beginning to strip down naked in front of anyone when we would all tumble into the water for a swim.

The river is our savior as the heat of midsummer approaches. Some of the group recognize that they will not be ready for the Stone Age journey this year and relax a little, enjoying instead the peace and acceptance that comes with the decision. The Canadian family— Annabelle, Michel, and Etienne—are among them. It's hard enough to prepare just for oneself, but a child also needs to be clothed and fed. They had been keeping their options open but will head home after the classes are over.

Marie has been struggling for months with an ankle injury that may end up making the decision for her.

During the next few weeks there is little spare time for those who are determined to be ready. The free time between classes is now a frenzy of hide tanning, berry harvesting, bow shooting, arrow making, and the multitude of other tasks associated with living an outdoor life removed from civilization.

As the classes build, adding new skills and knowledge, so, too, does the material wealth of the clan members. With seven classes behind us, treasures of modified rock, stick, skin, and bone are tucked into corners and bags around the camp. It's time to focus on containers to carry all this new stuff into the wild with us.

To create a durable, lightweight pack, we start once again by appealing to maple for her strong, flexible wands and to a rawhide deerskin that is cut into long strips for lacing and lashings. Thus we bind our world together; the pack basket style taught to me by one of my mentors, I now pass on with the little adaptations that I have made over the years. We see how culture is always evolving. Style changes, function remains.

Stripping the bark from the green maple we coerce the wands into graceful hoops. It is patience and care nature responds best to, not hurry and force. Ben is having trouble with the wands he has harvested; they break over and over. I see the smallest hint of frustration and am relieved that he is just a human, after all, like the rest of us. Ali gives him a couple of spares and helps him hold them while they are bound in place temporarily with the bark strips we have just removed. This assortment of hoops look like they might be props for some kind of magic trick, which I suppose they are. We put them aside to dry for a couple of days.

Turning our attention to the river we search the bends downstream for the clay seam that I have harvested from in years past. Louis finds it first and he calls us over, smiling broadly, his spindly arms aloft holding handfuls of sticky gray clay.

The test is performed. Can he make a clay serpent and loop it together into a doughnut without it breaking and cracking? He can and he does. We each gather a ball of clay roughly the size of a soccer ball.

Back in camp the magic show continues. When did our ancestors first discover that the drying and heating of clay changed its structure so it was no longer water-soluble? The archaeological record dates ceramic cooking pots as a relatively recent discovery a mere twenty thousand years ago. Probably people were baking food in clay long before pots were made and fired deliberately as cooking vessels.

The silky clay still has small stones and organic matter in it that we need to take out and then we actually add back fine-grain sand to temper and strengthen the clay before we start to build the pots. I encourage people to play with it for a while. Start something then smash it down and start over. Get to know it, learn its boundaries, its tendencies, its personality. By midafternoon the actual cooking pots are starting to take shape. A clay coil is flattened into a wedge and plastered to the preceding coil, nimble fingers smoothing and evening the surfaces. Too wet and it slumps, too dry and it cracks. It asks for sensitivity in the hands of its molders.

Gareth has broken his pot down a dozen times before the clay starts to yield in his hands and respond to his requests while Polly is already focused on adding intricate patterns to the rim of her perfect vessel. Falcon has sculpted the head of a bird onto a small bowl that she eyes with satisfaction, her long hair streaked with clay as she absently brushes it off her face.

At the end of the day an impressive array of pots of unique shapes and sizes lies in the safety of the shady workshop, away from the investigative whiskers of Thunder and Dragon. Once again we are the gods, building and shaping the world with our hands. Satisfied with our new invention, we let the pots slowly dry.

Creating ceramic vessels is to me the most profound act of elemental alchemy. Harvesting the earth element that must be mixed with the water element, that must be dried with the air element, that must be cooked by the fire element. They circle around one another in infinite intricacies.

The next day we pry sheets of bark from the spruce using sticks with curved, rounded ends. The shiny, wet wood below is pale and exposed. The tree gives its skin willingly before the heat of the summer clasps it tight again. We thank the trees and are conscious not to take more than a third of their circumference so they do not get too stressed. A couple of times I have found ancient cedars in the forests that bear the scars of native hands who removed bark for their own purposes. Hands of people long dead, while the trees persist. The patient trees.

The fresh bark is folded and sewn along the seams with the spruce's own supple roots. A gathering basket is born through the midwifery of our own hands. The giving trees.

Our maple pack baskets are assembled and laced with rawhide. Straps are added, and I encourage everyone to try them out to make sure they are comfortable when bearing weight.

On the last day of this week's class, the clay pots, now thoroughly dry, are prewarmed by the fire and slowly, ever so slowly, heated as the fire is brought closer before consuming them in a furnacelike blaze. The pots are barely visible within the inferno, glowing a dull red. We keep them covered in coals and ashes as the fire dies down. We won't know the successes and casualties until the morning after when we uncover them from their still warm ashy bed.

Next comes the clothing and moccasin class. Ben lies on his pile of soft smoked buckskins looking quite tired but blissful. "I feel like a millionaire," he utters with his eyes closed. His pile is big enough to make a long-sleeved shirt with a hood (three hides), a pair of leggings and a loin cloth (another three hides), a pair of shorts (one hide), a short-sleeved undershirt (one and a half hides), and a pair of moccasins (half a hide). Nine deer hides in total. He has also made a vest of felted sheep's wool.

Most people are pretty terrified when it comes to cutting into these hard-earned skins and I understand the dread, the sick feeling when someone realizes they just cut out two left feet on their moccasin pattern. The clothes are often marked lightly with charcoal and draped on their subject. When cutting proceeds, a sharp pair of metal scissors really are the tool of choice.

Thin buckskin thongs are cut from the outer scraps, and the clothes are sewn together by punching holes along the seams with a modified, tapered nail and laced with the aid of a bone awl. It's often difficult to convince the young women that it is better to be fully and plainly clothed when we head into the wilderness than to have just one exquisitely tailored slinky top and short skirt and nothing else. They will freeze. In fact, after so many expeditions I now have a list of items that everyone must have completed before being allowed to head off into the wilds.

After months of walking barefoot, the soles of our feet have become tough and calloused. The moccasins we make have double or even triple soles, but we use them sparingly because we know the effort we expended to make them. They are largely reserved for those cold mornings, the heavily laden hiking days on sharp, rocky trails, or when a foot gets cut or injured and needs some extra protection. There's no better footwear in existence—no comfort or security that technology has ever improved upon.

I vault onto my spotted horse Karma, and Falcon clambers up onto Christy's broad, chestnut-colored back beside me. Gareth is already astride Chaco and we trot down to their daytime grazing grounds bareback. Falcon is wearing her new buckskin dress, Gareth bare-chested in his clean new shorts. My own buckskins have long ago lost the shine of newness. I have mended them repeatedly. Tailoring is in my blood. My mother was a seamstress. The old clothes eventually wear out. With the time and effort needed to create this beautiful clothing they are lovingly maintained, seams resewn, patched, and when finally too tattered to serve their original purpose, they are cut up and made into something else. I have old buckskin work pants, stained and shiny with pitch that I am still wearing after twenty years.

We turn the horses loose and they toss their heads, kick up their heels and race to the bottom of the meadow, then turn and race back again in an exuberant circle before dropping their heads to graze. We three human beings walk back up to the camp together, stopping to eat a handful of saskatoon berries along the way. It's a good patch; the berries are sweet and perfectly ripe, and we will come back with our baskets and gather more later.

There are only two more weeks left before our designated departure date. In camp, berry cakes are drying on pieces of bark lain in the morning sun, and in the pleasant coolness Ali and Louis are already sewing buckskin bags from their leftover clothes scraps. Rick appears from the forest, bow strung and practice arrows in his hand. He's humming a little tune. With his buckskins already well used, they blend with the forest in the dappled sun-shadows.

Piles of carded sheep's wool lay at Ben's feet. He's still at the drum carder, turning the handle with one hand while slowly feeding the wool with the other as the fibers are teased and straightened into the soft, thick batts. Those who are making their blankets from wool start the process of laying it up today, while the people with the buffalo hides will be up to their armpits in soupy brain mixtures. Either way, both groups are in for many long tiring hours. When the blankets and robes are all complete, we hope to be nearly ready to go.

Everyone else has drifted off to their beds, leaving Falcon, Jenny, and myself at the main hearth alone. Falcon seems pensive and without warning tells us that today is the first anniversary of the death of one of her close friends. She goes on, telling us of how his body was found in a lake but there was no indication of his having taken his own life so it was surmised to have been an accident. A breeze riffles the pines and the moon appears briefly then fades again, rimming the clouds with pale gold. Wordlessly we study the dying embers. Impulsively I break the silence. "Let's go then, let's go say goodbye to him." The young women look up at me dubiously; it's nearly midnight and there are a million things to do tomorrow morning. "Let's go to Spirit Lake right now and you can talk to him, tell him how much you cared about him." We gather ourselves before the moment passes and head for the truck. As we roll slowly out the driveway, Falcon reveals more about the friend she lost and is seized with memories of their time together and his last days during which he had seemed so content. The drive to Spirit Lake takes no more than fifteen minutes up the potholed gravel logging road; we park close to the lake and are again consumed in stillness when I kill the engine. The night is balmy, the moon has come to us again, though a haze keeps it from bright illumination. Cricket song adds to the atmosphere and we unhurriedly disrobe at the end of the wooden dock and lower ourselves into the black tepid water with barely a splash.

I lie on my back floating, staring up at the night sky, transported back in time.

When I was a young child I learned to swim in a lake not unlike this, surrounded by forest in Sweden. The lake was named after the smallest coin. In the US we would call it Dime Lake, I suppose. It was icy cold but I didn't care. I would jump off the wooden dock, over and over, and paddle around until my lips were blue and I couldn't stop shivering. I knew nothing about hypothermia. All I knew was how much fun I was having and there was the promise of a big fluffy towel and a warm lap on the shore.

I remember a night in a small wooden cabin near that lake, too. I woke up in the silence, deep in the moonless forest, opening my eyes to find that not the tiniest amount of light was available to give me any shape or form in the consuming darkness. It's rare for us sighted beings to experience that total blackness. I was frightened back then. I finally found comfort in the faint points of luminosity shed by the numbers on my wristwatch. I was still alive.

But I had nearly died there on that small lake, before I learned to swim, following my big brother in the water . . .

. . . he is talking to his friend, they are both older and taller than me, of course, and suddenly there is a dip on the bottom of the lake and I can't quite reach anymore. The water starts to come in my mouth and I call out to him but he just keeps on walking without looking back. I feel panic, the water is too deep. I think I am going to drown and then he will be sorry. But the next thing that happens is that a strange man on the beach comes running out, picks me up, and carries me back to the shore where he puts me down. I go back to my family. I don't think they noticed.

I had a dream recently. I was going down in a plane. The crash was imminent. I knew I was going to die. A feeling of peace washed over me and I closed my eyes and started saying, "I love you, I love you, I love you," then the impact. So this was death finally? My words, however, continued but they had changed slightly: "I am love, I am love, I am love." I opened my eyes to find that I was not dead but awake.

Falcon and Jenny are sitting silently on the dock gazing at the moon that hovers above Spirit Mountain as I pull myself up out of the lake water beside them. There is a sense of peace between us and we drive back down to camp without any need to express anything. We embrace in a long threesome hug before heading off to our respective beds under the stars.

7

BLACKBIRD

Creating a clan is an act of faith that we will find strength and cohesion together. One never knows who will come or what will happen. One spring years earlier, barely a week or two into the beginning of the Stone Age immersion, I received a call from England: my mother was dying. And so, I abandoned my fresh batch of students with a distraught and hasty explanation and found myself on the next flight to England and twelve hours later setting up a tent in my sister's garden to begin the vigil.

Blackbirds change their song every spring. Lying in my tent on those following few mornings, I listened to the blackbirds' songs and tried to determine where a chirp or trill marked the beginning of the sequence again. But the songs are so complicated and I would lose myself listening, absorbed by the cadences, climbing, descending then an abrupt stop followed by an unexpected chatter midsentence and I am wooed and ready to build a nest and lay eggs myself.

Although I have spent all my adult life living outside of England, often as far as I could be from my childhood home, I tried to maintain a relationship with my mother. Through years of living off-grid and seeing her infrequently, we exchanged letters and spoke on the phone from time to time. She had birthed me and stood beside me as my own child was born. We had a pact, agreeing that when one of us died we would make contact with the other across the boundary of life and death.

Now the time had come, as my mother lay dying in a hospital near her home in Suffolk. I asked her if she remembered this and she whispered that she did. Early the next morning, the blackbirds in full chorus of this year's song, my sister received a phone call from the hospital. My mother was slipping away and no longer conscious. We were up and driving in less than a minute. My siblings and stepfather and I sat by her side. I asked her to squeeze my hand if she could hear me. No response. I got close to her ear and sang "Blackbird" to her. That beautiful and poignant Beatles song seemed so befitting for such a powerful transitional journey as this one. A few minutes later she breathed her last breath and I sat there. Still. Listening. Watching. Waiting.

———————◄

Her sign came on the fifth day. I had already traveled back to my home where my group of students had been left to fend for themselves in my absence. I was just coming up from the river, when into the meadow came one of my students, Lauren, radiant and heavily pregnant. Beside her walked a woman with a guitar slung over her shoulder. She was a visiting friend of Lauren's. I had met her once or twice before but didn't really know her. "I have a song to sing you," she said. And she sang "Blackbird."

By the end of the song I was weeping, I could feel my mother telling me she was still with me. I spent the following weeks with my students in a daze of love and grief.

When Lauren had arrived for the class, she had asked me if I would be with her for the birth of her first child. I felt honored. This time the call came late at night with a knock on my door and the message that her labor had begun. Twenty minutes later I arrived at Lauren's cabin where she and her partner had prepared a heated stock tank outside and she lay in the warm water moaning gently. The midwife and her assistant were already there, local women I know well. In the expectant hush, I greeted all and settled into the grass, wrapping myself in my buffalo robe to wait. Lauren started crooning a soft song and shifting her body uncomfortably as the contractions would rise and ebb. I couldn't stop staring at her. The air was cold. Clouds obscured and revealed a nearly full moon as they raced seaward and the dark silhouette of the mountains before us loomed dramatically. The midwife whispered to me to stop staring. "The watched pot never boils," she told me. I would be requested when I was needed. I took the hint and resumed my moon worship.

Lost and drifting with the clouds, I eventually heard Lauren call my name. I moved in close and sat by the tub, squatting on my heels, and Lauren took both my hands in hers, in a viselike grip. I was soon freezing in my awkward position but if I as much as wriggled a little to ease my numb legs, Lauren would grasp me tighter, urgently begging me not to go. She was so beautiful, so raw and real. Is there anything more stunning than a woman birthing? Witnessing this miracle as an active participant I was reminded over and over of my own birthing experience seventeen years earlier, when my child came into the world. Time stood still until Lauren's crooning became rapid breathy gasps and the baby was pushed down the birth canal from one watery world into another where she finally slipped out and was brought up to air. Rubbing her vigorously, the midwife massaged the limp being. *Breathe, breathe, breathe*, I silently prayed, waiting for that first gasp to usher in the new life. Then the squall as cool night air entered brand-new, never-used lungs. I sighed with relief as the midwife helped Lauren out of the tub with her baby, and I staggered on unsteady legs behind them into the cabin where the woodstove was burning brightly. I watched with alarm as Lauren's eyes rolled up and she passed out on the bed as an enormous amount of blood came gushing from between her legs and the baby was thrust into my arms while the hemorrhaging was stanched. These interminable minutes holding the tiny naked being in my arms, standing in front of the woodstove, cradling this new life, seeing the circle completed. Miracle, miracle, miracle. This was not my baby but we were there together bonding, keeping warm, pulling the fox furs close. *Be warm little one. Mama, come back; Mama, don't die.*

At last stabilized, after what seemed like hours, Lauren could finally hold her child again, and the midwife and her assistant packed up and left. The new father crawled into bed in another room and Lauren and I lay with the baby between us, our exhaustion no match for our wonder as the rest of the wakeful night slipped by.

At camp with my clan, my current students work feverishly to complete their last items while I drive to the other side of the valley to visit a friend. This annual, yet temporary community within the clan fills most of my social needs yet it's important for me to maintain friendships outside of my programs, especially with peers, family, and people I have known for a long time. As I leave, I tell Ali and Ben who are sprawling under Grandmother Fir together that I only intend to be gone a few hours to visit a friend I haven't seen in a while. But I'm uneasy. It hasn't rained for weeks, and the temperature has been steadily rising. The forest floor is crackly dry and the river and streams have dropped down considerably from their high mark at spring runoff. But now the air is unusually sticky, laden with the energy of an approaching storm. The last few nights, sheet lightning has eerily flashed between the clouds but not a drop of rain has fallen. A few wildfires have already broken out across the state as has become common in recent years of increasing summer heat. Over the last few days, we've been watching the sky as clouds build and dissipate, hoping for rain. As I drive, an ominous black cloud bank creeps in, obscuring the light. It's only midafternoon but it seems like night is falling. The wind starts gusting and just as I arrive at my friend's place the first raindrops fall, big, hard splashing drops that make me run for his door. I mentally go through all the things at home that I might have overlooked or left outside, but I'm fairly confident everything was in order and I hope my little clan is prepared for the onslaught that is just about to happen. The heavens unleash with speed and violence, the rain so heavy it obscures all visibility as my friend and I watch it in awe through the windows. I'm glad I'm not out driving in this. The wind screeches in the roofing as the deluge thrusts sideways. My concern rises for my clan who have just the open-sided Fire Lodge and outdoor kitchen besides their own tents and tarps for shelter. I expect they'll go down to my cabin or the workshop if they need to. A storm this big puts our puny little species in perspective. We're just dust in the magnificence of Earth's power. We really don't have any control as much as we like to think we do and we shudder and tremble when Great Earth rumbles.

In little more than an hour, the worst of the storm has passed. I bid my friend farewell, anxious to get back home to my side of the valley and see how my clan has fared. A few trees are down here and there, but nothing keeps me from driving to the main road that runs along the river. It's not until I get to the other side of town that I realize just how bad it had been over here. The road is covered with needles and small branches that have been blown from the trees, and here and there a large tree has been sawn to reopen the road. Thirty minutes later, with mounting alarm, I am at the top of my driveway and it's absolutely impassable. It doesn't even look familiar anymore. I jump out of the truck with a racing heart. I can hear chain saws. What of my people, my clan, camped down there in tents and tarps? I hurry across fallen trees and debris. The trees are broken off about twenty feet up the trunks, snapped like some celestial novice hairdresser has come down and whacked them off haphazardly. As I scramble over several large firs blocking the road I can see the neighbor's house that used to be nestled inconspicuously in the forest. A big tree has fallen on it. The chain saws are getting louder and suddenly there is Gareth cutting a swath to free up the road again. He kills the motor and greets me with wild excitement in his face.

"Is everyone okay?" I blurt out.

"Everyone is fine," he assures me.

A little later as we finally sit down to a quickly thrown-together meal I hear the tale of the monster that burst upon them. Ali explained how they heard a roar, like a tornado, that hit the corner of the property; it broke off the trees with a terrible cracking and splintering and one fell just feet from Gareth and Polly's yurt. They ran for it—everyone was running for the open space down near my cabin and the horse corrals. They told me how the horses stood together, backs to the wind and the driving rain as the branches were flung every which way. The phenomenal microburst jumped and bounced and sent more trees snapping like matchsticks about fifty yards on as it continued its path of furious destruction. We were lucky. My place was mostly spared but the neighbors' homes, just a hundred yards away, were raw and exposed, littered with the broken, scattered forest.

In the aftermath of the storm, we gleaned more information the following day. Several new forest fires had ignited in spite of the rains that evidently had not been enough to soak the brittle dry ground thoroughly. A little dazed, we tentatively continued our preparations for our planned departure. The group enters its own state of turmoil. There is anxiety about the fires, and the storm has left people jumpy and afraid.

Three days are left before we head out. The clan students have been up late at night sewing in the light of their headlamps. The still morning air has a muddy feel to it with a faint smell of smoke, and the sickly sun is a hazy orange.

The coming journey will be split into two phases; the first week we call "trial week," during which we head out with our Stone Age gear but we are allowed to take some of our modern stuff to help ease the transition. What we take is determined by what we can carry and usually amounts to some extra food and perhaps a metal needle, a nail punch, or a wool sweater for those who need to finish sewing the last of their clothes when we get out there.

Here's my list of required items per person:

Tools:
Stone knife
Quick blades
Pitch glue
Hide glue
Sinew
Rawhide and buckskin thongs and scraps
Knapping kit (pressure flaker, palm pad)
Bone awl
Bone needle
Fishing line
Bone fishing hooks
Fire kit (bow drill and hand drill plus extra cord)
Emergency tinder bundle
Small fat lamp

CLOTHES:
Long- and short-sleeved buckskin shirts
Long pants or leggings and loincloth/leggings and skirt
Shorts (optional)
Fur or felted vest
Fur hat
High-top moccasins
Rawhide sandals
Felt boots (optional)

BEDDING:
Buffalo robe/fur robe or felted blanket
Reindeer or sheepskin sleeping pad

CONTAINERS:
Personal small clay cooking pot
Gathering basket
Pack basket
Eating bowl and spoon
Water canteen
Tool kit rawhide container
Buckskin and rawhide food bags
Fat gourd
Quiver (optional)

WEAPONS (OPTIONAL):
Bow
Sinew, rawhide, or flax string
Arrows (6 sharps, 6 blunts)
Finger tabs
Wrist guard

DRIED FOODS:
Minimum 1 lb rendered wild animal fat (bear, deer, buffalo, etc.)
5 lbs wild animal jerky/pemmican/dry fish
5 lbs wild-plant-based foods (bulbs, tubers, corms, rhizomes, leaves, seeds, nuts, fruits, etc. [i.e., balsam seeds, pinon nuts, acorns, bay nuts, nettle leaves and seeds, plantain seeds, cattail starch, bitterroot, mariposa lily, spring beauties, yellow bells, lomatium root, wild onion, seaweeds, fireweed, wild rice, maple sugar, saskatoon berries, elderberries, thimbleberries, raspberries, blackberries, chokecherries, rose hips])

MEDICINE:
Plant salves, dried herbs

HORSE GEAR:
Saddle pads
Moose hide picket ropes
Woven horsehair halters
Saddlebags/packs
Picket stakes
Hobble ropes

MODERN EXCEPTIONS:
Glasses/contact lenses
Medications
Birth control
Modern bowstring
Journal
Pencil
Map of region
Camera (1 or 2 among the whole group)

Looking back over the summer months, there is a sense that the transitioning back to the world of the ancients has been gradual enough that the students are mostly ready. Armed with the list of what each person needs, they come to me one by one. I ask them to demonstrate their fire kit; if they cannot make a fire, they cannot go off on their own in the wild. If they cannot finish their basic clothes during the next few days, they cannot come at all. If they do not have the minimum weight of dried wild foods, they can only do the trial week. Now is crunch time.

I have a long talk with Marie about her injured ankle. She is unsure about the hike with the heavy pack basket and the unsettled weather and forest fires. I tell her it would be safer if she didn't join us. She needs to be able to run. Disappointed, she agrees; we decide instead that she will ride out with me and the horses for just one night and the rest of the group will follow the next day, driving out to the trailhead in my truck where Marie will meet them and drive back to camp as the rest of us start our journey.

After much deliberating, Gareth and Polly decide not to come, either; they feel unsettled by their close call during the storm, and James informs us that he is going to stay too. He met a girl in town recently and he's fallen for her. I'm a bit shocked; I thought he was more committed. That leaves only eight of us.

Early next morning, Marie and I saddle up the horses. I hug goodbye those who will be gone when I return next month and, with the tang of smoke in our nostrils, we ride up the road toward the trailhead.

PART 2

Searching

8

SMOKY MOUNTAIN EMBARKATION

I moved my buffalo robe in the middle of the night, ants crawling all over me. It had taken a long time to get to sleep under the trees in the thick forest just a few miles from home where Marie and I had pitched camp next to the trailhead. From Marie's regular breathing just a few feet away, I knew she was sleeping while I tossed and turned. What was that light flickering in the trees, the moon or the approach of fire? The knowledge of the wildfires burning all around us these last few weeks had left me uneasy. As the night cooled and the wind dropped, I drifted into dreamland with the horses moving reassuringly nearby, tethered in the trees.

The others drive up in the truck the next morning and disembark with their fully laden pack baskets. A nervous excited energy jumps down with them, permeating the still air. With cell phones, ID cards, and money left behind, it feels like we are each able to create an entirely new identity. Prayer is our insurance. Knowledge of the wild plants and the land, our first aid kit. Trust in each other and ourselves, our backup plan.

The truth is, a lot can go wrong wherever you choose to live, in the wilderness or in the modern world. We may not need to worry about the dangers of driving in hectic traffic or being mugged on the city streets but finding enough calories in a marginal environment or staying warm after a sudden rainstorm at high elevation are real concerns for us in the wilderness.

There is some last-minute fiddling with pack straps and tumplines; Falcon reties a knot that failed as she heaved her pack to her shoulders. Yesterday, Marcus weighed his in at almost ninety pounds. Although he is strong enough to carry it, I am sincerely hoping his pack basket is sturdy enough not to buckle under the load. We give Marie hasty hugs, anxious to start our journey. She's disappointed not to be joining us but with the heavy packs, long distances to cover, and her injured ankle, it's clear that it would be unwise for all of us to take the responsibility. Horses and riders start up the trail first. I ride Karma, with Ben on Christy. Ben, gentle and serene, instills confidence in the animals. Chaco, carrying the rawhide boxes that contain group gear and the dense, heavy pemmican stores, is ponying willingly behind Christy.

Ben and I walk and ride intermittently, the rest of the group following on foot, leaving behind the smoke in the valley, leaving behind the anxiety of the fires and the storm that flattened so many trees just days before as my people ran seeking the safety of open spaces. We're leaving behind the months of preparation for this experience. We can no longer prepare, for we are here. We stop and wait at the first stream crossing for the others to catch up. We don't talk much. Ben is calm but I sense an underlying enthusiasm bubbling under the surface. Jenny, Louis, and Rick are strong and in high spirits. Falcon arrives with a secret smile on her face; she appears to have dropped into this magical world with an immediacy that doesn't surprise me. Marcus and Ali arrive in the rear. Ali sits to remove a pebble from her moccasin. They both look tired. I know that Ali is concerned that she has fewer wild food supplies prepared than most of the others. We all drink deep and long from the stream, replenishing our body fluids, washing away the sweat that runs copiously down neck and brow. We don't carry the extra weight of water and are grateful for the clean-running streams and springs the land provides.

By the time we reach our first camp spot, it is evening and we are happy to just eat and rest, throwing out our beds to sleep at the base of a bare mountain, sparse of trees, free of smoke. Here, we consider, instead, the risk of sudden cold rain and rockfall. Ah, these raw elements that have taught us so much this summer. Our awareness brings new clarity and sharpness to the mundane.

We are alive. I inhale a deep breath of mountain air. Though fresher now, it is still tinged with the faint scent of smoke. Air, breath. Unconsciously we take in the air around us. The quality of the air we breathe and the way we breathe it will affect the quality of our lives. Inhale oxygen. Exhale carbon dioxide. That's what we creatures of the earth do. Conversely, the plant world inhales carbon dioxide and exhales oxygen. Perfect symbiosis. We take care of the needs of each other unconsciously.

Green.

That is the first thing I see when I open my eyes. Not something particular that's green, just green. It confuses me a little because I have my head under my buffalo robe and it is brown. When I peek out of the warm furs, I see that it is the bright green grass glowing in morning sunlight that penetrated the buffalo hide covering my face. Huddled forms of my companions surround me, someone stirs and lets out a sleepy sigh; perhaps they dream of the world they wish to create. I try to piece back my own dreams but they slip away furtively. The others slowly rise, grab a quick snack, rub sore muscles. We don't bother to make a fire, we will do it when we reach our destination.

We are happy, perhaps gloriously happy. Today's push over the narrow scree pass will set us up at our first base camp that we will come to call home.

Slowly we hike toward the pass. Those on foot shift the pack weight from shoulder straps to head tumpline and back again, gleaning lessons from the Indigenous mountain people of the high Himalaya. Gazing up to the saddle between the valleys, I feel a little trepidation for this next part of the journey that will lead us to our camp. The wildfires have become much more intense in recent years. I have a sense of responsibility for these young people; I am their leader, but I am hesitant, unsure with these worsening climatic conditions. The forest is below us now. It has gradually changed from thick, dense Douglas fir, much of it beetle killed and a virtual tinder nest for a greedy windblown forest fire, to dispersed larches, one of my personal favorite species with their deciduous needles that turn to gold and drop each autumn.

When we reach the tricky part of the trail, we stop to prepare it for the horses. Ben and I remove the awkward heavy panniers from Chaco's back. I go on ahead moving rocks and creating some steps where the trail has narrowed and broken away. We lead the horses across, one by one, rear hooves knocking scree that slides down the steep slope into the basin. A sudden false move would send them tumbling. With moccasined feet, we step carefully across ourselves. The difficult part is only about a hundred yards long but I breathe deep relief when we have passed safely. All is well. Falcon, Rick, and

Ben go back to bring the second load and we repack Chaco as he stands acquiescently for us. Dear Chaco, so strong, so willing.

Reaching the saddle between the mountains I look down the slope into the wild valley before us, high elevation meadows and alpine lakes teeming with wildflowers.

The scent of lupine sends me giddy with delight as we walk into a fragrant glade on the descent into the meadows. Blue gentians, barely blooming, red Indian paintbrush, splashing, boldly, brightly, with careless gaiety. Yellow composites, whose names escape me, purple asters and those already seeding, sending capsules of voracious longing to the four winds in hopeful optimism at the chance of life.

Gone are the frets and worries of life back home for the members of my clan; now only the simple needs that ask for food and warmth and water remain.

I know this valley and have been here several times before. I have wandered and explored more than fifty miles of this ridgeline and most of its valleys on both the east and the west sides. I usually scout the camps where we will stay for a while. They need to have a good source of water, fuel, grazing for the horses, and signs of game animals as well as plant foods to augment our prepared wild foods that we have so carefully harvested and preserved since the spring. Right now, we also need to have bare, open, rocky ground or a large lake to flee to in case the winds shift and fire does hurtle up the valley toward us. This valley has it all, including a series of lakes that flow into each other before cascading down a steep, narrow gorge and into the river below.

We choose a campsite close to the creek that comes seeping out from among the rocks just a short distance above us.

Water, hydration.

We thirst and we quench; we must or we die. The quality of the water we drink also directly impacts the quality of our lives. Our bodies and all the creatures and plants of the earth are largely made up of water. We drink, absorb, and inhale the moisture and the elements it contains; and we urinate, sweat, bleed, and weep it back onto the earth, exchanging and moving once more the waters in perfect symbiosis.

These clear streams, energized by movement as they tumble, are compelled by gravity toward the great oceans. The waters that surround us flow unimpeded across the land. The lakes, marshes, and streams run down to the rivers that flow out to the sea, where they culminate in their salty birthplace, evaporating and condensing into clouds; and with the assistance of the winds, they journey inland again, falling as rain or snow thus continuing an endless cycle.

Below the ground the earth's waters are no less miraculous, surfacing and disappearing in intricate unseen patterns.

Pollutants exist in all Earth's waters, but here in these pristine high mountain meadows all the surface water is drinkable. What a magnificent gift to be able to drink from any lake or stream. We are lucky. In many places that would not be possible.

Here and there small copses of larch and spruce trees provide us with plenty of fallen branches that we break into manageable lengths for the fire. The wood is dense and strong and will hold a coal in a banked fire all night long. There is plenty of open space, too, with rich, waving grasses that the horses munch hungrily as soon as we remove their packs and saddles. There is an advantage in being an herbivore; if only it was as easy for us humans to fatten and thrive on the abundance of simple green grass.

A firepit is scratched out on a bare patch of ground. I am not at all a fan of lining my firepits with rocks then leaving them dotted around the campsites throughout the wilderness. I prefer to scrape out a shallow pit, using a few rocks for balancing our clay pots on for cooking. Then clear it all away when we leave.

Rick pulls a fire kit from his pack and quickly drills an ember with the bow. He seems to have the most energy of everyone and entertains us as our little group relaxes around the fire, nibbling on quick, easy snacks of nuts, seeds, and dried fruits. Ali and Ben throw out their sleeping robes side by side. I have noticed for a while now how often they appear together in the mornings, surmising that an intimacy has grown between them. Although it's hard to imagine they might forge a long-term liaison, nothing could seem better for Ali right now than the care of this sweet man. It's common for these couplings to arise and now, seeing Falcon and Rick, cuddled up together, fingers interlaced, I wonder if they, too, are embarking on a new romantic exploration.

A huge smoke plume fills the afternoon sky to the north and, as the evening air cools at dusk, it colors the entire northern sky a muddy gray. The mosquitoes are out. Marcus and Jenny cook dinner in the big clay pot: wild rice, buffalo meat, and dried nettles. We sing together afterward, a strange concoction of animalistic sounds that belies our humanity. It's too late and I'm too tired to consider starting a shelter tonight so I make my way across the meadow, away from the rest of the group, and lie down in my buffalo robe sleeping bag. Even from this distance, I hear the renewed chatter of the young people. They are laughing and talking loudly and having fun. I'm glad for them, but I'm slightly irritated. I want peace. Now that the classes are over, my role as teacher and leader has shifted slightly; we are now essentially a group of friends and equals experiencing this journey together. They still look to me for guidance since I know these mountains and have at least twenty years more experience than most of them, but I'm tired of my role as teacher all summer. I need to rest and want to fall into the mesmerizing stillness that comes as we relinquish the busy thoughts that are tied to the modern culture from which we were so recently released.

Here is my holy land and I want to listen. Will she sing to me in the silence of darkness?

I awaken in the blue hour to the hum, the thrum of the earth. I hear her, high in these mountains, far from the polluting noise of our civilization. I match the tone and fall back to sleep, snuggled down in the buffalo robe away from the separate and distinct whine of mosquitoes.

I greet the first day. Sunrise. The air is warm, it caresses me. A few slow mosquitoes search for blood. Soft sounds of water flowing downward, downward, pulled by the inevitable forces of gravity. Slowly the mountains crumble. Whose voice wrestled through my consciousness last night by the dying embers? Mesmerizing in its foreignness, its truth, its power.

I have been reveling in my body, the comfort of movement, stretch, and gentle friction. A handful of soft ripe huckleberries, sensation after sensation as the sun rises higher and the ants grow active.

Movement. We were made to move, our bodies are exquisitely designed to run with the greatest persistence of any other creature on Earth. Without movement our muscles atrophy, our joints stiffen, our bones become brittle, our lymph and blood stagnate, our hormones and life force are depleted. It is to ourselves that we most owe the practice of regular stimulating exercise. We humans are lucky to have the ability to walk, run, stretch, swim, climb, and dance; and we are no less capable today of the admirable physical feats of our hunter-gatherer ancestors.

This is "trial week": the first seven days of our journey, the last transition of our rewilding. It basically means we can bring in anything we want in addition to our Stone Age gear; we still have to carry it, though, so it doesn't amount to much. Mostly it's nonwild foods, about ten pounds for each person. Dense, high-calorie foods like salami and cheese, which are quick to eat on the trail and don't require cooking. Most of us made up what we call energy balls or power mix that includes ground nuts and seeds, dried fruits and berries. They taste delicious. Mine has cashews, hemp seeds, cacao nibs, and coconut oil.

Food, nourishment. We fuel our bodies by the nutrients we absorb and digest. The quality of the foods we eat is no less important than the air we breathe or the water we drink. We eat, we defecate—this process is also symbiotic with the plant world, moving not only nutrients around but viable seed. When we disrupt this cycle, contain or condense it, the exchange becomes broken.

We love our foods and our habits and our preferences and addictions. What we eat and how and why we eat it is charged with so many personal reasons, traumas, and dogma. Our dietary health is directly proportional to the health of the land that we inhabit as well as the land where our food is produced.

Besides food, the group has some sewing supplies: needles, nail punches, and a pair of scissors. We will leave these behind after the trial week.

I have the commercially made packsaddle and two halters that I need to replace with rawhide or heavy moose hide rope before the week's end.

On the last day of this week, regardless of whether we shall physically move on yet or not, we cache all the nonprimitive gear for the rest of the trip with the exception of journal, pencil, one camera and batteries, extra bowstring, glasses, medications, and birth control. That's it. No phones, no matches, no GPS.

Our weather forecaster is the one who hikes to the ridge and comes back down to tell us what they saw. We watch and watch the sky,

noticing patterns, subtle shifts in breeze, temperature, cloud formation. Having lived for much of my adult life on the eastern slopes of
mountain ranges has taught me that the high, wispy cirrus clouds
can foretell the arrival of rain. They will often build in the afternoons then dissipate, then build again for several days. I have also
learned the folly of being too confident with weather forecasting. The
adage "If you don't like the weather, wait five minutes" is appropriate
in these mountains. Camping in this style does not allow carelessness; we have no plastic tarps to erect quickly in a sudden mountain
shower, and skin bedding and clothing must remain dry at almost
any cost. It would take days for a soaked buffalo robe to dry and risks
the hair slipping out.

The sun is up. I hear a horse nicker. It's Christy telling me it's time
to move her picket rope so they have a fresh place to graze. Chaco and
Karma are loose; they will not stray far from their lead mare.

I have had several horses in my life, but perhaps I will never love
another horse the way I love Christy. My first horse was a young,
sweet thoroughbred but he was so tall and a bit unfocused and
would often trip and stumble. When I sat my child up there on his
back it seemed like such a long way to the ground. One autumn
while my family and I were in Sweden, I got to ride a Haflinger, a
short, stocky draft breed, through some boggy, uneven ground. This
horse was the perfect size to put a kid on and his draft temperament
kept him steady as a rock. The Haflinger breed was developed in the
Austrian mountains, and these ponies are a mixture of the hardy
local mountain horses of that period and a single Arab stallion that
was the sire to the entire breed. Being small draft horses they were
bred to be versatile, calm, and easy keepers that could do small farm
work and the kids could also ride them to school. *Alas*, I thought,
these pedigreed horses are way out of my price range, but when we got
back to our home in Montana, a good friend had just started breeding

Haflingers and when I inquired he said I could buy a yearling and pay just $100 a month until he was paid off. I jumped at the chance and went to look at his herd and picked Chaco. I also borrowed a five-year-old mare for the winter while I did ground work with Chaco since he was still too young to ride. That's when Christy came into my life. She had been started in harness and under saddle with just a few weeks of training. Christy is a queen, the old-style Haflinger with short legs and broad chest. She has to trot to keep up with all the other horses when they walk, but what a trot. She is the most comfortable couch. I rode her all winter and was so in love that by the time spring came around, I knew I couldn't let her go. I found a neighbor who decided to buy Chaco instead, and for some years it was only me and Christy, together every day, learning, exploring, having our little tiffs and making up again. She has taught people terrified of horses to ride. I have put countless babies and small children on her back, up to six at a time! Four years after I sold Chaco, I got a call that he was up for sale again. He had been sold twice since he'd left my care. I went to check him out and was appalled. He was barely recognizable, thin, gaunt, depressed, his hair falling out. I took one look at him and said, "Don't worry, buddy, you're coming with me." I really wasn't sure if he was going to live, he had been so ignorantly neglected. He practically ran into the horse trailer to get away. I'm sure he could smell Christy all over me. Their reunion was marked with excited whinnies and exuberant racing around the meadow, which soon settled into a comfortable grooming session. So touching. Chaco quickly got his spark back with the good company and a lot of high-quality hay. I promised him I would never separate them again; they were in it for life. The gelded Chaco doesn't have the charisma of Christy, and his trot is just awful, the "butter churn" trot as I like to call it. But he's honest and dependable, a bit lazy but all around just a really good guy. In fourteen years with me these horses have done it all: been in parades, trekked in the desert, acted in a film, patrolled with the mounted security guards at a harvest fair. The only time I remember them really being upset was when two giant stilt walkers in flowing robes, fifteen feet tall, approached us at a parade and we had to steer a wide margin around such perilous beings. Compared to all their previous experiences, hauling packs on rocky slopes up a mountain in the wilderness doesn't faze them at all.

We have much to do on this first day at our base camp. Clouds in the early morning reminded me that I must look for shelter. Building a shelter in these high elevations using only natural materials and without the assistance of saws and axes is a time-consuming endeavor. The best option is to look for a tight stand of spruces whose conical shape and dense branch formation give natural protection from the elements. I decide to make a personal shelter. Last night, I encouraged the rest of the clan to focus on building, too, as soon as they can. This morning, they're quiet, still sleeping, and I sincerely hope they'll respond to my nudging that this dry weather will not last. Nor do we want it to. Please, let it rain.

Before I get to my own shelter building, I explore the area and familiarize myself with the resources and the lay of the land. Scouting the valley, I find an old trail that leads up toward the ridge. Compelled by the desire to see the endless peaks again that lay beyond, I follow it to the sun-glittering pass where a cool breeze and sharp rocks greet my bare feet. Glaciers and snowfields stretch before me; the mountains are my ocean, waves cresting, peak after peak as far as my eyes can reach. Twenty or thirty ravens swirl, tornado-like in the updraft. Who could not be moved by the magnificence of this land?

On the crumbling ridgetops a face appears with every angled contour, mighty beings, smiling, scowling, laughing, watching time, so meaningless, slip by through countless millions of years. And yet, each breath of wind that stirs the larch needles and trails a hair across my face is precious beyond all reason in this dazzling summer sunlight.

This is the mystery; it surrounds us constantly and we are part of it.

Would that every man, woman, and child entombed in urban cement could breathe a glimpse and knowing of this magic.

The trail continues down the other side and I make a mental note that it gives us another exit route with the horses from this basin in the event of fire. Below, from the direction of camp, I hear the sounds of branches cracking, telling me that the group is up and they've taken my advice to build shelter seriously. A wet storm and a drop in temperature are our biggest threats in this high country. Even in August while the sun is out, things can change suddenly. The wind blows from the northwest, from the fire across the river valley, and the air grows hazy.

I pile some slabs of broken, partially rotted fallen larch against a cluster of spruces as a shelter where I'll sleep tonight. It makes a little nook, somewhat protected from the possibility of rain. The trees are tall, though, and if a thunderstorm came roaring through it might send me scurrying out into the tempest. Many are the trees here that bear the jagged scars of lightning strikes.

———————————

The next morning, the wind has changed direction again. The sun is up, shining weakly through the smoky pallor. The earth is beneath me. Water springs from the rocks at the base of the scree and boulder fields, feeding lush meadows of lupines; but today the skies show no hint of coming rain and I lie here under my spruce shelter watching the smoke in the valley move in the direction of my cabin some ten miles away. It's hard to be present with the birdsong as I watch the smoke. I find myself thinking about whether I prepared everything I could back home for fire. Will someone move my truck? It has my driver's license in it and a few hundred dollars in cash. The art of my parents and friends on the walls of my cabin is irreplaceable. What would it be like to return to find the crumpled metal roofing strewn upon the ashy remnants of my home?

I wander down to the lakes. The first one has clear signs of people having camped and fished here before us. There are worn trails and bare ground and I wince at the rock-ringed firepits. It is deserted and I'm glad I don't have to explain myself and my unusual appearance or warily skirt the campers remaining unseen. The trail that leads on to the next lake is less obvious, and by the time I reach the lower lake another mile away, it's hard to discern a trail at all and signs of humans passing give way increasingly to the haphazard crisscrossing paths of the deer. I skirt the lake, heading for the boulders where the water is deeper, peering into the crystal clear pools and scanning the surface for the telltale rippling rings. I am looking for the fish. A month ago I was here for the first time, scouting for this journey, and the trout were abundant and less wary in this place off the beaten path so seldom visited by other people. I had gently and slowly reached beneath the water-drenched logs in the shallows near the outlet and stroked the silky bodies thinking to myself, *Don't catch them now, wait until we need them.*

Today the fish are absent, hiding in noonday sun, and I settle myself onto a soft bed of springy grasses and wildflowers. I wonder as I behold these strewn sharp boulders, if I were suddenly blinded could I find my way back to the meadow above where my clan, my food, my warmth and shelter would grant me another day? I half want to close my eyes and try but then I would probably stop at the fragrant flowers whose scent is so intoxicating and dwell in my sense of smell regardless of my vanished sight. My mind drifts away from this moment and I am roaming the faraway lands of my ancestors, lost in time, seeking that feeling of belonging, seeking broad, strong shoulders and calloused hands that are borne by a sentient being, seeking with mind the knowledge only heart can know.

I move from sun to shade seeking the cool breeze in the heat. Seeking, seeking, searching . . . Be still for all is here, now and always.

As a poet must, I love to string words together with intent to evoke the feelings of magic and wonder. And yet, I savor those moments of wordless awe and beg the words to give me another minute in priceless presence before they jostle for precedence once more in my unquiet mind. Rebel poet, know silence.

Back at camp my peaceful state is shattered by the commotion and activity of my clan, who are building a group shelter nestled under another stand of spruces. Ben is smashing branches against a rock to reduce their length and standing them side by side against the trunk of a large central spruce. It forms a conical design. Ali and Jenny arrive laughing, hauling armfuls of green spruce boughs that they have broken from several nearby trees. They take just a few from each tree to reduce the impact, then place them, shingle style, onto the walls to help shed the rain. Marcus, his vision obscured by a hefty load of poles, stumbles over Rick, who is prying rocks from the forest floor to create a flatter and more even surface to lie on. Falcon tests it out then rakes piles of needles and duff to make an insulative comfortable bed. All is happy, frantic pandemonium.

I love my people here. They are sweet and kind and young . . . but they are so noisy. They laugh and scream and yell so loudly sometimes that they startle me, making me think that something is wrong. I know why I resent this incessant noise. Civilization is so loud and brash and the mountains for me are the place to retreat, to leave the chaos behind. But here it is, still with me. Perhaps I should plan a solo trip for a full cycle of the sun from dawn to dawn or maybe one of the quieter ones would like to join me? I need to do it soon, though, to drop the old world and find myself in this new place, to be still.

I am twice the age of most of my clanspeople and I'm missing the companionship of more mature friends. Usually the immersion groups have a wider age range and there are often children who come with parents though it's rare for them to join the Stone Age journey. I wish Michel, Annabelle, and Etienne had joined us. It feels so much more like a village with children. The youngest ever to be part of the program was definitely Lauren's baby, who was in class within a week of being born! My most senior student was eighty-eight-year-old Uncle Lester who joined classes every week for the immersion phase. We used to pick him up with a horse-drawn wagon and drive him into camp since the trail was too rocky and uneven for the old man to walk in. He kept us in stitches with his silly jokes and I remember him saying that the key to longevity was to always learn something new.

———————————

The next day, Rick and I arise with the dawn, string our bows, and head up the ridge following pointed tracks on the dusty trail. The valleys surrounding us on every side are filled with thick smoke. Heading down another trail toward a distant meadow we know the tracks are fresh. Ahead of us we hear the pronking hooves of mule deer but we still don't see them. I stalk and shoot at a grouse but in a flutter of feathers it flies away. Sorry, grouse.

Ahead of me, Rick is hot on the deer trail, three big bucks with racks that show their wariness and age. They finally disappear into the forest. Ah, then the poor marmots, which we want to kill, but they are tough and quick and their holes are deep. Sorry, marmots.

We hunt in a wide circle that takes us over another pass back to camp. It was a fine day's hike but we bring no meat.

When I think food, I think meat. I think big game, deer or at least a fatty marmot or tasty grouse; even fresh squirrels are a fine addition to a meal. If the good meat is uncatchable, we will be sharing the mice we trap easily beneath our baskets of dried food supplies.

Grilled mouse, though not my first choice, becomes tolerable when hungry enough. First you gut the mouse quickly with a small razor-sharp sliver of obsidian (a type of glassy volcanic rock that has cooled slowly under the earth's surface). It's actually sharper than a razor. Then toss the mouse into the coals head, tail, and all. I like to turn it a few times to cook it evenly, then rub off the charred fur and pull off the feet and jaws so I don't chip my teeth on their hard teeth and claws. *Crunch, munch, munch*—three bites to a mouse. The head is crunchy and creamy, the middle is chewy, and the last bite is the best; we call it the rump roast.

The berries are scant. The pine nuts are off. The roots are finished. We must hunt and fish to supplement the greens that grow abundantly on every stream bank. In two days, the trial week will be over and we must start bringing in food if we are going to stay out here for many more weeks.

9

SUMMER CHILD

I peer over my round, swollen belly in an attempt to see my toes. They are obscured entirely. Nearly two weeks overdue and still no sign that this baby is ready to come out.

Clambering on my bicycle I make a little tour of the Swedish hamlet where we are staying at my mother's summer cottage: Klara's thorp as it is known locally, after the old woman who lived here and raised her many children alone. I try to hit all the potholes. If this baby isn't born soon, the doctors want to induce labor. "Come on, kid, let's go," I murmur, bumping along the gravel road. Up past the graveyard and old Klara's tombstone. Down through the neighboring farm, scattering chickens.

I came back to Sweden three months ago. I wanted to have my baby in a familiar place. I wanted to nest, I wanted to be near my mom. My partner, Ocean, the father of this child, joined me and we have been enduring a rainy Swedish summer, caught in that limbo, the waiting world where the coming birth event excludes all other thoughts, plans, and activities that aren't somehow related.

We went to bed that night, still no sign of imminent change.

I am suddenly awake. I check the clock, it's 2:00 a.m. Dawn's light seeps into the room from the small windows and birds are already trilling. A cow bellows in the distance. There it is again. A faint cramping in my abdomen. Did I imagine it? No, something has started. Ocean is still sleeping soundly and I get up quietly, careful not to disturb him. I pull on some clothes and creep out of the little cabin into the chill air. The sky looks promisingly clear. Dew covers the short grass and pools in the center of the lady's mantle leaves like drops of mercury. Over the rock wall, under the barbed-wire fence, I tread slowly, carefully, my bare toes wet and cold, then perch myself on a granite boulder that juts out of the grazed meadow. I turn my face toward the northeast where the sun will soon send its piercing shafts through the pine trees. "I'm going to have a baby today!" I can hardly believe it. Another tensing, gripping contraction pulses through me and I brace myself, holding my belly with suntanned hands. Am I ready to be a mother? Is anyone ever really ready? I'm twenty-seven, fit, strong, and healthy. My mind is unsure, but my body is ready.

I close my eyes as the first rays of sun spill over the hill through the branches and caress my eyelids. I feel the soothing warmth it brings, bathing my face in golden light. "Who are you, baby?" I secretly wish for a daughter, a daughter who may be as wild and reckless as she chooses, as free and supported in her passions and choices as I was not. I would never tell her she must restrain her impulses purely because she is a girl. The old neighbor couple are convinced I will bear a girl child but I am not so sure. I think that the being within me is probably a boy.

I will call him Thorsten, after the young man I'd known so briefly, who died at the age of twenty-six just four months after I met him.

The day goes on and on; every ten minutes my womb contracts, seized with mild requests for deliverance. I would prefer to give birth at home, creep into a sock drawer like a kitty and snuggle up in a corner with soft scents and sounds of the familiar. I am too scared to do it alone, though, and it's too expensive to bring a midwife home so we have opted for a birthing center, chosen a midwife, and invited family.

One thing I can say about Swedish birthing centers, besides being free, is that they are comfortable. It feels a bit like birthing in a midrange hotel with a personal Jacuzzi, the guests being myself, the father to be, my own mother and stepfather, my surrogate mother, Gullan, and Emma, who is now thirteen and still excited to hang out with me ever since our Jokkmokk adventure. On top of that we have two midwives who come and go as I labor in a not-exactly-cozy room, but at least there are pictures on the walls and it is devoid of hospital instruments. My guests take turns sleeping, showering, and eating. The expectant father has his own little bed in our room and is dozing.

I clearly remember the day I met Ocean just sixteen months before. I had been living in a tipi in a community in the Superstition Mountains in Arizona, learning plant medicine and desert survival techniques from Peter Bigfoot at the Reevis Mountain School of Self-Reliance. I'd come there after more classes at the Tom Brown Jr. Tracker School in New Jersey, arriving in the Sonoran Desert oasis some sixty miles east from Phoenix, literally following my dreams after one night's vivid image of an arrow pointing to the Southwest. It was during a period when I'd had a series of pertinent and provocative dreams. In one dream, I met my deceased paternal grandmother, a portly, practical little woman who in life was more captivated by British TV soap operas than anything remotely spiritual. She started telling me profound truths about the meaning of life that I couldn't grasp because her appearance was so contrary to the information she was transmitting. When I mentioned this, she said she only appeared in that form so I would recognize her but that her true form was entirely different, at which point she dissolved into a glowing golden egg. I awoke in wonder.

In another dream, I was back in the classroom at the Tracker School where I was informed by some nebulous forces that I had been chosen to be a healer but had to dedicate my life to it. I was given twenty-four hours to decide. What could I say? "Act now and ask later" has been a governing force for most of my life. I said yes, unequivocally, and made my commitment. From that moment in the dream I was sent to study with my mentor in the forest. Her name was Shuwa Awah and she was an Indigenous plant medicine healer. I was to live with her in her little shack and learn the art of healing. I awoke with the serene sense that my life's purpose had been sealed and I just had to participate in its unfolding.

For several years, as I embarked on my apprenticeship at Reevis Mountain School, I asked all the knowledgeable plant people I met if they had ever heard of this woman. They all said no, until finally, at a national Rainbow Gathering in Colorado, I met an esteemed author and herbalist and recounted my story. She looked at me kindly and said, "I think perhaps this woman you seek is the one that you will become yourself." I was shattered.

I recall the moment that Ocean came riding up to Reevis Mountain, a visitor passing through, on a gray mustang stallion, his long, curly brown hair streaming down his back and a beard to match flowing onto his chest. *I'm going to marry that man*, I thought to myself and was instantly, hopelessly drowning in incomprehensible longing to have a baby with him. Sitting by the river just two weeks into our love story, I watched the high spring floodwaters churning by and felt I was at the mercy of some invisible cosmic current because I was out of my depth and just trying to stay afloat for another gasp of air.

We were trying to make a baby. It was completely irrational but I was swept away by a will that seemed not to be my own. Ride it through, don't resist, flow with it.

Despite the apparent lunacy of our behavior, we were very conscious of conceiving a child in and with love. We talked to the spirit beings, invited one to join us, to teach us, show us, illuminate the world. There was no doubt in our minds that this invitation would be accepted and someone special would appear.

———————

The labor continues, gaining intensity, and a raw animal instinct takes control of me. I am clambering naked all around the room, trying to find a position that feels comfortable. I pace and lie down then roll around, then get up and pace some more. It is not moving quickly and I am frustrated and impatient when the midwife puts a belt around me to monitor the baby's heartbeat. They say I need to lie still but I don't want to. I feel like ripping off the monitor, snarling and charging, overcome by the power of it all. The hours tick by, my mother is beside me, breathing with me as the pain escalates and subsides for brief moments of respite. When at last the dilation is complete and the cervix is finally soft and open enough to allow passage, a wondrous change occurs. I am so expansive in every way, I feel as if I am connected to every mother who has ever lived or will ever live; we are linked across time and space, holding each other, understanding, knowing the mystery. It is sublime, complete, exalting. The urge to push comes with a rush of adrenaline. I am a lioness, I roar, I push, I roar. Then the women beside me are telling me to stop, the cord is around the baby's neck. With an immense effort I stall the pushing while the tight cord is released and the crowning comes with ripping and tearing, searing pain. I reach between my legs to feel the soft scalp of the infant about to be birthed. Another one, two pushes, extreme focused pressure, and the head explodes into the world, the rest of the tiny body slithering behind it in a gush of bloody fluids. Tremendous relief, I am almost laughing, but now we focus on the blue-colored being we will to breathe life, the gasp, the rush of color that instantly fills the little face.

Surprise, it's a girl!

I call her Klara-Liv; ready for life.

10

Last Frontier

When Klara was less than two years old I found myself yearning for clan. Just as quickly as I had fallen in love with Ocean, with equally alarming rapidity, I fell out of love with him.

That's it then, I thought to myself. *I'm going to be a nun.* But that sentiment dissolved with the meeting of a burly hide tanner the same summer. He smelled like chain saw gas and sour brains; I was hooked. Perhaps I wasn't going to be a nun after all.

We flirted with the idea of community and spent some weeks with friends arguing over whose turn it was to go to town and buy supplies (no one wanted to), then he and I and little Klara moved to his twenty acres in a remote part of northwestern Montana.

His place was in the foothills of the Rocky Mountains, off the grid, just a couple miles from the Canadian border, where the wilderness intermingled with logging roads and clear-cut forest. It is both wild and ranch land. Montana, the Wild West, the last frontier. For almost a decade, we lived in an eighteen-foot-diameter canvas yurt with a small loft that we built ourselves. We cut and burned firewood for heat and cooking. Simple living is perhaps an understatement—we weren't quite Stone Age—but we had no phone, no plumbing, and no electricity.

To connect with the outside world, we rode horses or bikes to the public phone at the Amish store three miles away. At least they had a hitching post there and doughnuts on Mondays. We wrote letters and mailed them in the mailbox at the bottom of our driveway. We had an old Ford pickup truck, but it didn't always run and we didn't always have the money to feed it or fix it. We had a couple neighbors and a good community of friends in the nearest town, but socialization was sporadic especially in winter when it depended on driving for almost an hour to get there.

We ate predominantly deer meat that we hunted ourselves and our own homegrown vegetables plus a few basic store-bought food staples and made a very small income tanning and selling hides.

My husband was a hunter and I felt it was time to learn to bring meat to the table myself. Before my first deer hunt, I made a prayer: "Teach me everything I need to know about taking life." It was a hard lesson, that frosty November morning in Montana, my feet crunching as silently as feet crunching can be, the first deer and the peace-shattering bullet that missed. Later, two does cut diagonally down the slope toward the creek, unaware of my presence. The raised rifle, the long shot considered, and the slow squeeze of the trigger.

The crisp November air fragmented into slow-motion scenes as the doe fell and started crawling desperately on her front two legs, paralyzed in the rear. I shot again, shaking, my shot missed. I shot a third time and missed again. I realized at this point that I had only one more bullet in my rifle. I ran down the bank and across the creek to get closer. Now I could see the panic in her eyes. I made careful aim at her head, pulled . . . *click*. Nothing. I had miscounted. I was out of bullets. Shaking and crying I thought about my prayer "everything I need to know about taking life." Would I have to kill her with my knife? Then, just as this grim reality started to sink in, I heard the sound of an angel coming to my rescue. The angel was driving a full-size pickup as angels tend to do on Montana back roads. I ran back up the hill and waved it to a stop. The window rolled down and a blue-haired, kindly looking older woman gazed out at me.

I blurted out my story . . . shot and wounded a deer and run out of bullets. I didn't really know what to expect. "What caliber?" she drawled. ".30-30," I answered. Incredulous, I watched her open a giant container full of bullets, rummage around and hand me one, then drive away without another word. The bullet does its job. I am spared. Blood stains the snow together with my tears.

After I killed that first doe, I skinned and gutted her there in the snow. I spent that entire winter using every single scrap of her body. Her flesh and organs fed my family; her bones became tools, beads, a flute; her hooves a rattle; and her skin part of a red buckskin dress that I still wear.

There was one winter I call the potato winter, where we were dead broke and the truck was too. We had a hole we'd dug underground for our root cellar and because we'd helped a farmer friend with his commercial potato crop it was stuffed with potatoes but very little else.

Since town was so far away, Klara was homeschooled. I had no inclination to set her on a bus for three hours a day, sending her off to what I considered a highly dubious education anyway. I taught her to read and write and then asked her what she wanted to learn and we would sled piles of library books up the driveway. Math was not my forte so when our arithmetic books got to a fifth-grade level, she was on her own. She was a self-motivated student, though, and it was more often than not that we would have to encourage her to stop reading and go and play outside. "And don't forget, if you see a mountain lion, pull your jacket up behind your head and look as big as possible."

The toughest part of raising a wild child was the social aspect. There was only one other kid nearby who was also homeschooled and they became friends by default. I often heard them bickering like an old unhappily married couple, "It's my turn to choose what to play, so it's army." That would be Charlie and off they would march into the trenches again until the next day when Klara would have her way and it would be dress-up, which made me chuckle because, unlike myself at her age, she actually loved to wear dresses.

Every morning, we two adults would start the day by running fifty meters down to the creek where we would bathe. In winter we kept a hole broken open in the ice. There we would plunge in for a few mind-stopping, time-shattering moments. I must say, there is nothing so conducive to finding presence than this. One cannot ponder or think anything at all. We did not have a thermometer, but winters in the Rocky Mountains could often drop below −30 degrees (around this point Centigrade and Fahrenheit come to a convenient equality). Instead, we marked the temperature with "nose prickling days" when an inhalation gives that prickly sensation on one's nasal hair or, even colder, "frozen hair days" when during the fifteen-second sprint back from the creek to the warmth of the woodstove one's hair becomes a brittle sheet of ice that could be snapped and broken.

I always rode Christy bareback, broad and comfortable like having a heated seat. Riding a horse in subzero temperatures has both benefits and drawbacks. On winter rides I would start to get frozen fingers, and I'd have to get off and walk or run for a bit to get the circulation moving again, but I often delayed that moment by letting go of the reins and just burying my fingers in the warm hair under her mane and against her neck. I train my horses to foot rein so with a gentle nudge on one flank or the other I can turn them in the direction I want to go. When it was really cold I just wrapped myself right over her to get as much body contact as possible. There were times when I'd become hopelessly lost in the maze of old logging roads that crawled around the foothills and then I'd just give in and say, "Christy, take us home," and she would. Horses have an uncanny sense of direction and even if their route is sometimes circuitous, they always eventually seem to know where the hay barn is.

When I rode Christy, Chaco would run along behind when he was a youngster. Once, when we were cantering up the trail back toward home, I noticed something lying motionless on the ground ahead of us. I pulled up beside a dead deer. I cast some furtive glances around the nearby trees. Dismounting and holding the reins in one hand I lifted the leg of the deer and saw that it was floppy soft, rigor mortis hadn't set in yet. This was a really fresh kill. I felt nervous standing there and that was when I saw movement from the corner of my eye, the flicker of tawny brown in the thick bushes not more than half a dozen yards away. Lion! No doubt about it. I slowly and deliberately climbed back onto Christy and rode away, talking to the cougar as we went. The horses must have known it was there, too, but they never spooked. My husband and I went back later with a rifle and gutted the deer out. Left it for the night to see if the cougar would come back for it or not, wondering if I'd scared it off, in which case there was a perfectly good carcass lying there for some other carnivores to eat. The following day we returned and though the gut pile had been partially buried, the rest of the carcass was untouched so we claimed it for ourselves. Thanks, cougar.

I trained the horses to pull, and they proved to be both our entertainment on horse-drawn sleigh rides, as well as our horsepower when they were used to haul wood and water, clear snow and get us out to the nearest road when the truck had long since stopped managing to make the trip.

We hitchhiked a lot. There is no better hitchhiking partner than a cute little five-year-old. When we heard the infrequent sound of an approaching vehicle, I'd say to Klara, "Get your magic thumb out." She would stick it out and blow on it, completing the spell, and without exception the car would stop and take us to town. It didn't even matter what direction they were headed, they would turn around and go back to town sometimes, beguiled by Klara's magic thumb.

Winters were long and dark. We dipped beeswax candles and burned deer tallow fat lamps for our light. Imagine a night walk in the dead of winter under a potent, bright moon. Beaver-tailed snow-shoe tracks undulating in your wake. Like the glitter of a thousand icy campfires, moonlight reflecting on each snow crystal.

I had skied as a kid in Sweden, but it wasn't until I moved to Montana that I really fell in love with the snowy winter landscape.

My husband and I took a class one year and made ourselves a pair of skis from birchwood. They had simple leather bindings that one strapped to one's boots, which didn't make for very effective turns, but to steadily glide across the snow with such a pleasing rhythm—pole, swish, pole, swish, pole, swish—was a kind of meditation as well as exercise and a fine way to see what other creatures were moving about in the forest.

I have a picture of myself aged about four sitting in the snow with a tangle of skis and poles around me. My first pair of skis were red. I'd received them for my birthday. My uncle took me to a ski hill in Sweden where I clearly recall that inaugural slide, no time to learn to slow or stop but with the enthusiasm of a four-year-old and the certainty of success, skis pointed downhill, I gained momentum and ended jubilantly wrapped up in a small fence.

During those winter months, while my mother sat inside crying over her recent separation from my dad, my uncle played with us: my sister, baby cousin, and myself. I can still hear my tiny, exuberant voice yelling, "Let's build snow horses! I want to build snow horses, then we can ride them." He built us all a snow horse. It's no surprise that two of my favorite things to do in my adult world include skis and horses.

I still love to celebrate my birthday skiing. One year, when the truck was still running, for a special treat we drove north and crossed the border into Alberta for a change of scene. As usual, we didn't have a really specific plan, just hoped to find some logging road heading up a mountain somewhere and then get out and ski. Pulling slowly around a corner we were confronted by a large cat sitting on the road. A really large cat. In fact, a lynx cat. We stopped and the lynx, without any great hurry, got up and trotted to the bank, jumped into the deep snow, and disappeared into the forest. Wow! A lynx for my birthday. That was the most memorable of birthday presents and still the only wild lynx I have had the fortune to meet since taking on my name in my twenties.

Our mailbox was at the end of our driveway, which was about two miles long. One winter morning I put on my skis to head down to check the mail. It was a mild day and it started out just fine, but as I neared the mailbox a thick, heavy, warm, wet snow began to fall. This kind of snow sticks to the skis and stops the slide and glide altogether. I made it to the mailbox and turned around in what had become a serious snowstorm. Now the joy of gliding back to the yurt with a pocketful of letters had become a slow, exhausting trudge as with every step a heavy, sticky layer of snow pressed onto the undersides of my skis. These layers built up with each subsequent step until I was compelled to stop and stamp them off only to repeat the process all over again. I tried removing the skis and carrying them but the snow on the trail was deep and I quickly realized that postholing through thigh-deep concrete would wear me out long before I reached home. It's strange how quickly conditions can change with snow and make what was usually a twenty-minute jaunt into a laborious and exhausting trial of a couple of hours. I seriously wondered if I would make it home at all, and by the time I got back I was so beat, I collapsed.

11

Cave of Angels

On Smoky Mountain, the morning dawns and the spotted horse nudges me, her nose under my buffalo robe. I yawn and stretch, ready for a new day. I watch Karma as she grazes peacefully close to me and recall the remarkable way that she entered my life. I have always loved horses. I love to bury my face in the coarse hair of their manes as they methodically graze between clumps of fresh grass, their unique earthy scent mingling with that of the grass that their chewing unleashes. The language of horses, as prey animals, is not always gentle. I have learned much about hierarchy and acceptance by watching them control and dominate each other. They challenge me to think on animal terms instead of human ones and they, in turn, invite me into their way of seeing the world. I have owned many horses but I have felt a special bond with a certain few. Christy is one. Karma is another. The events that caused our paths to converge were seemingly unrelated but cause and effect are not always obvious until the story has come full circle.

———————<>———————

One prophetic loop in the endless spiraling circle came when I finally was able to buy my own piece of land in Washington State on the Twisp River. I had thought to myself, *Now I can stay here forever*. But no sooner had the end come into sight, the dream actualized, when the insatiable wanderlust stirred me again and lured me off to new lands and adventures. There are so many mountains to love. So many valleys to roam. After years of teaching in the US, some of my European students convinced me to come back and teach. So there I was finishing up teaching a class in the forested mountains of eastern Italy in an undeveloped cave known as the Cave of Angels. There's a local tale that a goblin hid a marvelous treasure there. A man dreamed of the treasure and took his baby son to go dig it up. Laying his baby on the floor of the cave he started to dig intently but as the hole grew deeper, his baby sank to an equal depth without his father even noticing. Finally the man found the treasure and saw that it was in fact the face of his son. Looking up with alarm he saw that his baby boy had disappeared into the earth, only a tuft of hair remaining. This, too, vanished as the man realized the true treasure he had lost.

On the last day of the class, I led my students on a drum journey in the entrance of the cave tunnel. One of the students had brought a simple hand drum. I had never led a drum journey myself before and it was with an impulsive urge that I now prompted the students to close their eyes and let the drumming take them. I, too, was transported.

That night, I knew I would make my own sacred drum someday. I was capable of building it myself, but it felt important to have a guide to assist me. It felt bigger than just the act of physical creation. But finding my drum mentor would come years later in the Arctic regions of Sweden. For now, I was fascinated by caves and by the rhythmic beating deep within the earth.

Alone in the cave, after my students had left, I took the lamp that

I'd made from clay and filled with the fat of the sheep we'd killed and butchered a few days earlier and crawled up the slippery narrow passageway. I wanted to give thanks within the womb of the mother. I had not been this far inside the cave before, but I had heard from locals that there was a maze of tunnels that went deep into the mountain and some of them dropped suddenly in places making it rather dangerous. I squirmed up a particularly slippery slope holding the lamp before me. As I reached level ground, I found myself in a small chamber with several tunnels leaving it in different directions. That was when the wick of my lamp slid down into the molten fat and extinguished, leaving me in pitch darkness.

I had a moment of panic. I had no other light, nobody knew I had come in here, and I could no longer see the tunnels around me. Which one would lead me back into the daylight?

Biting back fear, I took a few deep breaths and reassured myself that I had just crawled up from the tunnel that was closest to me. I reached my bare toes out in the darkness and touched . . . a wall. Slowly feeling along the wall, I located an empty space; surely this was the tunnel from which I had come? I forced myself to stay calm and uttered my thanks before gingerly making my way back down the slope. I was naked and the soft damp clay covered my body as I slipped and slid in both wonder and fear for several minutes until the dim light of the world penetrated this earthly womb.

The experience in the Cave of Angels, coupled with the power of the drum journey there, led me on a string of cave visitations over the coming years. I had been drawn to the region of Dordogne, France, a World Heritage Site, home of numerous prehistoric painted caves, and there found the perfect place to run some of my own programs. I posted my desire on my website to find a teaching location in France and was contacted by a man who took it to heart to find that place for me.

A couple of months later I was standing in a meadow in southern France, Ferme de Fonluc, a place steeped in my DNA. A magnificent limestone rock that looks like a mammoth stood before me. It sheared off the cliffs, who knows how many thousands or millions of years ago. The man who was giving me the tour of his land had a ruddy complexion and weathered good looks. He was the steward of this place along the river. When we first met, I wondered if perhaps we might have known each other about twenty thousand years ago in some past life.

I always wonder whether a single event can change one's life path and whether it is predetermined, choice or chance? The first meeting with this man who rapidly became a dear friend and whom I secretly call the Gypsy Warrior was one such event. He spoke with a thick German accent, telling me the mysterious way that he came to be here some thirty years before. His English made for some amusing and sometimes confusing anecdotes and his perspectives weren't confined to the boxes that shape the ideas of the masses; for example, when I lost my voice once he told me, "Ah, very good, you have said some important things and now it is time to listen."

It was the Gypsy Warrior who told me to talk to the trees. "The trees you see, their branches are like antennae reaching into the sky and their roots are all connected beneath the soil. Find one and whisper to it what is your heart's desire and your words will ripple out all around the earth."

Even now, when I consider which tree to speak to I am drawn to the elders, those that have stood the passage of time and the whining saws. Surely the old ones will carry my message?

"This is Mammut." He pointed with a calloused farmer's hand at the monolith with ivy growing up from its base accentuating the form of legs and trunk. "The people used to hunt them here. I have found old spear points when I raked the meadow." He spoke in a way that made me half believe that we had traveled fifteen thousand years back in time. We walked up a slope alive with joyful blooming primroses and the glow of sweet chestnut and hazel leaves to stand beneath a great overhang, protecting the dusty ground at our feet from rain and storm. The cliff above us was layered with shelves that could be reached only by a series of ladders. "Imagine a cave lion," said the extraordinary man beside me. "He cannot climb these ledges and the clan will be safe here during the night." He pointed to the rough poles that could be used to ascend the first tier and added, "You never forget the first time you see a cave lion!"

There were many unexcavated caves in the area. We continued up a forest trail, along another ledge, and arrived at a cave that penetrates the rock and clay behind it, petering out some forty yards within where he and his family had been digging, wondering if another prehistoric treasure might be awaiting rediscovery deep within.

Looking out over the meadows beside the muddy brown meandering Vézère River, we watched his herd of spotted horses grazing peacefully. I thought of my own dear horse friends Christy and Chaco, back home along the Twisp River getting older, and wondered how much longer they would be able to follow me into the mountains. We stood there looking over the valley and fell silent. I closed my eyes and called forth in my imagination a spotted horse, a young mare. She was so vivid in my mind that I sensed her warm breath on my cheek and envisioned us galloping bareback across these meadows. "Imagine this valley, a haven during the last Ice Age, no trees but vast steppes populated with herds of migrating reindeer and horses." The Gypsy Warrior took me back to a distant time, and I shivered as goose bumps rose on my arms. Something was happening inside me.

I spent a week exploring the forest nearby and visited a cave called Font-de-Gaume near the village Les Eyzies. It's one of the last prehistoric painted polychrome caves open to the public. A guide led our small group inside and along the narrow passageway. When we reached the first painting of two reindeer, one tenderly licking the face of the other, I pretty much just fell apart. Tears streamed down my face and didn't stop. Seeing the way the artists used the rock formation to add depth and form, imagining being here with the flickering light of a tallow lamp as I had in Italy, and considering the animals leaping into life as the light and shadows played them into movement. What brought our ancestors to such a place to express themselves like this? Were they illustrating scenes witnessed in dreams or reality? Teaching or entertaining or remembering? Praying or honoring? Could they have been manifesting their reality by giving life to the beasts on the walls before the hunt? We can only wonder, imagine, and be touched. If anyone has ever doubted that the ancients were not as fully human or capable as our modern variety, they must witness this. Bearing witness, I feel my perception of reality in time and space shift.

———————◄————

I cannot get this place out of my head. The Gypsy Warrior and I plan my class at Fonluc. Standing alone beside the head of the monolith Mammut, I pick a small piece of limestone from his craggy side and place it into the medicine pouch around my neck. Sealing my fate, I ride one of the spotted horses and write a song for the horse who will come to me, for this land, this rock, and this legendary human being, the Gypsy Warrior.

THE SHAMAN AND THE MAMMOTH
Chestnut trees, damp leaves,
Frost lies on ancient lands,
Broken spears, countless years,
Stones uncovered by time-traveled hands.

What is gone lives on, shrouded in sacred mystery,
The wise one, he listens, recounting our history.

Layered in rock, layered in time,
What's lost in one realm is found in mine.
Graceful curves carved in limestone ceiling,
Painted beasts in caves revealing.

Bring me a spotted horse, with no saddle,
Bring me a wooden boat, with no paddle,
The mammoth smiles his secret smile,
The shaman walks his hundredth mile.

Bring me a spotted horse with no tether,
Bring me a wooden boat in unsettled weather
Watch me ride the wild wind, with no fear.
Watch me sail the rugged waves, for a million years.

At his feet, I speak his name . . .
Mammut, Mammut, Mammut.

Two weeks later I am back home and I have found her. I call her Karma.

Karma is a sweet, young Appaloosa filly, envisioned on the other side of a great ocean. I knew she was coming. "Bring me a spotted horse with no saddle . . . " I read *Pippi Longstocking* as a kid, about the strongest girl in the world. She had a spotted horse. I wanted to be like Pippi. Guess I still do.

So upon my return to the American West from France, I went to look at a herd of Appaloosas. She wasn't the prettiest of them all, this gangly, unbroke teenager, but she came up to me. She liked me. I wanted to check her out, away from the others, and see her move a little, get a feel for who she was. The only way to take her that day was through a barn that had about thirty huge barking dogs penned up on both sides of the aisle. She had never walked through there before nor even ever been away from the herd. I whispered in her ear, "If you are my spotted horse, will you follow me through this?" It was a big deal. It was intense for me, too. We walked through the gauntlet together, she trusting me. When we came out the other side, I had tears running down my face; she'd chosen me. "Let's go home."

<hr />

During the months that I teach my wilderness skills courses in France, I live in the cave known as the Neanderthal cave at the farm of the Gypsy Warrior. I use it mostly for my personal space to retire to after long days of teaching and human interactions. There are several caves and rock overhangs on his land and the aesthetics of these natural shelters, coupled with the practicality of being outside and still remaining dry, make them perfect natural classrooms. A dozen or more people can craft by the firepit, cook, play, and sleep in their generous spaciousness. Although it is just a short walk to the heart of the village and the sounds of farm life and roads are amplified by the reflecting walls above and behind us, it is still easy to imagine this place long before our current civilizations' noise and bustle. All the evidence of modernity can be diminished by delving deeper into the cave interiors where sound and light is finally obliterated and replaced by absolute darkness and silence or the faint dripping of subterranean water. These waters have carved out the limestone in their sometimes slow but eventful play. What an exquisite carver the underground waters have been, patiently eroding the soft limestone over millennia to produce these magnificently decorated caves that are often purely adorned with the marks of nature. Stalactites and stalagmites, sometimes meeting and creating majestic pillars of glistening calcite. No wonder the ancient hunter-gatherers who hunted these valleys added their own marks to many of these cave walls some thousands of years ago. As far as anyone living knows, the Neanderthal cave does not bear any ancient paintings or engravings, but who can tell how far down and back this cave actually goes? The excavation of sand and clay in the tunnel behind me has been minimal over the last thirty years and ancient works of cave art are constantly being rediscovered.

I have several different areas in the cave that I choose to sleep in, depending on either the temperature or my mood. When it's cold outside, I retreat deeper to a flat place where the cave has narrowed and the warmth of the earth penetrates the air around me. Usually, though, I sleep close to the entrance or outside it on the ledge that is still shielded from the rain by the overhang above.

The ground is sandy and though the humidity is high, I remain more or less dry in spite of the ambient moisture. Regularly I must hang up my bedding and sleeping skins to let them dry out a little in the airflow.

Awakening in the predawn light with the other inhabitants of the cave still active, I flirt with the bats. I like to stick my arm out of my bed and feel the air ripple past my hands and face as they feed on insects with their erratic flight patterns until the light becomes too bright and they retreat to their own sleeping quarters in the dark chambers and fissures behind.

One morning, I lay musing just inside the cave in one of my customary favorite places, quiet and still, not yet ready to arise. As I was studying the shapes on the rocks around me a movement came suddenly into my peripheral vision. I remained motionless as a roe deer entered the cave and in an absolutely calm and unhurried manner walked past my bed, barely a few feet away; without giving me as much as a glance, he disappeared around the corner into the tunnel of the cave. I then sat up to peer after the animal, admittedly rather surprised by this unexpected visitor to my bedroom. Just a few moments later he returned and now fixed his attention on me and came closer to study the being that had manifested itself in such a short time. I sat stock-still in silence, and we had a second or two of mutual appraisal before the deer continued in his steady and unhurried way back out of the cave.

Just before disappearing again from sight, having apparently not yet sated his curiosity, he turned again, and came back to study me a little more. Finally satisfied and convinced of who knows what in his deer mind, he calmly left in the same direction from which he had arrived. These kinds of encounters always make me wonder if there is some message hidden in them.

Beneath the limestone cliffs there is an ash tree that the Gypsy Warrior calls Yggdrasil after the Tree of Life in Nordic mythology. The mythological tree has three wells springing from its base, representing wisdom, fate, and the source of rivers. This ash tree here also has a spring nestled between its vaulted roots, and in the fall the salamanders come creeping out and head into the forest. Around here there are fire salamanders, big, flashy black-and-yellow creatures, prehistoric amphibians that are so befitting this land with its ancient history. One damp night as I lay in the brown leaves shielded from the persistent rain by the enormous limestone overhang known as Roc Simon, I heard scuttling around me. Turning on my headlamp I came face-to-face with two salamanders that were locked in what could have been either an embrace of love or conflict. I watched them, mesmerized, and some minutes later became aware of another one close to my head, then another and another. Finally, I was surrounded by seven salamanders moving slowly around and over my bed. I didn't know what to think; the tussling had ceased and they no longer seemed specifically interested in each other. Somewhere in my mind I thought I recalled that one shouldn't touch fire salamanders, that they exuded some kind of poison on their skin as a protective mechanism, but they seemed so at ease, not at all worried by my presence or light, and after a while I reached out and stroked one. For a couple of hours I lay there caressing and talking to these mysterious amphibians and finally asked them to move from my bedding so I could go to sleep without fear of crushing them. Throughout the night I would wake periodically and find one not far away watching me. *Send me a dream salamander*, I said. *What message do you have for me?* And the salamander did.

I was in a building with many local friends and neighbors. I was a young Frenchwoman. Tension was palpable and a wave of distrust swept through us as two German soldiers entered and demanded that we all produce and show our identification papers. I was gripped in fear. I had papers but I knew that showing them would be my undoing. My companion took my arm and told me it would be all right, just give them the papers. The soldiers moved among us, checking each person, and when I was finally obliged to show my own, he paused and scrutinized them closely then pulled me toward the door.

I woke up with a racing heart.

I was confused and shaken and took my experience and dream to the Gypsy Warrior as soon as I had a chance.

He listened to me thoughtfully then told me that during the Second World War people had sought refuge and hiding among the cliffs and caves at Roc Simon; it was an area where the resistance was active due to the natural shelters and abundant wild foods. Perhaps the fighting salamanders were reminding me of another time? Another life?

Time travelers, what is back and what is forward? Is there any such thing or are we spiraling in an infinite, eternal cosmic dance, the in breath and the out breath of God?

With my clan at Smoky Mountain, as I have come to call it, we circle every night to eat and recount the happenings of the day. Some days we walk alone, but often we craft or do little projects together. Falcon has been sewing herself a fur hat and I sit with her while I mend my moccasin sole, restitching it with sinew and a bone awl.

Community, belonging. We are not solitary creatures.

Even in these days when basic needs are easily met for the lone individual in Western civilization, no matter how self-reliant one feels socially, without connection to other human beings, sharing workload, ideas, concepts, touch, and love, we will wither and shrink in some core part of our beings. Cooperation as a clan, tribe, or perhaps even a species gives us an enormous advantage in almost every way over the individual. Elemental resources are much more easily obtained within a group whose size is proportional to the abundance that the land has to offer. Moreover, tedious or strenuous chores are more pleasantly and safely experienced when shared by a group of communicating individuals. Having empathy for each other, the thoughts and vocal ability to express complex concepts and feelings may sometimes give rise to miscommunication but overwhelmingly serves us in the greater picture of collaboration and cooperation.

There is abundant time and space to act, discover, rest, or play in company or solitude out here for our little clan. Tonight we meet in the group shelter.

We speak of death and the afterlife and mysterious, inexplicable things.

A question is posed by Louis, "Do we come here to this pristine and fragile environment to just take? What do we have to give?"

Everyone speaks in turn. Everyone has a slightly different intention, but in wholeness we are one. To kill or not to kill?

To see the direct impact we make on the land or to acknowledge the indirect impact in our daily civilized lives?

To share thoughts and emotions or to sit quietly alone with them?

Purpose, meaning. What is the point of being alive? Our lives must have meaning or purpose whether it simply be to raise children, feed our families, and enjoy the small moments of peace and tranquility or we might just as well not exist. These larger existential questions seem to have always baffled and troubled us giving rise to innumerable religious, spiritual, and hedonistic propensities.

Having a focused purpose provides a reason to be, to get up in the morning, to continue through the moments of doubt and sinking desperation. To toil through the anger, sadness, hurt, and fear that our lives are also subject to. Whatever one's spiritual inclination, we still need something to hold sacred. It's part of our humanity.

This land, this world away from the madness, brings up uncertainty, deep questioning, and introspection. We act like society's refugees. We are in shock, suddenly unable to function in this new land.

After so many weeks, months, of busy preparation, it can take time to shift into the new pattern of just living, moment by moment, day by day, week by week without a goal or agenda. This discomfort can last a few days and has to be pushed through. Have patience, I say as much to myself as to them, it will come.

It's not unusual to feel untethered as we slide into Stone Age mode. It has taken many years for me to accept that there will be an adjustment period as we adapt to this way of living that usually comes around the fourth or fifth day for most people.

I call it the "adjustment day slumps." Gone is the euphoria, the peace, tranquility, and passion for being here. The coming weeks seem like a sentence.

One can feel lonely and depressed, uninspired, unmotivated, sick of eating dried meat, fish, and berries and stringy onions with gobs of fat thrown in.

I'm not immune to these feelings, either; sometimes I'm just crazy for distraction . . . fresh greasy meat like lamb, tantalizing tastes and spices, a cuddle with my sweetie, a good book or even going out to a movie.

Right now, I don't want to see another flattened mouse or another seven-inch trout. I imagine a trip to town, an ice cream bar, a big wad of millet or rice pasta dripping with olive oil and garlic with grated Parmesan all over it and hot sauce.

Food fantasizing, it gets to us all at one point or another.

I don't want to poke my bare feet on sharp sticks. Give me sunshine, blue skies, and energy to explore.

I want to look outside of myself again and see beauty and purpose. *Oh, please, let this be food adjustment that will settle down in a day or two.*

I sit with my clan. The night stillness and silence is broken by voices singing, first deep and low, harmonies layering one upon the other, jumbled as the jagged rocks. Stories unfold, thick as mosquitoes, of distant lands and lost times. Jenny tells us about the meditation retreat she made in India some years ago, how she notices parallels between the long hours of quiet meditation and being out here without the distractions of the world. She says she's starting to feel her mind settle. Marcus remembers a trip he made to Mexico with his family when he was a young boy and how the poor children begging on the streets had upset him, and he couldn't understand why his parents walked past without noticing them. Without doing anything. He wonders out loud what would happen if we had brought homeless people from the city streets out here, how would they react to this wilderness? Is it our privilege that allows us to spurn our cultural upbringing? Our thoughts return to the fires burning nearby and a new theme develops. Rick tells us a story of how he and a friend, in their teenage years, had been out camping and how accidentally their campfire got away from them, started burning in the surrounding brush, how scared they had been as they had tried and finally succeeded in putting it out and how supervigilant he has been ever since. One of the students has a tale of youthful ignorance, how she and the neighbor kids built a straw bale fort in the meadow on a friend's farm, how they had lit a candle in it, left it burning as they ran off to play and the resultant bonfire, though harmless, scorched a tremor of fear in her ever since.

I recall running alongside my father, my little hand in his, as we went to look at a house that had caught fire near our street. There was a crowd of people standing and watching. It was evening and the flames and sparks flew wildly up into the night sky. How the fire truck came screeching in, sirens wailing, to put it out but they couldn't and it all burned down to the ground. I had never seen such a fire. The strangest thing of all, though, was remembering my father's wristwatch that was right in line with my face. It didn't have any numbers on it, just the hands, and I couldn't tell the time yet. It had a red-and-black-striped strap and while the house was burning I was wondering if he would let me wind it.

The element of fire demands respect, each of us has learned through our intimate connection with it that we shall do well to heed its demands.

We sing to the moon as she arrives pregnant and glowing.

--------◄

Louis, Falcon, Ali, and Ben sleep in late, long after the sun has risen. I let them be, they need it.

Sleep, rest, and relaxation. I'm not sure how long we can live without the restful rejuvenation of the body and mind. Without regular sleep we become anxious and start to lose grip of our sanity. Lack of sleep causes judgment impairment and we're more likely to choose unwisely, behave poorly, erupt in anger, be careless and sloppy, and succumb to avoidable accidents. Without proper sleep we cannot give the nervous system its necessary cycles of deep sleep and REMs that keep us healthy, active, and positive.

Living in a modern environment that is full of stimulating noises, lights, and frenetic activity is certainly not conducive to deep rest. I've noticed that many of my students when they come into the woods to live want to sleep. They are also surprised at how vivid and numerous their dreams become, easily recalled when they have time to awaken naturally and slowly. I believe that consciously recalling our dreams is vital to the recognition and understanding of our subconscious fears, needs, and desires and that we have much to learn from the time we spend sleeping.

We are such sensitive beings and I have noticed over and over that when you bring an urban person into nature they don't notice much at first; they have been so conditioned by necessity to numb their senses to all the stimulation that surrounds them. It's a protective measure—they have to or they'd go mad. After a while, though, and it can take a few weeks, they gradually relax and become aware of subtle movements, sounds, and changes in the environment, nuances we would have had to be aware of in our ancient, natural human state where we must hunt to eat or be eaten. All predators and prey in their natural state have razor-keen senses as a matter of survival. Unfortunately, when those refined senses are dropped back into the madness and stimulation of daily city life, they quickly become overwhelmed and are forced back into numbness to maintain some form of sanity.

———➤———

In the morning, my doubts, cravings, and despair of the previous day have vanished. In an instant they're replaced by excitement. A doe is licking my pee spot, within shooting range. She wanders off a little, among the horses. I dress in wild cat furs, string my bow, and grab stone-tipped arrows.

Then we dance. We dance—deer, horses, and huntress. She wants salt, they want grass, and I want meat. I can get close, very close with my grass-eating buddies beside me. I pretend to nibble on the grass myself, crawling at the edge of the meadow. Not close enough. The doe will come back for more salt tomorrow and I will be more ready.

Jenny, Falcon, and I ride the horses down to the lake to fish. First we hunt and catch grasshoppers for bait. They're slower in the mornings. Slowly swishing our feet through the yellowing plants, the grasshoppers leap before us then we creep up on them and pounce. Pulling off their heads we string them on stalks of stiff grass or they would, even headless, still hop away. We cast our handmade dogbane line with the grasshoppers tied with sinew onto bone hooks into the still water. The fish are not interested, we are too late in the day. We make a quick fire and cook the rest of the grasshoppers and eat them instead.

The horses bear us back up to the main camp where we find Ali sewing up still more holes in her buffalo robe. Louis is always hungry.

He's eating again, though he is already rail thin. I hope he doesn't lose more weight. I can see every rib on his pale, slender chest. Everyone always seems to lose some weight on these projects, especially in the beginning when people are trying to ration their food, but as we acclimatize to the wild food diet, the intensive activities, and the unpredictable conditions, the weight generally stabilizes after a couple of weeks. Marcus and Rick, still robust and well-muscled, are busy straightening arrow shafts that they roll above the fire's embers. The sun shines down through the hazy air, burning our thighs and shoulders. We are still an island in a sea of smoke.

The occasional plane or helicopter reminds us that another world exists down there in the smoke. Here we feel like we are in a fantasy novel filled with mythic beings—heroes and demons, wizards and goblins, giants and elves—while the lower world burns.

Red moonrise. I awaken to the deer in the moonlight ten feet away, my bow unstrung.

Red sunrise. The smoke gets thicker. I feel it now in complaining lungs. I pee in the same spot, string my bow, sit and wait in the dense air. How would I feel about this hunt if the town below was gone and everyone burned? How would I feel about anything, if everything in the world as we know it was gone?

I remember my teenage dream in Amsterdam, of running to the forest to watch the world coming to an end, and with a shock realize that this is actually what I've done: I've run to the forest and have been watching it end ever since.

12

QUEST

I spend the early morning on Smoky Mountain waiting for the doe to return, slowly sweeping the trees and meadow edges with my eyes searching for movement: flick of ear or tail or the snap of a twig. Light twitter of birds all around and the heavier thud of horse feet. An arrow rests against the bow in my lap.

I have been hunting for many years now and in the reflective mood that accompanies the innumerable hours of sitting and waiting, still and silent, past, present, and future start to overlap. Memories and ambitions combine, merging into a kaleidoscope of abstract impressions flowing unimpeded through my consciousness. I am transported back to a hunting trip the previous year . . .

———————>————

I am a woman.

I lie in long grass, yellowed by the passage of summer. It is the same color as my hair. Clouds drift solemnly from the west, blue sky, dappled with white. Close by, my spotted horse, black on white, tears at the yellowing grass. Beside me a yellow bow. I wear a red buckskin dress. I am waiting for the deer.

I haven't said my prayer yet or made any offering. These things are important to me. What shall I give? My breath, my blood, skin, flesh? I have offered each in times past but what will move me today I do not yet know. The wind rises and falls. I hear it coming in the tops of the green pines and then it is upon me in the grass, passing by, and another gust builds in its wake. The yellow bow is unstrung, hanging on a branch together with a quiver full of arrows.

The bow tells a story. I made this bow myself.

Bright yellow curls of wood fell to the ground, steadily scraped away as I shaped the seasoned stave. The stave became a bow. This bow has taken life but it has not taken a deer.

With my knife I cut a swatch of my yellow hair, and with a piece of fading yellow grass tie it onto a branch in the tree that I lie beneath. My prayer is for a clean, peaceful kill. I have shot a few deer, three to be exact, but with a rifle. It's very different, the shocking violence of the explosion. I clearly remember all three of them. I could go to the exact spot that each fell and tell you how they died.

I am a daughter.

All of us women are, whether or not we know or love those who gave us our bodies. I will still be a daughter when both my parents are gone from this world, held in the divine embrace of the great mother.

I was born in a city far across the ocean.

Blue.

The ocean reflecting the sky, the same color as my eyes. My mother was a textile artist. She met my father on a boat going to England from Sweden with a friend. I have seen photos of that journey, that first meeting, the young women and the young men, smiling and laughing. I can easily imagine the smell of the salty air, the cry of gulls, the spray of the dark North Sea. There is excitement in their faces. I, too, have traveled that same route many times.

With the big sky above, I lie down in the grass, wriggling into my sleeping bag, throwing my coat over my feet. I know the dew will soak me. My clothes are piled under my head for a pillow. A bright star is visible, a planet probably. Suddenly, as if by consensus, the familiar patterns leap simultaneously into the sky. The Big Dipper, pointing north, no surprises, I am familiar, at home in this land. Tonight there is a moon, waxing in its third quarter. The hills glow across the river, illuminated. The blue sky turned to black, yellow grass to gray. I hear the deer all around me, grazing in the moonlight.

I am a mother.

Not every woman shares the story of carrying a child within her womb or expelling a slippery body in a gush of blood.

Blood.
                Red.
                            Red is the color of my dress.

Yes, I am and have a daughter. Her hair and eyes are the same color as mine but that is another story.

My dress is red.

The morning air is still, a faint brightness on the eastern horizon. The dew in little pearls all covering the flattened grass around me. Some deer stamp and snort nearby as they catch my scent or hear me rustling as I turn over. My bow is still unstrung beside me. I dream some more, the comfort of the ground beneath me, the cozy warmth of my bed.

Now it is light. Pale, rosy red clouds grace the sky. I sit up and look around. A doe is looking straight at me. I duck back down below the tall grass, reach for the yellow bow and string it with difficulty, staying as low as possible. Pulling an arrow from the quiver and slinging the rest over my shoulder I crouch-crawl to the cover of the pines. She doesn't stop looking at me. Slowly the white flag tail goes up. She snorts and starts the cautious, deliberate pacing away from perceived threat. No overt panic or flight, but she is not going to stick around.

I walk the tree line on the edge of the clearing, my moccasined feet now soaking wet. In this same meadow a few years ago I drew a thin line across my shoulder with a sharp-edged flake of obsidian. Red drops fell upon the grass with my prayers, like the dew today. I clear the meadow and meander up a familiar trail making a big arc. I see half a dozen more deer, one even in range, but they are all hip to me and bound away before I have a chance to string an arrow.

I am a mother, I have birthed. It is not my instinct to kill. I believe that men were made for that task. Women bring life into the world. Men take it in order to sustain us all. Yet I eat and love meat; I want to take responsibility for life, and so I walk this autumn morning, bow in hand, hunting.

I am a goddess.

Cocreator of my destiny. I wrote a song about that once, calling it "When I Am an Old Woman." About Shuwa Awah, the name I heard in a dream. Maybe I will become her someday. All the verses in the song are filled with the things that I want to do in my life. I wrote them down so they could start being arranged in the Universe. That's the way to do it, you know: just think it up, speak it out, write it down, and watch it unfold.

When I am an old woman I'll be friends with the trees,
Climb high in their branches of needles and leaves,
And together so softly, Shuwa Awah
They will tell me their tales of their power.

I look at the green firs and pines around me, conifers . . . evergreen. Green is my favorite color.

I hear a rustle behind me. I turn and a deer, startled, bounds past me, barely twenty yards away, a muley doe. She stops and I sink into the grass, nocking an arrow. I whisper almost inaudibly, "Are you offering yourself to me? Come closer." She walks in tight circles, stiff-legged, curious, on high alert. She moves a little closer, sniffing the air. The wind is in my favor . . . nineteen, eighteen yards, still out of range for my wooden bow. "Will you give yourself to me?" Gradually I crawl toward her, I feel utterly feline, limbs smoothly, stealthily inching closer, mind, single-focused, absolutely present. She backs off, high stepping, stiff, tight little circles. Slowly I rise to my knees. I've gained ten yards and lost as many. A pine tree shields me from her view and I take a few quicker steps. "Are you?"

She is not.

She bounds, four legs in the air. She is not giving herself to me. Not now, not today. All the while I was wondering . . . Would I take you even if you offered? I still don't know the answer.

When I am an old woman I shall run with the deer,
I'll talk with the eagle, the fish and the bear,
And the animals call me Shuwa Awah,
And the grasshoppers sing, Shuwa Awah.

I look around me at all the colors: yellow, blue, red, green, and all the shades and hues and textures. The kaleidoscope separates and I am once more just a being, holding a bow in a bright new morning.

13

Rain

Today is the last day of trial week, then the rest of forever begins. In another week or two it will feel like this is all I've ever known, the past a distant dream from another lifetime. These weeks in the wilderness to listen and speak to God. Yes, God in the wind, the sun, the water, the trees and plants, the fish, the birds, animals and insects, God in the reflection of human eyes, God in the starry sky and on the smoky earth. Forgive us, how should we proceed?

A quiet day of fasting, rest, and self-care is what I plan. With the inactivity that fasting accepts, a clarity can enter the mind and questions posed find simple answers. I comb my hair with the antler comb and tie it with a buckskin thong. I brush my teeth thoroughly with a willow twig and pick them with a bone needle.

I move the horses to the lower meadow to graze. Ben and Falcon will tend to them while I am gone.

I hike for an hour or so into another valley away from my clan and pick a rocky outcropping as the site for my solo sit and fast. It's time to pray for rain to settle the smoke and quench the thirst of the dry land. It's time to stretch and drink and nap, conserving energy, to sit alone and listen and give thanks for my life. I am easing into the transition that will mark the beginning of the second phase as we drop the last of our modern gear and return to the Stone Age. It seems somehow holy. I watch the smoky mountain and sing.

As I settle down I take the bear claw from my medicine pouch and place it as an offering on a boulder for one who has gone. It is for Jim, an old logger who was my neighbor just a couple of miles down valley. He was born there and spent his whole life hunting and fishing these mountains, lakes, and rivers. A logging accident took both his legs and for the last ten years of his life it was only memories that brought him back to these secluded lakes and meadows. *I am glad I got to bring you out here with me even if it was just with words and pictures. Thank you for the inspiration you gave me. I know your spirit is free in these mountains you loved and knew so intimately.*

It seems there are some clouds now and not just smoke although it's hard to tell. They are coming from the southeast but still it's calm and warm down here on Earth. The last week has felt eternal and I know this next day will bring another eternity as I rest upon this giant flat boulder with nothing more than a small gourd cup, my clothes and bedding, pencil, journal, and unquiet mind. Perhaps I will find peace.

It's warm, too warm on my exposed rocky bed, where I sit to fast and pray. It gets smokier and I find it hard to get a fully satisfying breath of air. I get up and look at the mountains in the dim light that have all but disappeared in the smoke.

I tuck my face into the gaps between the boulders where cool air and water issues forth from the earth. There it is easier to breathe. For the first time I wonder if we could actually die here, not from the fire itself but from the smoke and lack of oxygen. I have no experience of a fire of this magnitude, and I feel a little prick of fear that reminds me of my childhood.

When I was a small child I would sometimes wake up in the night with my throat constricted, unable to breathe. My parents would rush me into the bathroom and turn on the hot water filling the room with steam. I was terrified. I think they were scared too. I wondered if I was dying and asked my mother; she would say, "No, not for a long, long time." I wanted to know where we went when we died but nobody would tell me. I had a complicated thought for a child of that age that maybe there were many worlds and when we died in one, we woke up in another and carried on as if nothing had happened.

Now I think of my clan in the valley over the ridge and hope they are okay. It's dark but not too dark. Do we need to move to higher ground or cross the ridge? I had planned to stay here on this rock throughout the night for my solo, but I am gripped with unrelenting worry due to the fire. At last, unable to quell my anxiety, I throw my buffalo robe under the shelter of a huge rock and start the ascent on the dimly moonlit trail back over the pass with smoky, laboring breaths.

In the camp in the meadow the air seems cleaner. I awaken Marcus in the group shelter; he's calm and levelheaded as I express my concerns. I am comforted by this strong, pragmatic man and we stay up talking for a long while watching the faint moon behind clouds we hope will bring rain. I tuck myself up in my own shelter without my robe and fall asleep.

The following morning I set out to retrieve my buffalo robe and then hike to the top of the nearest mountain to survey the smoke and fire situation. The valleys to the north and south are still dense but a southeast breeze has cleared things a little so I can see where one fire is still actively burning. It is clearest to the west but to go there would require dropping into one of the smoky valleys first. If it were to worsen, our only way out would be to take a trail to the east and hope for the best. I am glad that I know this country and understand what lies in each direction.

I sing to the rain spirits and ask for a rainstorm that is not too intense . . . and please, without more lightning. I sleep the rest of the day.

———————

The next morning, two mice are flattened under the deadfall trap, but no one seemed particularly interested in eating them, so I guess I will. It's good to keep trapping the little rodents by the food caches, though, or they will eventually start chewing holes in everything.

Jenny wanders over as I pull their charred remains from the fire and offer her the first bite, the crunchy one. She looks at me as she bites into it, like she has just been initiated into a very exclusive club. We smile at each other and she giggles. An unspoken barrier is torn down between us. It has taken quite a while for this to happen, but now I feel that a new equality is emerging.

Rick and Ben come back with squirrels they have shot and share them with the rest of us. Squirrels are tasty, so much more agreeable than the mice. Deer would be even better. I string my bow at dusk. I have a short moment of panic when I see that the horses are all gone. But they've just moved to another meadow. I feel a rush of relief. I walk with my yellow bow, but the doe is nowhere to be found and I return tired to the fire and enjoy the meal that has been cooked by Ben and Ali from our precious stores of dried roots and buffalo jerky. The saxifrage greens that grow along the creek make a delightful additional salad. Ali is in high spirits; she has a growing confidence that is evident. She gives me a warm hug when I sit down beside her.

That night, as I start to drift into slumber, the first patter of rain begins. With slight trepidation I lie awake waiting to see what blows in but thank you, Spirits, the rain is gentle and steady for most of the night. My shelter remains fairly dry with just an occasional spatter that sprays in upon my face.

The next day, the rain continues calmly. Exactly what we need to settle the smoke and damp back the fires. I hear a few rumblings in the heavens, but it seems that lightning was sparse.

At some point soon I hope for a lull in which to check on the others and see how the food, hung in baskets and covered by the somewhat water-resistant bark-tanned hides, has fared.

Louis went out on his own solo last night; I hope he stayed dry.

I hear horses whinnying so I know they are still in the valley.

The rain ceases midmorning. Muddy tracks coming down from the pass tell me Louis has arrived. Cold, wet, and a little scared after a night alone in the storm without much cover except his blanket and clothes, the tall young man looks like an angel.

We light a big fire, no longer worried about the parched conditions as we dry our clothes, bedding, and food bags all day. It stays gray and misty but breaks up toward evening to a mostly blue sky.

Watching big white cumuli drift westward, I am satisfied that it is no longer smoke, though it's hard sometimes to tell the difference.

As I prepare for sleep that night, I think about how we must soon consider a change in base camp as the grazing diminishes. I hate to leave this valley, though. I feel I could continue to explore it for another week or more. Over the years I have discovered that changing camps, even a camp rich with resources, about every ten days prevents stagnation among the group. I still don't know if it is restlessness that prompts this nomadism or something deeper, imbued in our cells from our hunter-gatherer ancestors that demands a change of surroundings and fresh resources.

I awaken at dawn.

The sky opens with a fork of fire followed by crashing thunder. The storm is instantly upon us.

The slow patter of rain . . . Minutes later another rumble, though this time it comes from the mountain on the other side of the valley; with a great tearing, the rocks come shearing from the face of the cliff and tumble to the floor below, my pounding heart in unison.

Ah, raw nature from which we cannot hide. My frail body finds comfort in my bed of soft needles and the skins and furs of animals past and the cover of this rough, quick shelter from the skeleton bones of larch and the living, spreading branches of spruce. I quickly pull inside all my food bags and quiver full of arrows still damp from yesterday's rain.

We are never safe.

No, we are never safe. At any moment the earth can rend open and cast us to her belly's depths. The ground can shake and the winds can rip, uprooting mighty trees that crush us as we run or sleep. The heavens can open with fire or flood, burn us quickly or slowly, drown us or smash us with instant mercy. The sun can dry and scorch, the ice and snow with silent numbing fingers suck away our feeble warmth.

No, we are never safe, but still we try to tame this world in which we live. When the jaws of all big predators have fallen to dust, the great trees slain and hewn and reassembled into boxes we call houses, the earth's very innards removed and reforged into steel and concrete, still we will not be safe. Instead I ask the grace and mercy of this living wonder to grant me another day in paradise.

Some more rumbling and the rain comes down in earnest. I run out to free Christy who is tied to the picket line in the open.

Some birds have sought refuge under my spruce, and I watch them fluff their wet feathers an arm's length from where I lie.

The earnest rain turns to a deluge for a while. I try to keep my buffalo robe out of the drips and make up a little song in a language that comes to me:

Oh heché vo, imeno, imeno va
Oh heché vo, imeno Imana
Oh the rain coming falling, falling here
Oh the rain coming falling to Earth
Oh akani vo, allana, allana va
Oh akani vo, allana sapomi Imana
Oh the sun coming, warming, warming here
Oh the sun coming, warming, drying Earth.

There comes a ceasing. The horses, all untethered, are halfway up the trail to the pass. I bring back my little mare who, once freed, incites desertion and I tie her up again.

Most of the clan appear from their shelter and together we seek out dry tinder, and Falcon spins a coal from an unsoaked fire kit.

We stand beside the blaze cooking in clay pots as the rain begins again. We steam and turn and steam and turn again, trying in vain to dry our damp buckskins and warm first our bare toes, then our faces. With a pot full of hot water I retire to my nook to eat and rest and sing some more.

Here is the madness of mind. Mind, grasping for distraction. Every rumble is horse hooves, thunder, rockfall, or airplane. Every slow drip in the shelter in which I have lain all day is a source of mounting angst. And it's only been one day of rain. Oh, where is my presence? The mist covers everything, and even when it is not actually raining it is dripping. Now is when I want to flee but we can't, not without leaving everything here. Oh sun, come shine on us.

Again the rain ceases, and my clan lifts my spirits beside the glowing hearth. Jenny says the hearth is the heart of the camp. Hearth,

Heart, Earth. I never thought about the profound connection of these words before but suddenly it seems obvious.

We sing of storms and thunder. The night sky clears to brilliant stars and a late waning moon. Karma, the spotted horse, a specter moving softly past my shelter door.

A new day dawns cloudy again. The fire is revived from a mound of coals. I air my bedding then quickly pile it back into the shelter with the first spit of errant rain. I sit and watch the mountain. From the east the clouds come on their solemn march.

Rick and I seek cover in the boulder fields where we make arrow tips with bone and stone, sheltered by a great rock fallen from the cliff above. All day the mist rolls in and out, obscuring and revealing the peaks by which we're flanked.

The next day I awaken slowly from the warm embrace of a forbidden lover that in dreamtime does no harm. Bright sunshine on my eyelids. Blue!

The entire clan lays out their treasures of wild foods, skins, and baskets to let the magnificent sun do its work. We lounge and craft and eat with little or no clothing on.

I jump on Karma bareback and ride her up to the pass.

Smokeless hills and valleys.

Big relief.

I meet Falcon at the drinking hole by chance. We are drawn there simply by thirst. We sit by the water for a long time, sipping periodically, talking and watching the travesty of a hapless ant that gets shipwrecked on a rocky island in the middle of the stream. I think about how rarely I would take the time in my "normal" world to watch such a scene for so long, being always driven by doing. Here I feel like I am writing a script for my life. I can make anything I choose happen, introduce any character I wish, and create whatever relationship I desire.

The story is never dull. It is as rich and vibrant as Earth itself.

Like a butterfly emerging from its chrysalis, wings damp and fragile, I am transformed with each new moment wondering who I will become next.

After a fine dinner of reconstituted buffalo jerky, wild onions, bitterroot, and *Bryoria* lichen, I string my bow once again, make a few practice shots, and wander up to the ridge. On the way a ground squirrel meets the tip of my blunt arrow with force. A rock finishes the job. I feel saddened. But life cannot exist without death and here in these high wild valleys there is little to eat except greens and animals. Thank you.

As a last snack before retiring, we roast and share the squirrel body, crunching the small, cooked bones to extract as much nourishment as possible. I work the skin until dark then wander up to my shelter.

In the predawn I am awoken with great thirst and heat. I drink again at the stream, barefoot on the dew in cool moonlight.

These simple things . . .

Tomorrow we plan to leave this basin. I repair the horse panniers with rawhide lacing and make a couple of simple halters from strong tanned moose skin, then ride down to take a bath at the lake.

Impossibly blue and icy water races up to meet me as I dive from a pointed rock. The fish scatter and I am reminded what it means to be right here in this absolute moment. The sun warms my tingling skin and a delicious sense of well-earned fatigue envelops me as I lie upon the larch needles.

The energy of the sun turns to grass. The grass feeds the horses. We spare our own energy by riding the horses to and from the lake. Energy is so direct and transparent out here.

The clan is ready to move.

After my swim, I eat a pancake for breakfast. Not the usual kind you might think of with butter and syrup but another flattened mouse caught under the deadfall rock. Gutted and cooked, bones, skin and all, the fur singed off in the bright coals.

Clouds again form in the southeast, a slight patter of rain then the sun in a sucker hole. All afternoon the clouds swirl from every direction and cluster in marvelous shapes.

Two bright stars appear on the eastern horizon. Like eyes they pierce the predawn, and in the last shred of moonlight the deer grazes quietly in front of my shelter door. I watch her shadowy form barely two bow lengths from my bed, but any slight rustle will send her bounding off. I wish her a wonderful day, roll over, and invite more dreams.

I shall miss my nest beneath the spruces. Thank you.

We circle at breakfast and lay out an offering to the land that has held us. Each of us places a morsel of food on a flat rock: a few red berries, green edible leaves, a sprinkle of fatty pemmican. It is beautiful. We circle on the knoll and we sing our thanks. We cry our gratitude. We touch the edges of wholeness, of who we are, who we long to be.

Before we leave our camp, we burn the coals to ashes, douse the firepit carefully and then disperse the rocks and leftover piles of firewood. Finally we fill in the pit to soften the impact that our presence has caused. The last of my unpacked gear lies strewn around me. Our presence here has been erased except for a short piece of buckskin thong, a shard of broken pottery, a flake of foreign stone. Flattened grass and softly worn trails remain but these, too, will soon be scarcely more than a quick breath in the memory of the earth.

PART 3

Transformation

14

Smoky Mountain Absorption

When everyone is packed, we begin our climb at a painfully slow pace to the ridge. The horses are antsy to move too, but with the steep trail and a lively wind, the rawhide pack boxes strapped to Chaco keep slipping. We adjust and retie them a dozen times. It frustrates and exhausts me, but I am grateful that his steady temperament keeps him calm when the packs slide all the way around his ample girth.

We make a few miles with the heavy loads and camp not far away from the trail. We wear our moccasins that give more grip and stability than the rawhide sandals while we are hiking. The feeling of Earth beneath moccasined feet is reassuring. One can sense the terrain and yet be protected, so different from the separation that occurs when a foot is clad in stiff leather and soled in rubber. The connection is literally lost by the insulation of the rubber, no magnetic energy can be exchanged. If there was only one thing that I was able to tell my fellow humans, it would be, *Take off your shoes and feel the earth.* Our feet are designed for this connection.

Three drops of rain keep me awake during the first night. Camping so completely in and with nature, we are forced to become aware of every change and nuance in the weather. With no tarps or matches, stoves or plastic food containers, we must be constantly alert to opportunity in the form of immediate shelter and dry firewood for fuel. Setting camp takes several hours instead of a few minutes with modern gear; campsites must be carefully selected, firewood gathered, fire made with bow drill, food cooked carefully on coals in clay pots.

Fortune offers us another dry day to move; we slowly hike up and over the final pass, and arrival at the new camp goes smoothly. I have passed through here and camped before, too, and know that it offers grazing and access to some other lakes. I call it Ancestor Basin. We are farther from the well-marked trails and the signs of hikers are scarce. Once we have walked for more than two days from the trailheads, signs of human influence fade.

In spite of our fatigue, two new shelters are erected. It is necessary if we plan to be here for at least a week or more. Jenny, Marcus, and I make a lean-to under a particularly sheltering spruce. They are the quieter members of the clan and we are comfortable sharing time together often in silence. The others create something similar not far away but bigger to accommodate them all. Our bedding, being our primary concern to keep dry, is only laid out when we are ready to sleep.

Before we all retire to our respective shelters, we eat together and speak of diminishing food supplies that are scantily supplemented from the land. Some of the clan—Falcon, Jenny, Marcus, and myself— had prepared more dried food than the others. Since we take turns making our daily meals with our own food supplies, we cannot go on long this way. Ben, Ali, Louis, and Rick will run out of food. Now we come to a unanimous decision: the pre-prepared wild foods that we have all brought with us are no longer to be considered personal. Those of us who have more are eager to share with our kin who have less. We agree that it is more important to stay together even if it means an earlier return. Rick's eyes moisten; he's deeply touched by the small sacrifice. We are together, we stay together, we share. We leave when we must and we realize we do not yet have to rely on nature alone; our society will catch us when we have to return. We all recognize the privilege that gives us choices, and once more touch the edges of reality.

A mouse scampers through my hair in the night and even sandwiched between my two companions I am slightly cold. The intolerable mosquitoes begin their plaguing whine about my face, repeatedly violating the breathing hole through the hair of my buffalo robe. With vengeance I crush their tiny bodies.

I wake up earlier than Jenny and Marcus. I don't really want to get up, but I do anyway. After crawling over them, I string and flex my bow. I pat and whisper good morning to the little mare Christy and walk.

The ground is cold and wet with dew that dampens my moccasins. I head down the valley with every living tree squirrel sounding their forest alarm at my approach like beacons. A grouse takes wing, and quite probably every creature in the connective sensory web becomes aware that a predator is at large and on the stalk. Would that my own senses were that keen. Every little bird yells, "Hunter, hunter, hunter!"

I am so lost in my thoughts and my words. I can see the beauty of the web. How can I become part of it? The shift happens subtly.

I track deer along the ridge, startle a hare. I take no shots.

Returning to camp, I am physically depleted and spend the remainder of the day eating and resting.

We light a ceremonial fire at sunset and make prayers and offerings to the spirit of the deer, asking for a successful hunt. There are only four of us who have our bows and are actively hunting: Rick, Ben,

Marcus, and myself. Louis, Jenny, Ali, and Falcon choose to focus their attention on fishing and gathering the wild plants instead.

From this high vantage point at the ceremonial firepit we can see for many miles across the Cascade range. Looming in the far distance is Mount Baker, one of the venerable active volcanoes in the Ring of Fire. Tonight it glows in the sunset. We beseech the night to bring us dreams, to give us a clue to where we should go to hunt.

Next morning, slightly appalled by my civilized mind, I recall a dream, indeed not of the hunt with wooden bow and stone-tipped arrows but of shopping for meat at the local butcher.

When I get up, I feel dizzy, light-headed, ethereal. I'm drinking water, ate plenty yesterday, and, today, had a good bowel movement, slept well, was warm . . . Body, what do you need to feel grounded, vibrant, energetic? I can't understand what my body needs except for fat. I envision thick juicy steaks cooked rare with a layer of dripping braised fat.

It was just last year, during our Stone Age excursion, that I had been camping in this very basin with my clansmen and we had planned a side expedition, down to a large, deep lake eleven miles away. Though it's a remote area only accessible by trail or water, it does have a daily ferry that brings visitors from the recreational town of Chelan some sixty miles south who spill onto the dock at the head of the lake to take pictures, hike the trails, and swim in the cool clear water. Most of them hop back on the ferry to return a couple of hours later after a snack at the little café. For us, though, coming from our base camp, this involved an arduous nine-hour hike with a steep drop in elevation. There were four of us—myself and three clan members: Stephane, a solid man from Switzerland; Miles, a youngster from the East Coast; and Danielle, from a dairy farming family in Wisconsin and the only other woman of that year's Stone Age clan. We packed food for three days and headed down the valley with minimal traveling gear. This lake and its surroundings was for me a very special destination.

I spent the summers of my early twenties in Chelan with my "hike-till-you-drop" boyfriend. It was in the Northern Cascades that I had my first multiday wilderness hiking experiences. And it was then that I first armed myself with plant identification guides to learn about wild edibles. Twenty-five years later, my three companions were as excited as I was to explore the different, drier environment of a lower elevation and we set off on a trail marked on the map as unmaintained.

The first few miles went easily on the old, abandoned trail, the tracks and scat of deer, moose, and bear accompanying us. No sign of humans having passed here in many moons. Following another trail we suddenly found ourselves in a tortuous obstacle course of burned and blown-down forest. We entered the burn. Sick forest cleansed by wildfire. Needles covered the ground; buckskin colored, we blended in. Charred moonscape, blackened towers loomed above and around us. There, among the ashes, the brittle bones of a casualty of flames and smoke.

Two and a half miles became an arduous six-hour hike; sometimes we were crawling, clambering under and over giant ponderosa and lodgepole pine scattered like pickup sticks. We were blackened by charred wood and streaked with sweaty grime as we continued on even though we couldn't be sure what awaited us.

Parched from the difficult descent, we heard the illusionary trickle of water at every turn on the trail. When finally the real stream appeared, glistening on rock and moss, we quenched our thirst greedily. Mountain water: sweetness, loveliness, life.

With much relief we rejoined a repaired trail and moved swiftly again, but the sun was sinking and we were losing daylight. We killed a rattlesnake lying across our path and tossed it in a basket to add to the evening meal. Though cut, bruised, and aching, we finally arrived down at the lakeshore trail many hours later. Desperate to find a camp spot to sleep, we found ourselves on bluff after rocky bluff. Step after weary step. The sun set and the crickets started to sing. The moon rose, then was gradually obscured by clouds as we moved on.

In a strange way, despite the fatigue, we were loving it. How often does one get to move through such an inspiring, beautiful landscape into the night on an epic journey? It is the punctuation of these powerful moments that give life flavor.

When we finally laid out our robes and collapsed beside the lapping water at our feet, too tired to make a fire or cook, we slept deeply. In the low elevation and warm night, funny dreams woke me up laughing, sad dreams woke me up crying. The richness of my experience filled my being. Memories flooded back from half my lifetime ago when I first loved these torn and craggy peaks.

The following morning I woke beside the glittering water with a mission.

I decided to head toward the top of the lake, despite the daytrippers who would be flocking there, with an empty gathering basket and hopes of blackberries. But the berry patch I remembered had now been posted with No Trespassing signs so I continued on grasping the little pouch around my neck that contained my intention rock and prayed. For meat. It felt absurd but I prayed not for just any animal, but for elk steak. Then I modified my search power to include deer and moose just to play it safe and hiked into the dock area just as the ferry boat, having discharged its passengers, pulled away. My appearance drew stares from both locals and gaping tourists. Worn and weary, covered in grubby buckskins sullied by the burned forest, I felt like I had stepped into a glaring cartoon filled with characters charading with absurd mannerisms, chemical scents, and sparklingly clean clothes.

I was dizzy and depleted. I sat with a group of day hikers and nibbled dry salmon and berries while they drank cold, fizzy beverages that held no appeal. I fantasized of juicy, bloody elk steak, I couldn't help it.

Walking farther up the valley, I was driven by the vision of elk steak. I was insatiable. My mind had no limits, my conscience, no boundaries. There is a small settlement near the lake of around sixty year-round inhabitants and I knocked on the door of a secluded ranch and explained to the surprised woman who opened the door how I longed for a piece of elk steak. Unbelievably, or perhaps not, given the altruistic nature of the Universe when coupled with positive intention, she went to her brother-in-law's freezer and as I stumbled back to camp in the moonlight many hours later, I had in my pack two pounds of elk meat, blackberries, purslane greens, and four fat feral apples. I had covered fourteen miles barefoot and, at times, in rawhide sandals and the cost was happy utter exhaustion.

I anointed my feet with fat that they gratefully absorbed. That night, belly sated on lean elk steak, I laid my weary body down on a bed of prickly sticks, covered my head with my jacket, and fell instantly asleep.

Thanks again, Universe.

A few drops of rain sent us scurrying under sheltering trees in the middle of the night. I slept very badly, restless dreams and discomfort. Awakening in the morning I did not want to move, but we motivated ourselves with our gifts of sustenance and ate more succulent, blood-dripping elk. My companions were rested and ready to hike, but I lay around procrastinating. The hike that lay ahead was straight up, no shelter, through another old burn. It wasn't the same trail we had come down on but I was still dreading it.

Finally we set out. I tottered along uncertainly. I asked Stephane to walk behind me in case I should pass out and roll off the trail. It became evident that I couldn't hike as planned and needed a rest day. So we all stayed another night in a new camp by the lake. I fell upon the pale, dry grass on my buffalo robe. The wind whipped up big waves on the water, trees swaying wildly like my thoughts. I was gripped by an irrational irritation with my male companions. I wanted to blame my miserable exhaustion on them for snoring and keeping me awake at night. I watched the thoughts come and go: they are dear men but I hated them anyway.

I realized just how quickly one can starve. Protein alone isn't enough. Protein without adequate fat or carbohydrates can actually cause protein poisoning whereby the urea buildup in the body reaches toxic levels. The hunter-gatherers of the far north have traditionally eaten high-protein diets with little or no plant-based carbohydrates. They kept an equilibrium of nutrients by consuming large quantities of fat and raw organ meats. We needed five thousand calories each to climb back to base camp, and we probably didn't have that between us. An old apple tree and more blackberries provided some carbs and entertainment for the tongue but my withering body cried fat, fat, FAT.

Here, in the high mountain basin one year after that long day on the trail with my body clamoring for fat, I continue to dream of last year's elk steak and wonder if I will be able to go with the hunting party this morning. I'm not sure. I can hear Rick, Ben, and Marcus gathering up their weapons and discussing a hunting strategy, eager yet focused. They do not seem like boys to me anymore; they are the men of the clan, capable and sincere.

I lie back down, my face in the flowers, white and purple. It is so still and silent I feel like I have been placed upon a painted landscape. Slowly the world comes alive, sun creeps onto the ridge above, breeze stirs the larch needles, a pika squeaks. Cool air, no mosquitoes!

Falcon cooks up a breakfast mush of acorn flour that she had prepared and brought with her from England. She adds generous spoonfuls of precious bear fat and a handful of dried berry mix into the large clay cooking pot. I devour a large bowlful. Increased consumption of fat and lots of rest equals increased energy. The equation is simple.

As the three hunters set out, I am feeling better so I quickly pack my gear and follow them. They wait for me at the pass. The four of us are packed lightly with two days of food and bedding. We climb the ridge and drop into a new valley.

We are on a scouting mission. Huckleberries, grouse, fish, deer, nuts—we search for a new camp that will feed us.

Gone is the malaise and I trot the trail behind them nimbly. Thank you, body. My heart chooses its deepest desire. My brain figures out how to get there most efficiently, instructing legs and feet with precise directions, great speed and skill; this rock, that rock, jump, wait . . . now! Ah, those feet and legs, so willing and compliant, rarely complaining even as they are scratched, bruised, and tired. My back and shoulders bear the load, shoulders grumbling occasionally, bickering between each other like surly siblings. *You take it now. No, I had it longer.* They shift the weight back and forth. My faithful hands, resting as we go, leap into action when we sit and take a break, rummaging through bags for food, rubbing sore muscles, producing maps for my brain to ponder. What a wondrous organism, truly miraculous, every cell playing its part in this great and unique embodiment.

An Irish fiddle tune pops into my head as I hop and leap down the rocky trail, the movement coalescing into an erratic, whimsical dance. I am alive.

15

BECOMING

Our Smoky Mountain hunting expedition proceeds ominously. Clouds begin to build. Rain is imminent. Rain, even in September in these high elevations, can mean dangerous cold and a halt to activity while we wait for it to cease.

All day we walk, climbing passes, snacking on our meager rations and the berries we find. A rock well tossed from the hand of Marcus provides a grouse; fresh greens and berries round out our meal when we finally pitch camp beside a large, deep lake.

We discover the shelter from some of last year's clan, add to it, and gather a pile of firewood before the rain sets in. Once more, shelter becomes the highest priority. This is the site where one of our clan members shot a deer last year. It truly felt like an offering. The fearless doe stood and waited. She had been circling the camp hoping for something salty to eat. The hunter, incredulous, got up and strung his bow, just yards away, all the time she was watching him, waiting. He made his shot in the failing light and the deer bounded a few steps and fell. We had rejoiced and feasted, satiating and filling our growling bellies.

Tonight, just before dark, a giant tree comes crashing to the ground not fifty yards from our campfire. We watch it fall and marvel.

Exhausted, we bundle and sleep beneath the spruces. Comfort is a matter of perspective. I am just glad to lie down in the pitchy needles and close my eyes. A brief patter of rain wakes me momentarily then fades and I return to my slumber.

The moon sets and as the sky brightens in the east I hear a waking whisper and feel a gentle shake. Ben is squatting beside me. His cheeks look a little hollow in the accentuating, shadowy dawn light. We all arise and string our bows whispering few words in the cold morning air. With steam floating above the deep lake, first frost glitters on the lupines.

I stalk to the corner of the meadow and settle beside a large stump where the coming sun will warm me. I am content to watch the glow of sunrise touch the western hills with hues of red and orange and gold.

With the yellow bow strung and ready in my hands I know this Earth that I love so fiercely would destroy me with utter certainty were I left entirely to my own devices to feed my hungry belly.

Not only do I lack the knowledge of my ancestors, but we are challenged by the dwindling of once abundant food resources and the regulations designed to protect them.

Add to this the result of a species veered from the path of natural selection through modern medical intervention and we are faced with a perception of humanity, weakened and in excess, competing for limited resources.

At no other time have we been more in need of Grace.

I say my prayer.

"Deer People, I thank you. Could your flesh become my own? Is there one amongst you willing to sacrifice your life, your body?

"I ask with humility, ready to accept your answer, whatever it may be."

I close my eyes.

The trail is before me. Only I don't call it that. I don't call it anything, it's just that opening, that easy way down to the big water and meadow where the sweet grass grows. I don't have names or words for any of these things. They just are. As necessary and permanent as the being that I neither call "myself."

The stones make a clatter beneath my feet. Something tickles my leg and I thrust nose and teeth into silky hair and rub. All is pure sensation and I am fully alert. I smell the damp forest and it is bursting with information that I absorb and recognize without analysis: the sweet, sticky sap, the flowers, the wet earth scent, the denser water scent of the lake. I don't name any of this but I keep walking down, stopping to nibble the grass along the way. I hear, too, the winged ones and discern without thinking which of their calls should alert me to danger. My sensitive ears twitch in every direction gathering the nuances of sound that permeate the forest.

Down at the edge of the meadow I pause, look around, sniff the air, and listen. All is as usual. I know this place well. I do what my instincts tell me, I eat the grass and other succulent plants that smell and taste so good. I do this all without thought.

I drift toward the running water where I drink, where my hoofprints from yesterday are still sharp in the mud.

A noise, an unusual loud "twang" and a blow . . . a sudden sharp pain in my side. I don't think. I just bolt. But oh, that pain, it hurts so. Then a scent . . . a danger scent . . . the upright creature nearby. I must run to safety, get away, but, oh, that pain is worse. It's hard to breathe, I don't understand, I don't question it but I must keep running. There to that thicket. Something snaps and falls from my side and the wrenching pain again. So hard to breathe . . . can't fill my lungs . . . have to go lie down and rest . . . yes, there the thicket . . . oh, the pain . . . it's turning dark now, I am driven by fear and pain but I hear no new alarming sounds and the scent is gone . . . short breath, rising darkness . . . the thicket . . . lie down . . . rest. My legs buckle beneath me; I will lie down, I cannot run. I cannot breathe. There is darkness enveloping me. It does not hurt anymore, I am lying in a warm, sticky puddle, but I hardly notice anything now; my eyes blur as the darkness consumes me. I am going on a journey . . .

The sun is upon me and I open my eyes. Words flood my mind and I wonder how it must feel to just be without them, pure consciousness, wordless being. No deer enters the meadow except the one that I imagine. No deer lies in a pool of blood in the thicket.

Why?

Why do I do this?

I am not a hunter and yet I hunt. Cold and tired before the rising of an autumn sun, I hold the stick I call bow that has never taken the life of a deer.

I do not want to kill the deer, I want to BE the deer, but this form that is my body has its own demands. It is the same force that reaches for the rifle when I recognize my lack of skill and patience and shatters the peace of the forest, robbing another of its existence.

Later a doe does walk close to camp, but the eager hunters scare her back in the direction from which she came. I settle in the rain below the camp hoping she will circle round and try to pass us alongside the lake. She does not come and I get cold and return to the fire.

16

Ishi

My first Stone Age Project was at our home in Montana. We spent some weeks in the lead-up to the project building a Stone Age camp across the creek from our yurt. "Our" land was in the traditional homeland of the Ktunaxa, whose territory ranged from the north Kootenays in what is now Alberta and south to the Tobacco Plains where we lived just across the US border. The Ktunaxa people, as they call themselves, are often referred to by their Anglicized names: Kootenai in the US and Kootenay in Canada. They have been separated by the national border and, as the familiar story goes, pressed, coerced, and forced onto reservations. Conformity and assimilation at best; abuse, torture, and genocide at worst.

In the Ktunaxa native tongue there are no possessives. As with many Indigenous languages there is no way to express ownership. One can only belong. Belong to land, belong to tribe. The inspiration for my very first Stone Age Project was my yearning for this sense of belonging that seemed so unachievable. In preparation for our inaugural project, I went to a one-day introduction class to the Ktunaxa language. The man teaching it, himself a native struggling to revive his ancestral language, was learning from the last handful of fluent speakers left in the world. There were only eight of them. With the inevitable extinction of a whole nation's language there would also disappear one more reminder of Indigenous wisdom: we may not possess the earth and its resources and inhabitants; we can only participate in a brief journey through life and belong to the infinite web of creation.

I had invited a number of people from various parts of the United States and Europe known for their knowledge of primitive technologies and ancient living skills to share with one another their experience and try to spend up to ninety days living "Stone Age." I didn't receive income. I didn't teach any students. I wanted to see if we could live on an all-wild foods diet in this land. Would it accept us? What would happen to our bodies, minds, and spirits? Some who came were my friends and others I had just heard about but never met. None of us were natives of the land in this corner of Montana. We were all white people who lived spread across the continent from Wisconsin to Oregon. There was also a Dutch man. The participants ranged in age from eight to fifty, Klara being the youngest.

None could leave behind their modern lives for a full three months to see what might happen. So they came and went as it suited them, and the energy brought in from people arriving from a long road trip with the smell of bacon and eggs on them was unnerving to those of us who had been subsisting for weeks on berries and squirrels.

Everyone had to bring all their own tools, clothes, and wild harvested foods; they didn't have to have made them with Stone Age techniques, but we relinquished everything that was made from metal, cloth, glass, or plastic and all refined processes such as matches or nonwild foods with a few notable exceptions: eyeglasses or contact lenses, medications and birth control, journal and pencil, and a few books that we dubbed "The Elders." They were mostly plant identification books, to help us when we found something we thought we might be able to eat but weren't sure about, and "how to" manuals for various Stone Age technologies. We felt like lost children without guardians. We hid the books away in a hole in the ground and brought them out just one day a week to answer any questions that might have arisen.

The project was based on the modern Neolithic period, after the introduction of horses but before the widespread use of iron. I chose this period because I wanted to include my own animals but there was only a brief period of history during which the horses that escaped and became feral after the Spaniards invaded native lands to the south were then tamed and traded by the tribes and moved northward more rapidly than the metal tools that the Europeans had also brought with them.

The first phase of the first Stone Age Project was "camp life." It had a total of seventeen participants who came and went, most of whom stayed for just a few days at a time. It was a huge learning opportunity in how a person responds not only to a sudden change in diet and lifestyle but also to the social upheaval of thrusting together a group of virtual strangers into an intense and unfamiliar situation.

During this phase, shelters were constructed across the creek, just a few minutes' walk from our yurt, but the camp felt cut off from our home life, invisible until one stumbled on it, a little clearing in the forest surrounded by birch, larch, spruce, and firs. My husband and I had built a spruce bark tipi, peeling the bark from living trees in a soon-to-be harvested logging section. This method of bark harvesting, girdling, and taking the whole circumference of the bark will kill most trees since the cambium layer is the layer that transports nutrients and water to the leaves. The exception to this rule is the harvesting of birchbark. Removing sheets of the white outer bark but not the inner cambium will disfigure but not kill the tree.

During the camp life phase, we harvested and prepared plant foods, largely roots, seeds, and berries, for eating and storage; small animals were hunted and trapped; and a whole bison was slaughtered and processed. We made pottery and fired it aboveground. We also made tools and utensils all with Stone Age technologies.

We began the project the day before Klara's eighth birthday. As part of her homeschooling she was encouraged to write a daily journal. Her second entry read, "Today is my biffday, I et worms for brekfast, my mom made soup wiv them." Despite this culinary experience that most eight-year-olds avoid on their birthdays, the activities of the children happily reflected the activities of the adults. Charlie, the neighbor kid, would sometimes join us and another friend with a little girl of a similar age came for a week. The kids were all clothed in buckskins and ran around playing shelter building, bows and arrows, berry picking (though most of the berries went directly to the mouth instead of the basket).

During these weeks one of the most interesting and notable phenomena I observed was how obvious it is that people need each other to prosper or even sustain themselves. After one month, with most of the participants gone, we still needed just as much firewood at our hearth, just as much water hauled, and nearly as much time to process, prepare, and cook our food. Those general maintenance tasks were virtually unchanged, though with fewer people there to help, it seemed impossible to sustain while I spent the whole day just maintaining what we had without having the time to replenish our supplies.

> *There are no camas on the Tobacco Plains*
> *And the bitterroot barely itself remains*
> *Where will the native people go*
> *When their hunting grounds fall prey to the plow?*
> *It's illegal to be a hunter-gatherer*
> *Illegal to be a hunter-gatherer.*

The buffalo, too, are all but gone
And the rancher's cow has no season.
Mining destroys the Indigenous lands,
Logging is taking the earth from our hands
It's illegal to be a hunter-gatherer
Illegal to be a hunter-gatherer.

And who is responsible for this sad state?
Yup, it's you and me, buddy, and the food that we ate.
We drive in our cars and we build out of wood,
We love all our metals and plastics are good.
It's illegal to be a hunter-gatherer,
Illegal to be a hunter-gatherer.
Or maybe we can do something different?

After one month I reviewed our progress and learning. I was alone now for most of the time although my husband and daughter would come by and "visit" at the Stone Age camp across the creek from our other life in the yurt. I realized that the social dynamics had been greatly flawed by the fact that people didn't know one another at the onset. Having people come and go was the most difficult, especially when they left. Everyone agreed that when we had a larger group, dynamics were better, subgroups could develop, and variety was greatly appreciated.

Ishi, I wasn't born here, native of your land
I come from far away across the big sea.
And now I call your land my home.
Ishi, would you understand me or I you

Across the chasm of time, space, and blood?
I'm living in dreamtime, Ishi,
Maybe, perhaps, just almost touching your world.
Do you feel my presence reaching back?
Do I feel your loneliness?
Just a drop in the ocean of your loneliness?
As I dream across time, back into the Stone Age.

By day thirty-five I was scribbling in my journal in a haze of disappointment to a historic figure named Ishi. Ishi was the famed "last" Yahi Indian found in 1911 in a small California town. Starving and bereaved after losing his entire tribe to the rapid onslaught of Western civilization, he was befriended by an anthropologist and lived out his final years, a living relic in a museum before succumbing to tuberculosis. He showed his white friend many of the techniques that his people had used in their material culture but he never again spoke his true name. In his language "Ishi" just means "man"; when the last of his family had been killed or perished naturally, his name must have died with them. Even a man raised and taught by his elders in their native land could not endure the endless toil to sustain himself while hiding and evading his antagonists. I had taken to addressing him as I watched my "tribe" gradually disappear and wrote:

"Well, it's you and me, Ishi, and the others who are still here getting ready to leave are like ghosts passing through our dream."

Once ancient, if just in play
My body seeks the divinity of Earth
Earth, close to me, touching me, filling me
With her soft urgent voice.
Alone on the hill with the mother of us all
Lights across the valley beckon me,

My people, calling me, luring me
Back to the world.
I would that these two loves might someday
find the time to meet and fall in love,
As surely they would
Bridging the gap between culture and conscience.

The second phase of the project was a ten-day journey of approximately 150 miles across the Purcell Mountains and into Idaho by foot, then returning on horseback.

As with the first phase, I started with a couple of companions, but near the end, I found myself alone and wondering *What now?* I was still alive and feeling quite healthy and I didn't want to end life in the Stone Age, but as a social experiment it seemed like an utter failure. Despondency set in.

After this first project was over, I found myself back in my "normal" life living in the yurt with my family. Since I had been experimenting all summer with living Stone Age and hadn't been teaching or working, I was acutely aware that we needed money. I sold Christy's yearling foal to buy hay for our other horses and we made it through the winter on deer meat and potatoes.

The following year, an acquaintance wrote to me and suggested that I do another Stone Age Project but this time train students for it, request a modest sum for the privilege, and in this way I would be earning a living doing what I loved.

Pretty soon I had four students who were willing to live with me for a year, through a Montana winter in tents, and take a weeklong class each month in preparation for a new Stone Age Project.

The year of preparation turned out to be way too long and the initial group all decided to leave just a few weeks before our anticipated start date, but a couple of guys, Tony and Chris, had joined us in the spring; and a friend who had been with us the first year, Alice, said she would like to go. I also invited another girlfriend, Anna, who wanted to try it out for a limited time.

And so began the trip we later dubbed the Starvation Project.

We planned a monthlong immersion into Stone Age living with strict parameters regarding our food allowances and took with us only regional wild foods. Our stocks of dried meat had to be animals taken by bowhunting or trapping, no roadkills, no purchased animals. We had very few high-calorie foods at the onset: a few dry squirrels, a rabbit, and about a pint of marmot fat between us.

On the first day, the boys took off hunting in one direction and I in the other. I startled a couple of deer, a grouse, and several squirrels. I missed a chipmunk and continued on roving and taking practice shots.

It was cool and I noticed how hard it was to shoot with cold fingers. I was hungry and feeling a little weak and had trouble pulling my bow to full draw.

Rain kept us from hunting with our sinew bowstrings, which can't be used wet; they will stretch, weaken, and fail.

One day, after about a week, sitting by the river alone with thunderclouds brewing, I started upon reflection. What was our purpose? Yesterday we stated our intent for this experience and it seemed that we are all seeking harmony, searching for something to fill the void within. I wanted to kill a deer, a good clean kill, grateful for the lessons and the filling of our bellies.

That evening the boys and I went looking for rabbits that we'd spotted feeding in the clearings. We split up and I lost an arrow shooting at a squirrel in a tree. A costly mistake. Reconvening at camp Tony had two squirrels and a grouse. Fine hunter. We feasted.

But the next day, everyone's energy was even lower, we simply weren't consuming enough calories. I'd also been feeling a little dizzy and had a slight headache. We went out again hunting before dusk but all returned empty-handed. Anna had made dinner; she called it "Everything Soup," having put a bit of everything from our food supplies in it.

The nights were getting cooler, and the boys were having trouble staying warm.

We made dinner the next evening that tasted mostly like *Bryoria* lichen slime even though it had avalanche lilies, onions, and a dried squirrel thrown in. I couldn't find the salt in the dark, which would have helped a lot. My scat on the trail the following day looked like *Bryoria* slime with berries in it. Dinner had looked like *Bryoria* slime with berries in it, hardly any difference really.

Back at camp, Tony, gloomy and apathetic, was seriously thinking about splitting. He noticed his arm shaking while he pulled his bow to full draw. He'd been missing all his squirrel shots and his confidence was diminishing. I'd been preparing for a year to do this, so my incentive was far greater. I wanted to learn, gain insight, and connect with the ancient hunter's spirit. I knew that this transformation was hovering just out of reach.

Homo sapiens, upright hunter, where have you gone? I asked. What is it that possesses me, obsesses me to return? Squirrels chattering, scolding me for my presence as I sit amid the young forest with words failing me. Soft-eyed does and spotted fawns, strong, elegant bucks, you elude me. Often we see each other, usually you see me first, stinking and crashing through the forest as we must seem to do. I search you out. Sometimes I watch you from above, my scent wafting away high on the light breeze, and you step closer, unaware; your delicate feet snap a twig, and I am the hunter, waiting, heart pounding, daring you to move into range, arrow nocked, hand almost trembling, belly rumbling.

How timeless these moments seem. Thus far the promise, flickering, recedes, a branch between us, position not quite right; wind changes direction, and you wander or flee out of sight.

Again I sit alone, viewing this mighty creation, remembering the time when I was one with God.

That night as I watched a mouse creep around in the rafters of the conical lodge we'd built and covered in green spruce boughs, I reflected on the reality that our diminished daily calorie intake meant that we were slowly starving.

Chris was feeling sick to his stomach. I caught him eating the fat out of the fat lamp the day before. He looked guilty but I couldn't blame him; I was hungry too.

I spent hours in my tree stand each day, watching the thoughts flow by. My hunger was replaced with a gnawing emptiness. We were learning, but I realized that if we had double the calories we could be learning a lot more.

Insufficient calories produce lethargy, forgetfulness, carelessness, weakness, dizziness, and stupidity! I understood that the longer we went without food, the less capable we became of obtaining it.

A couple more days of being wet, cold, and hungry and we decided with consensus that it was time to pack it up and go home. I vowed to be better prepared next time. I had learned so much about what not to do.

17

AFLOAT

The next year I determined: we were not going to starve this time! Understanding from the previous year how we limited our learning by our constant state of weakness, we bought and butchered a buffalo and spent much of our preparation time gathering wild foods.

Our group consisted of nine adults and three children (Klara was ten years old now and my friend Tom had come with two of his own children).

This Stone Age Project had a river excursion as its goal. I wanted to learn more about primitive boat building and boat travel, of which I knew almost nothing, so we endeavored to build traditional watercraft.

I had met an old Kootenai native up in British Columbia who had built several traditional canoes, only covering them in canvas instead of pine bark, and we consulted with him as we proceeded to build ours. I remember asking him what to stuff in the big hole between the keel and the end battens after we had fixed the bark to the gunwales. He said, "I usually just stuff an old sock in there." We were trying to do it with Stone Age technology so we used moss instead. Without him, though, we would probably never have put the canoe in the water.

The great pine tree we had slain to build our boat was a sacrifice. We had spent a long time searching for an appropriate tree to choose.

I asked one of my students to cut a tiny piece of my skin from the back of my arm as an exchange for the bark of the living tree. She sliced it off with a razor-sharp blade of obsidian, and I wrapped it in a small buckskin bundle and offered it up to the forest. Living skin for living skin, each a sacrifice but of different proportions. Though we both bled, mine was just a little wound leaving a small scar that reminds me of the great tree whose life we took. The sticky, clear sap, lifeblood of the tree, poured onto the earth as we pried away her skin. It was sweet to taste and we often stopped to lick the pale exposed wood.

And when the deed was done, it became our sweat that stained the earth. As the great pine was transformed into a canoe, my transformation was within.

It felt important to ritualize the felling of a four-hundred-year-old tree. We would skin a huge sheet of bark off it to make our sturgeon-nosed canoe. There is only one other traditional canoe shaped this way in the world, far away in Asia in the Amur River basin. We didn't know why the shape was important until we found ourselves out in the lake with a rising wind. A common shaped canoe would have blown all over the place and been very hard to handle. We also built a cedar board pirogue, but the boards had started to buckle so badly from swelling when we left it in the water that we had to pull all but one of the bottom cleats and replace them with thicker, stronger ones that we screwed down with brass instead of the pegs that hold the rest of the boat together, an exception to the Stone Age.

We sealed the seams with birch tar and the rest of the boat with bear fat and added seats. It had no leaks and though slow with its wide, flat bottom, it sturdily served as our well-loaded barge.

The bark canoe, just the opposite, delicate and fragile, also required its many cracks to be repitched, and still there was another slow leak that we couldn't find. Light and unstable, sitting high on the water it sped along, cutting the gentle waves happily with its ram ends.

All the other boats were modern, plastic and fiberglass, gray and green. Though this wasn't a totally primitive trip—I never expected that it would be with the plastic boats and life vests—the gear was comprised of simple buckskin clothes and felt or skin blankets, and all wild foods.

As part of the preparation in the spring we had paddled the whole Kootenai River in segments from where it crossed into Montana from Canada and existed for the first seventy miles as the Koocanusa Reservoir to where it doubled back to Canada from Idaho. Portaging the dam and the falls we got an idea of what we might expect when we repeated the journey during the summer in the Stone Age.

When it was finally time to go and our boats were loaded, we set out, seven canoes and a kayak. The cedar board pirogue was looking fine now after its reworking. The reservoir was still calm and inviting, the day warm, sun blinking off the rippling surface.

We had all spent considerable time throughout the spring gathering and preserving bulbs, berries, mushrooms, and the buffalo we had processed, so our stores of pemmican and berry cakes were impressive and heavy. Much more than we could carry if we were hiking.

After days on the water, I stopped counting them, preferring not to number them, quantify everything as my race is so apt to do. Here, the most important things were the wind, the sun, and the water.

The eagles were important too; we saw them daily, golden and bald eagles. I found a large wing feather and picked it up and examined it. I watched for the eagles and wondered what messages they had for us.

It rained our first night on the shore so we built a shelter and it stopped raining. The fire was banked and started again from coals in the morning. We paddled heads to the wind as the first little whitecaps curled over. Watching an eagle flying with the wind, I noticed that we didn't need to fight it; we could stop and wait in one sandy cove, or the next one. There was no agenda here. Eagle would lead us when it was time to go.

I fell in love with the bark canoe. Its patches of pitch covering opening cracks grew daily, but I covered them all, would have covered the entire boat if necessary, to keep that big tree alive with us. Crafted with our own hands, both the bark canoe and the pirogue gave me such pleasure to see on the water. They had spirit that the modern boats lacked.

Vivid impressions of that trip include: thunder rolling through the canyon while we get our gear and selves under upturned boats in just the nick of time; a spotted fawn swimming ahead of us; the water like glass reflecting cut banks and forest; cars stopping on the portage road to give us a ride that we graciously decline; yellow jackets; eagles; and rain—lots of rain.

One day, in a strong wind that brought a halt to the group, Tom broke and lost half his paddle blade as he battled some ferocious gusts; Klara was a passenger in the bow of his boat. They disappeared down the river, hurtling toward the Kootenai Falls that we were planning to portage with a safe, wide margin the following day. As the rest of the group huddled by the shore in a severe bout of driving rain, I set off frantically after my missing child, paddling the bark canoe hard to keep it facing forward in the wind. But when I spied them on the opposite shore, my daughter stashed safely under a cedar tree out of the rain, I was both relieved to find them and impressed by the bark canoe's maneuverability. I stopped fighting the wind and returned to shore.

We had plenty of food, we had a wonderful community, but the rain was relentless and people got edgy being forced to stay put to stay dry. The group grew as restless as the weather. The river flowed by, oblivious of our thoughts and words. The rain misted through the boughs of our sheltering fir—maybe it didn't care. Hopefully our presence there fed and nurtured it in return, ashes from our fire and our pee at night on the needle-covered ground. With our abundant supplies, we could have gone on but the weather kept us bound to our shelter. Our pace was out of our control.

With each project I was learning, recognizing essential foundational truths, but the list seemed endless. I now understood that movement was a key element of success. We are nomads at our core. Another project that reinforced this was spectacularly successful in terms of physical sustenance. This one we called Peace Creek Project.

We had made and set up a conical fish trap on Peace Creek and placed it at the apex of a funnel we constructed with rocks in the shallows. The first fish were caught efficiently by driving them downstream from the upper pools, splashing noisily and slapping the water with sticks. They fled and were funneled directly into our trap. We then left it there to work passively overnight.

On that trip, everyone brought fish back to camp with them, caught by net, hook, trap, or our bare hands. Fishing with a bone hook that has no barb is no easy task. Often one must fling the fish out of the water, lightning fast with the first strike. The grounded, gasping fish would try to flop back toward the water as we gave chase. I have seen them hanging in trees or cast far behind me and lost in the forest duff.

We made elaborate dinners: dozens of trout cooked to perfection on the coals and filleted on rocks; stews of roots, seeds, meat, and black tree lichen, adding plenty of fat since the trout contain so little. We fried the heads and ate the brains then cooked the skeletons to a crispy snack like potato chips to glean as many calories as possible. I made a list of observations while watching the fish for hours at a time:

1. Fresh grasshoppers stay tied to a hook longer than dried ones.
2. Stream fish seem hungrier after a cold, damp spell.
3. Jerking fish out of the water with surface strikes appears to be the best way to hook them.
4. Rib bone hooks are easier to manufacture than other bones but can be weak. Thorn hooks float, bone hooks sink. No one has yet caught fish on thorn hooks.
5. Abalone lures inspire interest but no strikes.
6. Unweighted lines are hard to cast.
7. Stream fish lose interest when the sun starts to shine on the water.
8. Fish tend to escape by swimming upstream.
9. Fish face upstream.
10. Fish are easily startled by shadows and other disturbances.
11. Fish have a sharp learning curve.
12. Fish have memory.
13. Do fish communicate with each other?

That Stone Age excursion lasted the customary month. We had not planned to hunt big game and focused our attention on fishing instead. Our group had the difficult dynamic of nearly all of us having spouses or partners who were not participating with us that diffused the energy and sent it outward instead of in toward the center of our clan. Though we were successful in our fishing endeavors and many of the clan members were highly skilled, I felt we lacked something not quite tangible. Was it just me? We didn't sing together, and I found myself making up songs with harmonies that I had to sing myself.

Now, some years later at Smoky Mountain, we had a clan that was so tightly knit and eager to find our way together. What we lacked in knowledge and experience we made up for in affinity and cooperation; we talked, laughed, cried, prayed, and sang our hearts out but the challenge of the elusive game in the aftermath of the disquieting wildfires cast its own shadow over us as the sun's shadows also grew longer with the steady passing of the season.

This high country is not a place for people to live. To journey through, to hunt, to pray on the bare windy mountaintops closer to the gods, yes, but not to live. The river valleys are where the ancients lived, where our ancestors have always lived. The valleys have always been where the roots and the berries, the fish and the deer are more abundant. But the once wild river valleys are now flanked by choking industry, streams of gridlocked roads, teeming with people that swarm like ants. What have we done? Forgive us, what have we done?

18

FIRST PEOPLE

In the deepest, darkest part of a Montana winter, stagnation can lead to despondency. In these twilight zones that demand focused and conscious practices to avoid succumbing to depression I recognize the importance of community, fresh air and exercise, good nutrition, sleep, and dream recollection. Dreams and their messages are pertinent, our subconscious giving us clues to navigate our waking world. I now know deep winter is actually the perfect time for introspection and reflection. Without the purification of this time, the death of old and stagnant energy and ideas, there can be no space for the conception of something fresh and new.

But as winter finally started to wane and the first Chinook winds blew in a thaw followed by another freeze, my second husband—the hide tanner—and I would find ourselves ready for a change and would leave our homestead to take a road trip south to the desert lands to teach at a primitive skills gathering and spend time exploring. In March, after a month in the Arizona sun, we were usually in no great hurry to get back to Montana for the fifth season we called "mud season." One winter, it was just the two of us—Klara was staying with Ocean—as we started the long drive north again in our truck. I noticed a dotted line on the road atlas that led to a place called Supai on the Havasupai tribal lands near the Grand Canyon. I love maps and the juicy sensation of discovering a new place, and dotted lines on road maps can only mean one thing, a trail! A road map with a trail marked on it is something noteworthy, so I suggested we go there and check it out. My husband thought it was way too far off our route. I concurred and switched to a playful technique I have for spontaneous adventures, involving spinning the map and with eyes closed dropping an index finger on a destination. I opened my eyes, and there was my finger, once more directly on Supai. We decided that this was too great a coincidence and chose to see what providence would bring.

Arriving at the end of the road just as night was falling, we pitched camp and peered down the trail wondering what would lie ahead.

Next morning, we gathered supplies, packed up our backpacks, and started off. Coming up the canyon path was a man riding a mule with a pack string behind him.

We peppered him with questions, which he answered patiently: "Yes, there is a village, a few hundred people live down there, it's about eight miles, and this is the last mule mail train in America!"

With that, the mail carrier continued his journey ferrying mail for the United States postal service and we, even more excited now, trotted down into the canyon that mostly followed a dry wash. In desert country such as this, one could see why there was no point in having a road descend into the canyon. With the steep walls on both sides it was easy to imagine what would happen if a heavy rain were to fall anywhere in the vicinity. All that water would course into the nearest wash, fill it, and go gushing down the canyons to the river far below. I had experienced the power of flash floods in the desert lands of the American Southwest. One night when Klara was a baby, Ocean and I had parked our truck beside a tiny stream to camp for the night. We had built a simple little canvas-covered wagon over the bed of the pickup and, as we were going to sleep, it started to rain. I knew there was the possibility of flooding, but the stream was so tiny, I could hop over it easily with a baby in my arms. All the same, just to be safe I suggested we drive up to higher ground for the night, which we did, and fell asleep to the lullaby of steady rain. When we awoke the next morning, there was a loud roar; looking out of the back of the truck I was horrified to see that our little stream had become a raging torrent about forty yards wide and where we had first parked was about four feet under a brown turbulent river. If we had stayed where we were, we would have been hit by that wall of water and washed away, no doubt about it. Since then whenever I'm hiking in dry canyons, I always check for escape routes. Even if it's sunny, a microburst many miles away can be upon you without so much as a warning.

It was a beautiful warm Arizona day in mid-February and the Montana winter we had left seemed very distant. It was good to be exploring this land.

About halfway down the trail, on the top of the canyon wall we saw a raven pecking on the quill of a large feather. He released the feather and we watched it drift twenty or so feet down to the trail. I walked over and picked it up while Raven just sat there looking at us.

I placed the feather on a good-size boulder in the middle of the path. We walked a few yards farther, and I yelled back to him, "Here you go, Raven, here's your feather back."

At that point the big black bird flew down to the rock, picked up the feather again and flew directly toward us, dropping the feather as he passed above our heads. We looked at each other as Raven flew away. I picked the feather up again, sticking it in the headband of my wide-brimmed hat. This was a gift! We walked on. As we dropped in elevation the canyon widened and big trees appeared beside the trail and we heard the sound of water rushing close by. Suddenly from out of the canyon wall, a creek magically appeared. It wasn't a little trickling spring, it was a great volume of crystal clear water with a hint of turquoise that gushed from a fissure in the rock. What other strange and wonderful occurrences would happen next? We followed the rushing creek until we came to the gates of the village. A museum and visitor center was built right at the entrance and we paid a small sum, entered, and looked around at the Havasupai artifacts exhibited there.

Havasupai—the "people of the blue-green waters." They are one of the tribes to be living on a remnant of their traditional lands, having lived both in the canyon as well as upon the rim seasonally for at least eight hundred years. Since the European invasion their territory is now less than a tenth of the land that their ancestors roamed. An ongoing dilemma for the Havasupai in modern times is how to generate income from tourism in the small area that the canyon provides without damaging the fragile ecosystem.

I had seen on the map that the trail continued down toward the Grand Canyon for a few more miles where this flashy turquoise tributary made its final spectacular arrival at the great river with a waterfall named Havasu Falls. We walked purposefully along the broad, dusty trail passing a deserted primary school, a general store that seemed nothing more than a tired shack with faded advertisements, and the post office from which the mule train we had met at the top of the canyon had originated. Scruffy prefab houses with bare yards were scattered haphazardly and dogs lounged with lolling tongues in the shade of the few trees. Some horses wandered listlessly seeking out tufts of vegetation. The scene juxtaposed the magnificent backdrop of sculpted red rock cliffs and spires. Along the canyon walls derelict stone houses from a previous era aesthetically blended with their environment.

We were dressed in our customary buckskin clothing and walking barefoot. We had leather backpacks that we had made and my hand drill kit poked out of a pocket in my pack. I carried a gourd water canteen, supported by a buckskin thong. We were not your average-looking tourists. I always felt especially self-conscious when on Native American tribal lands dressed the way we were—I didn't want to seem to be pretending to be anything I wasn't—but these were the clothes we had. This was in fact how we dressed, so we couldn't change anything anyway. It was morning and people were moving about the village. We asked the first few folks we passed if there was anyone here still making traditional items like the ones we had seen in the museum. We were met with suspicion and felt thoroughly uncomfortable. "Where you from anyway? California?" one man asked us with barely disguised derision. "Nah, Montana." Being from Montana is a bit like having a special key in certain situations and it helped, but we still didn't feel we were very welcome.

We decided to bag the trip to the falls and head back out of there. On the way, more people stopped and stared at us and it wasn't until we reached the village gates again that a man engaged with us without our questions or prompting.

"What's that you got there?" he said, motioning to my gourd canteen.

"My water bottle."

He got up from the bench he was sitting on and started to walk away.

I don't know what possessed me right then, but before he had gone very far I ran after him and pulled the feather from my hat that Raven had given us. "I'm not sure why," I said a little breathlessly, "but I think this is supposed to be for you." I offered him the feather and he took it from me, studying it silently for a few moments.

"This is a feather from a fallen eagle," he said finally. "Come with me." My husband and I exchanged a quick glance and we followed him without speaking.

He told us his name and took us to his little stone house, built with local rock, a welcome change from the government-issue houses that had been helicoptered in for many of the village residents.

He showed us his own buckskins that he had tanned and explained that there were still people in the village who worked to preserve and protect the traditional ways. They were known as "the Guardians of the Grand Canyon." They opposed the meddling of the government, they didn't want the helicopters bringing in tourists and cheap, poorly made infrastructure. They were saddened by the continued practice of removing their children and sending them away to boarding schools when they finished their primary education in the village. Even there, the teacher was an outsider, not a tribal member at all. His honesty and openness contrasted with the initial responses we had received, and after our visit with him we decided not to leave, but head back down toward the falls after all and stay a while longer.

We said goodbye and retraced our steps from the morning, only this time everything was different. It felt to me that Raven had whispered into the eagle feather some kind of charm that now hovered about us as we meandered back through the village. This time we were met with friendly greetings with each encounter.

One old man asked about the hand drill fire kit poking out of the pocket in my pack. "It's a fire kit," I told him.

"See that ruin up there, that's where I was born," he told us, pointing to an old stone dwelling perched on the cliff, built safely out of reach of any flash flood as the old ones always knew.

"Now they say we should live down here beside the river and they bring us these new houses," said our new acquaintance. Then he asked us to show him how to make fire with our kits. We were stunned and deeply humbled to be asked to resurrect the practice that was so recently lost in his culture and so long ago lost in mine. He said he remembered his uncle making fire, but never learned how. Now he wanted to teach his grandchildren. We followed him and sat in the dust outside his home, where skinny dogs lay panting in the sun, and took out our fire kits, encouraging the man with his knobby arthritic fingers twirling the drill and taking turns. Between us we coaxed a coal from the slender fire sticks and blew it to life there in the yard. He was delighted and thanked us profusely. We packed up our gear and continued on our way, a gaggle of little children following us, laughing and playing in the warm, dusty sand.

We entered the shade of tall trees that flanked the marvelous creek once more and came upon a small group of men hauling long branches of firewood. They greeted us and asked us where we were going and we told them we were headed to the falls. The sound of a helicopter clattered closer and they looked up at it with fierce anger.

"We are Guardians of the Grand Canyon. We are going to sweat—come join us."

Once more we aborted our mission and helped them drag more wood to their little sweat lodge by the creek. Some of the teenagers were home from boarding school and we were once more invited to make fire with the ancient and traditional fire sticks. The boys jumped in, sticks spinning faster and faster, brown hands that were of this land and white that were not. Together, the sacred fire was lit.

"What kind of Indian are you anyway?" somebody asked me.

"A Swedish Indian," I replied and they laughed.

We sweat. They are traditionalists and the honor was all ours. They sang their songs and then asked us if we had a song to sing. I closed my eyes and sang to them a song of blood and water, stone and bone, with all the feeling that our present situation inspired and waited somewhat timidly for their response.

"It is a good song," they said, nodding approvingly. Crawling from the lodge and immersing ourselves in the turquoise waters, I marveled at the change of events that occurred with the one simple little act of the offering of the eagle feather.

"Come back and see us again," they told us as we finally parted.

We never made it to the falls, but somehow that didn't matter anymore. The connection with the tribe was what really mattered.

The story of invasion, conquering, and displacement of Indigenous peoples leaves a trail of blood and tears that no amount of time will ever erase. We were visitors, uninvited guests, and we left that place, and those brave, beautiful people, with full hearts.

———————————◄

It's November, springtime in the Kalahari Desert of northern Namibia. My visiting group of European and American students is spending a whole month in the village. There are a couple of San tribal members who speak some English and act as our interpreters. We spend hours asking the elders to tell us how it was before the borehole, before the settlement, when they would roam, wild and free. It was not easy, they tell us. The romanticism is marred by the death of children without water, starvation, and scarcity. A young Swede in our group asks the old chief who is talking with us if he ever had the feeling of kinship with the animals he has hunted that made him want to just watch them instead. The translation is completed and the old one's reply is brief. "The old man says: when he sees an animal, he wants to kill it." There is no room for sentimentalism in a wild world such as this where to eat or be eaten is simply the reality. In the West, our culture has set us at the top of the food chain, having destroyed nearly all the large predators. Our awareness has disappeared alongside them.

Named days drift by meaninglessly and I begin to understand why these people of the bush have a wholly different concept of time. I ask one of the trackers his age and he answers, "I was born in the rainy season."

In the searing midday sun, the Kalahari sand scorches unprotected feet and a little blue butterfly stops for a drink of sweaty moisture from my toes. Even the shade gasps for another breath of ruffled breeze.

This morning, after several hours of tracking, we climbed gratefully into an elephant water hole, its earthy, musky, slightly sour scented water pleasurably evaporating and filling our senses. The giant tracks of the elephants themselves show they have left the water hole just hours earlier. After our dip, I follow an older elephant trail for a short way, jumping from one large track to the next, delighting in their immensity. Something catches my eye in the track ahead; pressed into the baked mud is a stone. This in itself is an anomaly; the vast Kalahari Desert consists of interminable sand with a notable scarcity of other rocks. I bend toward it, my curiosity turning to wonder as I pry it from the track and turn it in my hands. Mine are not the first hands to hold this stone, for it is an artifact, an ancient relic flaked by a human being hundreds if not thousands of years before the elephant ground it into the mud with her heavy foot. I do not usually take these old tools, but I carry this one in my hand for a long while before setting it gently back down on the sand where it may sit for another hundred thousand years.

The little people still know every track and bush, still dance and sing the traditional songs, but hidden between the claps and smiles of the beaming children one starts to discern snippets of rap in uncomprehended English. Cell phones dangle from the outlet at the water pump and when the creased faces of the smiling people break open, browned and rotting teeth are revealed. Discarded soda bottles lie on the outskirts of the camp, and when we gently suggest that the sugar is harming them, they reply that they need it for energy. Without dependable access to their hunter-gatherer diet of wild meat, fruits, and vegetables, the people are now issued bags of GMO corn, noodles, and sugar.

We plan a hike across the desert with some of the villagers to guide and protect us. We will sleep out for a couple of nights without tents and it is with much excitement that we set off. Ten from our own group and eleven San: two of the village's best trackers and hunters and their wives and babies plus a handful of teenage boys who are up for an adventure.

We whites fill multiple water canteens, thirst being just one of the fears competing with snakes, lions, scorpions, and the countless desert creatures that are potentially harmful.

We depart early before the sun is too hot. Clouds have been building in the afternoons for the last few days and the long-awaited monsoon makes the air dense and sticky.

The two San hunters carry their tiny bows with the deadly poison-tipped arrows; the women carry their children bound in brightly colored cloth, and they sing as they tear berries from the bushes that we pass. I lure the babies to trust me, the great white monster with yellow hair and strange blue eyes, by pressing more berries into their chubby, dirty hands.

A youth carries a long pole with a hook at one end used for poking down rabbit holes and skewering the unfortunate rabbit if one happens to be hiding there. We come across a land tortoise that the hunters eye with relish and put upside down so it can't walk away but one of our group turns it loose when no one is looking. This brings up a heated debate among our group: "Who are we to take away the food of these people if they find it in their own land?" The San seem wholly unconcerned. The sun beats ruthlessly down on us and we migrate toward some large trees that will offer us shade for the coming hours that will be so unbearably hot. A great cry and commotion is let loose among the San. A black mamba snake lies in one of the trees where we were about to sit. A mamba bite is a death sentence and I hastily shoulder my backpack again thinking we will move farther on, but the San are in full assault mode and throw stones at the deadly snake that with lightning speed departs its tree and breaks cover on the ground. I look toward the women to decide what to do and they run as fast as they can away from the snake's last sighting. I do the same. It's mayhem with everyone running and yelling. Then the snake climbs another tree and the assault begins anew. Eventually the snake is torn from the branches, mangled with the rabbit pole, and left on the baking sand, unmoving. The excitement dies down and we settle ourselves in the now-safe shade to wait out the heat of the day. We learn that it is a belief among the San that if they kill the first snake on a walkabout, all the subsequent snakes will leave them alone. I can't help wondering if it wouldn't have been safer to just find a new resting place instead.

We continue our hike after a few hours of uncomfortable repose. I ask !Toma, the tracker, how he knows where we are going. With the sun now covered behind a leaden sky and the endless Kalahari stretched flatly before us with scrubby bushes and trees that all look more or less the same, there are no visible landmarks, trails, or signs to my uneducated eyes that might determine our location. !Toma, unbearably thin and suffering from tuberculosis, smiles his sympathetic shy smile and tells me, "I just know."

This is the difference between people who belong to the land and people who believe it belongs to them. !Toma and his people are inextricably linked physically, spiritually, and ancestrally to the land, which makes them a part of it.

Sweating profusely, we foreigners are drinking our voluminous water supplies but we each carry more than a gallon. The young San boys carry their water in small plastic bottles. When they run out, they dig for the enormous fleshy water roots under the baking sand that they mash and squeeze to extract the slightly bitter liquid.

We stop and study the tracks of steenbok, kudu, and hyena; a long shot is made from one of the Bushmen's little bows at a springbok antelope but misses. Clouds are gathering and the temperature drops, and our guides decide it is time to stop for the night. The thirsty boys soon disappear, pushing on to the water hole and leaving their bags while we make camp. We gather a large pile of dead wood and build a fire, carefully raking away the dry grasses, conscious of how easily the wind could pick up even the smallest ember and set the bush ablaze. The clouds move in fast. Heavy, dark cumulus clouds and minutes after a light tarp is erected for shelter the first splattering drops of rain start to fall.

Simultaneously, the boys return still thirsty with empty water bottles after an elephant bull chased them away from the water hole. They dive under the shelter with the rest of us; twenty-one beings from two wildly opposite cultures knit together by the storm that unleashes itself with unrestrained power. In the deafening roar of wind and rain, I consider the strong likelihood that we will all die together, struck by lightning, huddled in the pool of water that floods steadily under the tarp whose edges we grip as the magnificent Thunder Beings hurl bolt after blinding bolt of lightning onto the thirsty Kalahari sands.

I wonder how many of us send out a silent, whispered, or even shouted prayer, for who among us would hear over the deafening roar of thunder and the pounding, torrential rain? Yet I recognize that I am not afraid to die here, not afraid to call these my last moments. I am almost exultant in the possibility. However, after an hour or more we have not exploded in a blast of heavenly electricity, nor have we drowned in the accumulating waters. A puff adder, displaced by its own inundated home, slides slowly by and peacefully away, and our shivering is eased and dispelled by the hard-won rekindled fire. Kneeling in the muddy darkness, shaving bark off rain-drenched twigs and enormously grateful for a dry paper bag smeared with oily skin salve. Nobody bats an eye when the boys add their plastic water bottles to the pyre, willing anything that might combust in these suddenly reversed conditions. The rain continues for several hours; some snatch sleep propped up on each other in the shelter, and the wettest of us use the fire to warm the water that saturates our clothes and blankets, as we watch out for lion eyes that might appear on the periphery of our sodden camp. An incongruous yellow umbrella appears from someone's pack and we take turns pretending that it really helps. The hours slowly pass in a kind of dreamy motion picture way and as the rain slacks off, one by one the trackers, sleepy-eyed, appear and tell us stories of the hunt. The tiny woman whose name I cannot pronounce sits with her swaddled infant on a pile of damp bedding. She becomes my new heroine; perhaps it is her serenity and accepting grace. I can't say exactly why, but I am in love with her round face, her wide-set eyes and unflinching demeanor. The baby squirms and I hold out my finger for him to grasp.

Having survived the storm together, we journey on to the water hole where the boys spear bullfrogs and the rest of us take a well-needed nap before we are picked up by the truck that has come to take us back to the village.

That night we sit with the villagers and sing together. There is a new camaraderie between us.

As darkness falls, a terrible wailing comes from the villagers' camp. At first I think it's an animal of some sort but as it persists I realize it's a woman lamenting. The wailing is joined by men's voices shouting, angry and accusing.

Our worried-looking interpreter comes to our camp some hours later asking us if we've seen his wife. She had evidently been in town at the bar with some of the others and had disappeared into the bush. He tells us that two brothers have gotten drunk and been fighting and one attacked the other with a broken bottle.

I sleep uneasily.

The following evening the villagers join us at our campfire for the last time before we leave tomorrow. The interpreter's wife is among them, quietly composed.

The old healer man enters the circle from his usual place at the periphery and starts to encourage the women to clap and sing. Both San and Europeans are interspersed around the circle and as I realize that a healing ceremony is about to begin, I try to drop out from among these dark-skinned women but am pulled back into place by the strong hands of the two who flank me. I cannot clap the complicated poly rhythms that they are making, but I do my best as the voices swell around us and the healer starts to shake and gyrate within the firelit circle. He staggers toward one of his kinsmen and appears to pull unseen threads from the man's body. I am aware that this is not a show put on for our benefit but a real ceremony and we are now included. The healer then performs a similar exorcism on another man from the village and I understand that these are the brothers who had been in conflict during the night that the drunken wailing broke out. The clapping and singing of the people causes a shift in perception and the trance state of the healer infects us all. He is whirling erratically within the circle and eventually falls dangerously close to the fire of which he seems to have no awareness. Sure and gentle hands of his kinsmen pull him to safety where he lies spent and twitching.

The First People know they cannot go back but instead are forced to leap "forward" in such a swift and sudden bound across the span of so many thousands of years to meet our broken, disconnected culture.

We offer them misguided aid without asking them what they actually want and need. I witnessed the disastrous consequences of a well-intentioned NGO who installed flush toilets at the tourist campsite of the San villagers' living museum. Two months later it was broken and disrupting the water source to the village itself. In another unforeseen miscalculation, the villagers were given goats and encouraged to become pastoralists. They were told not to eat them before they reached a sustainable breeding population. In the meantime the goats devoured all the wild plants the villagers still relied upon for their own sustenance. Assuming Indigenous peoples will respond in the same way that we might to our voluntary assistance is arrogant and narrow-minded.

What can we offer them that is honest, whole, and beautiful? The feeling of leaving these people, so embodying their land, reminds me of the time with the Havasupai Guardians and once again my heart is torn.

19

PILGRIM

It is so rare that we sit still and in silence, without distraction. I know how my mind will do almost anything to stop deep contemplation and stay in control with unrestrained busyness. In the stillness, ego loses its grasp, fearing the flooding truth that may take its place. Such is the gift of grief. Six months after my mother's passing, I had decided to make a pilgrimage to Nepal, as a way to say goodbye to her, starting on her birthday in November.

My family, I often felt, did not always understand me or why I chose the life that I did. But my mother and I connected on a spiritual level although we led very different material lives. At the beginning of this journey, I didn't have a plan beyond the expansion of my mind and soul, so I wandered in a way that I had not done on my travels in many years. The void left by loss gave me the courage to explore beyond the familiar habits and places that I had grown accustomed to. At the time, I was already living on the banks of the Twisp River. Besides Klara, the most important being in my life was gone and the emptiness of my grief was somehow liberating.

Klara was seventeen and living in Seattle. When she'd turned twelve, she made the decision to try being a "normal" kid and went to live near her dad, on an island in the Puget Sound; she wanted to go to school and see what the outside world was up to. I didn't want to force her to stay with me, it would have made me the enemy. So I had to let her go, but I felt like I was losing her to the culture that was my enemy instead. Now, though, on the cusp of adulthood, Klara was a confident young woman who could bridge both worlds. I had invited her to come with me to Nepal, but she was as busy with her life as I was with mine at her age.

My first impressions of Kathmandu are of chaos: strange noises, scents, and visions. I am split wide open and feel such a significant freedom of mind that I'm awash with unexplored potential and opportunity. The familiar ways of the West have been left behind and I am acutely aware of my foreignness.

I plan to take a bus from Kathmandu to Pokhara. I've been warned against the perils of the local buses. Everyone recommended the tourist buses instead that are much safer. By this morning I was convinced that I should take the tourist bus but found that it had already left so here I sit in the local one. I'm told it's better to ride on the roof but we are not allowed up there until after the police check station. It's illegal. From the roof, if the bus should go careening off the mountainside (a highly possible scenario), one can at least jump and potentially avoid certain death. This, I think, will be an interesting journey.

A young boy with a toothbrush in his pocket took my pack and put it on the roof. As the bus crawls through fume-choked streets with hordes of youngsters jumping on and off, I wonder if it's still there. There are no bus stops. The boy with the toothbrush and another young man hang out the door yelling "Pokhara, Pokhara, Pokhara . . ."

We stop, still not outside the city. People talk on cell phones everywhere by burned-out vehicles and disintegrating piles of trash. It seems that the boys are trying to fill up the bus. They go out and encourage potential passengers. Some climb in and look around, then get off again, evidently not impressed with what they see. Did I get on a bad bus? Urchins selling water and snacks climb on as well as beggars. I look down at my journal and keep writing. I could go broke real quickly. A little boy with huge brown eyes and a filthy shirt stands before me, hand outstretched. I try to ignore him, I can't stand it. I give him some bread and he continues through the bus munching. We are still only half full, other buses look packed.

We roll on.

Images so fascinating flit by constantly.

A man and woman on a motorbike with their two kids, the little one dangling precariously from her mother's arm. A handsome Gurkha soldier sits next to me, wearing a mask to filter out some of the poisonous air. The city goes on and on as it picks up passengers. The bus is nearly full by the time we finally start to climb and terraced fields appear. At a police checkpoint, we stop and start, choking on gas fumes.

Off in the distance I catch my first glimpse of snowy Himalayan peaks hovering like specters above the gray hazy air. Now we are hurtling down the steep narrow mountain road amid a cacophony of other honking buses. I am the only foreigner aboard. My eyes sting, my head aches, and yet I wouldn't trade it for the insulated tourist bus that I see up ahead of us. I'd love to get on the roof but we keep seeing police, and I hear there is a hefty fine. My traveling companion's name is Menon, meaning "gentle mind," a good name for an officer in the world's toughest mercenary army. I wonder, *What happens when I need to pee?* I dare not drink anything.

Our bus driver's judgment is flawless as we scream around the corners at breakneck speed. Our lives are all in his hands. I trust him implicitly. Dark clouds build as we near Pokhara but we arrive alive. Even my pack survived the trip on the roof. Since angels are obviously protecting me, I accept a ride with the first person to offer me a cheap hotel room. Barely hesitating, I clamber onto the back of this stranger's motorbike with both backpacks and no helmet and as the rain comes down, I trust him, too.

I've arranged to meet a guide to take me to the mountains, into Gurung territory. These people, the last of the Honey Hunters—who for centuries have subsisted on their ability to climb cliff faces and ancient trees, lull the wild bees with smoke, and remove pieces of the enormous hives for the rich and valuable honey—have until recently procured their bounty with only the most rudimentary of tools and gear. As always, the skill and ingenuity of the mountain peoples fascinates me.

My guide, Tenzi, is Sherpa. He feels like an old family friend; his name means "the Beginning of the Winter Season." Tall and slightly built with a scant, scant beard, his face cracks into an easy smile.

———————⋗———————

It's our third day on the trail. We toil up the stone staircase; it's slow going. Sweat pours off my face, and I feel it running down my back and legs. Tenzi tells me a word in Nepali: "It means going uphill," he says.

I ask him what the word for "downhill" is and which he prefers. He smokes a cigarette and coughs. "I don't like going uphill *and* I don't like going downhill," he tells me. I tell him he should live in Kansas. We see no other foreigners. Everyone asks where I am from. Tenzi gives me a crash course in Nepali . . . My name is Lynx . . . I live in America . . . I made it myself . . . I feel a bit like a circus entertainer; they smile and laugh and ask Tenzi a thousand questions.

I realize I am much too hot in my buckskin pants. It stays warm and balmy into the evening. I buy some traditional cloth to wear for a skirt. Tenzi and I walk the streets of the village into the darkness. The children follow us chanting "Namaste, namaste, hello, hello!"

After dinner I wander alone through the rice fields to the river. The moon is full, her face the only familiar one I see in all this strange world. I am glad for it. The tree beings, the plant beings, the rock beings, all waiting to become friends as we learn one another's language, together with these black-haired, smiling-eyed people.

We walk, now where no road exists. We cross a rickety bridge and climb to a beautiful farm above the river. I make friends with the three little kids and we eat the best curried fish with our rice and lentils. We decide to stay the night. The old man there is sixty-seven. He came here when he was twelve and his father built the place. His wife is buried on the hillside. They had four sons, one of whom, Shuk, now lives here with his wife and two children. There is another family that lives here too, with their four kids. The man, Pasad, is mending a cast net; he says we can go fishing with him. Down the stone staircase to the river, he wears socks but no shoes to keep traction on the slippery rocks. Pasad throws the cast net sure and nimble in the fast-flowing water. It's breathtakingly beautiful but there are no fish. He says they used to catch many.

At dark we return without fish but with eggs from the neighbors downstream. The men drink Chang (rice beer) and rakshi (corn liquor). I try some, it's good. Pasad pulls out an ancient musket and asks if I want to go to the jungle to hunt. I answer, "Yes, tomorrow, without the rakshi," and they all laugh and start singing songs that they make up while beating on a plastic bucket for a drum. I crawl to a flat grassy area on the hillside above the house and sleep like the dead.

Back on the trail again. Across the hills, terraced farms appear in impossible places. After three hours of arduous climbing we reach one of these unlikely villages. Women in the fields harvesting rice and millet with small-toothed sickles call me to come help. I go down and give it a try.

The sky clears, and the Annapurna range leaps into sight.

Upward, upward, interminably on. We decide to stop at a village. I sit with an old man and a bunch of chickens and baskets. As I write in my journal, teenage girls look over my shoulder two inches away. I give them my photo book with pictures of my home and family to look at and it gives me a little space. Tenzi, my saint, answers their questions. I am beat.

Here I receive my first major trial. There is no privacy. Every time I look up there are ten black eyes watching my every move. I wait for darkness, but then they shine a light on me. I know they are just curious and well-meaning but it starts to drive me crazy. I get up to find a quiet place away from the village, but the old man is worried about thieves. Finally we reach a compromise and Tenzi takes me to a room in the back of the house away from the prying eyes.

It's better but I still feel like crying.

This is cultural immersion and I am drowning. Tenzi is my lifeline.

We have seen no other foreigner since leaving Pokhara. All this is exactly what I asked for and wanted and now I long to blend with the crowd. Do I? I don't know. It's just like the period on the Stone Age Projects that I call "adjustment." Someone peers at me through the crack in the door.

I used to think I was tough, but I am humbled. These people are tough. All day long it seems that our destination is three hours away. It doesn't matter how many hours we walk, how many steps we climb, the elusive village is never quite here. Finally, we're told it's one hour away and three hours later we reach it only to find there is a permit checkpoint here. I do not have a permit to be in this region, didn't even know I needed one, so we wait till nightfall. Then, with my basket and my traditional wrap, my yak scarf covering my head, we enter the village and pass the now empty checkpoint shack in disguise.

The stars appear, the fog has lifted, and there is another old friend: Cassiopeia, at the foot of the Himalaya where I have come searching.

Silent dawn. Soft pink light of alpenglow graces Annapurna in the distance. We head back to Pokhara today on a mountain bus ride to await the permit that I have now applied for to hike in the Annapurna range, alone this time. I must change my perception of "impossible," since the impossible is a daily occurrence. Tenzi says we must walk back to the last village to get on the bus. He asks each person along the trail and we get a variety of answers: "There is a bus today," "There is no bus today," "The bus has already left," "The bus is waiting for us."

The bus is in fact waiting for us! I ask the bus driver, who looks about fifteen years old, if I can ride on the roof. He says no. I ask him why not. "Very dangerous, your choice." I climb on the roof and ride a little way holding on very tightly, then I join everyone else inside. It is indeed very dangerous; you could either be scraped off or bounced off!

As we slowly make our way down the side of a steep mountain that yesterday I would have deemed impossible, I sometimes bounce four or five inches above my seat. The boy driver plays loud Nepali pop music, and my arms ache from clinging to the seat in front of me. I peer over the side of the mountain; I'm not scared anymore. It's best

to approach all this with the Buddhist philosophy that everything is
an illusion. I have had five years' worth of new experiences in the last
five days, and my head is spinning.

———————————————

Now, back in the bustling city of Pokhara staying in a hostel for a few
days to gather supplies and rest my weary limbs, I see a sign advertis-
ing a Buddhism course and, on a whim, I wander in and sign up for it.
What could I have to lose? What might I stand to gain? Do gain and
loss have any serious import in the grander scheme of life?

I am in deep investigation into the mind. When I walked into this
place I couldn't find a living soul. I wandered around and around until I found one of the staff members. I am in the right place. I feel it instinctively. Although this is only a three-day course, an introduction
to Buddhism, I know that I will be pointed in the right direction as I
leave. There are nine people in our group. Europeans, North Americans, and an Israeli. Just one token man. I am the oldest. I am open.

Our teacher, the venerable Yeshe, is an American monk who has
been teaching for thirty years.

He is clear and engaging in his method. There are teachers everywhere, but is there someone particular I am still waiting to meet while
I am here? Question: "Who are you?" This is what our teacher asks us
to consider. We discuss it before our evening silence as we eat dinner.

Who am I?

I am perfection in the Universe . . .
I am the perfection of the Universe . . .

This is all I come up with. Questions demanding answers beyond
words. Then more pours out . . .

I am everything, I am nothing
I am the beginning and the end
I am momentary and eternal
I am substance, I am formless
I am light and love in darkness and fear.

We sit in the gompa with its red floor and yellow walls while he asks us all this question.

"Who are you?"

There is confusion and flustered responses. Concepts of self, dissolving, looking at the ever-changing essence of being. I start to smile, and feelings of overwhelming love come over me. My whole body tingles, I spread out of my body, I feel like I might cry, I smile some more, I laugh, I tingle. "Who am I?" I don't mind. I just am . . .

20

Hidden Lakes

Ben is snoring quietly as I wriggle out of my buffalo robe. I crawl over Marcus as carefully as I can, trying not to wake him, but he opens his eyes sleepily and rolls over. Rick's sleeping robe is empty, his bow and quiver gone.

No deer fell before us yesterday and as I now plunge into the lake's water for my morning dip I see the fish are surface feeding and sending out concentric rippling rings far offshore.

Later, when I toss in a line with a squirming grasshopper, the wind has come up and the window closed. Despondency. How can I learn to live and eat in this wild world?

How can I live and eat in the modern world when I see its monumental cost?

I feel dizzy and walk slowly back up the trail to the hunting camp, bow still strung. I need something to literally fall before me, so incapable I feel as hunter.

Rick comes back from fishing, scarcely more successful than the rest of us. Just one fish between the four of us. He lays it on the coals and studies it quietly while it cooks.

Oh, fish, finned and flecked with glittering spots, your slippery bodies shining in the sun. Fish, fast and flawless, discerning eyes summing up the situation: leap and strike or flash and run. Watching you I have gained such respect for your beauty, your grace, and yes, today your sagacity is greater than ours.

Time is different here, punctuated not so much by the occurrence of sudden events but by the slow cycles in the changes of nature. The weather holds. It's cooler, and as the sun filters through the forest canopy a light breeze stirs the leaning trees that creak and groan like ghosts. Warm, bright days turn to frosty nights. Soon the inevitable changing of the season will render the green to brown, the plump to withered, the humming of the insect air to silence. The plants are yellowing in the meadows. Bears have moved higher with the ripening berries. The mosquitoes are all but gone. The sun is sinking farther south on the ridge.

Modifications in our minds and bodies are taking shape. I consider what might be my role in the group? I feel suddenly inadequate and mediocre at best. Who would I be in the tribe I yearn to belong to? I can do everything a little but nothing really well. I am irritable as I deliberate on this question.

"The Keeper of Ceremonies." Could that be my special gift? It gives me a sudden sense of purpose. But the Keeper of Ceremonies has no place in a community that shares no Creation Story, for all ceremony, if it is to hold any power, must be held together by common belief. These transitory groups that I pull together year after year do not persist into perpetuity. We are all lost, seeking, yearning.

Moon blood has come. Will there finally be an end to this excessive sensitivity? The sound of large branches crashing this morning reminds me to be conscious of where I leave my blood and to be scrupulously clean. Some bears still linger in the valley and we don't need to attract them any closer.

Anxiety. Noncircumstantial, purely chemical. I can deal with the discomfort and it will pass.

A few drops of rain fall as we pack up at the lake and reluctantly prepare to retrace our steps on the long hike back to the rest of the clan. The mood is somber.

Jenny is gathering firewood, piling the dead broken limbs together and wrapping them with a thick, strong leather thong. Intermittently she looks up from her task toward the pass where the returning hunters will appear. She dares to hope they will bring meat. She is tonight's cook and as she gathers wood for the fire where the clay pot sits simmering with spring roots, she feels something akin to what she believes another young woman might have felt waiting for the return of a hunting party: a mixture of hope and expectation, acceptance and belonging. When finally the four hunters appear on the pass, she scrutinizes the distant figures for the shape of a carried burden, evidence of a fruitful hunt.

Half an hour later the hunting party returns filthy and exhausted to the valley. Ben tosses a fat ground squirrel not yet gutted beside the hearth and drops down beside it. Jenny smiles at him and gives us all a warm hug then slices it open with a simple flint flake deftly removing the guts. "This will be good in the dinner," she says. Ben nods tiredly; we know that we all wish it was a deer but nobody says anything. We are content to be together, we own nothing individually anymore. The sharing has become complete. We enjoy and we suffer together.

Falcon notes we are more than halfway through our project. She says it with a wistfulness, like she is one of the gradually seeding gentians, knowing its fertilized blossoms are fading. I feel like I am just tasting the land. I want to know it intimately. I want to feel its joy and sorrow. I want it to know me. This high country, so long covered in snow, now erupting with final, desperate life before the new, cold blanket arrives. What is this insatiable desire to wander? Why do I feel I have only just arrived?

We eat the food we brought: dried deer meat, roots of camas, balsam seeds, wild rice, acorns, and dried mollusks from the distant ocean, adding the small game, berries, and mushrooms that we find. Our bodies cry for salt and fat.

A waxing moon is now visible high in the sky. The sun sinks over endless mountains.

The air is noticeably cooler but again the mosquitoes whine.

A rock clatters down the scree slopes and we look up like startled deer.

The night clears again to stars and cold air. We sleep wrapped in animal fur and piled in a puddle like puppies; I feel warm and safe with my littermates pressed close beside me. With soft breath and faint stirring I lie awake, piecing back together my dreams. The trees and sky, black and white turn to green and blue as color seeps into the fresh morning light. The frost lies crisp and white on the lupine leaves. The sun burning through the saddle of the pass thaws it. We start thinking about "bed rotation." Everybody wants the middle of the puddle.

Arising, I rekindle the fire from sparse coals and soon a lively dance of orange and gold crackles beside me. I eat, then lie down and go back to sleep again. I am awakened by a couple of grouse that mock me but have flown away by the time I have restrung my bow.

I hear footsteps approaching and Louis sticks his head in the shelter opening. He says he wants to leave tomorrow.

Always the same, food runs low, time to go . . .

Some of us could last a week, maybe more, without a deer but will the first to leave pull all of us?

I hate to say this word but are we slowly *starving*? Is it just calories we need or is there a vital nutrient missing or lacking? My stomach has shrunk for sure and I begin to see the weight loss in the faces and bodies of my kin. Are we still transitioning? I feel like I'm eating quite a lot. What do we need to regain energy? Or maybe it's something else altogether, the knowing that this isn't forever. This experience and this clan has an end and it's soon. Are we starving in advance for something that we have but know we are about to lose?

That night, I do not sleep. I don't know why. I am comfortable and at peace. "Relax. Enjoy your life" is what spirit tells me. I shall do this.

I know it won't be long before we must head back to the other world that is so noisy and frantic. I will enjoy the rest of our time here in the peace.

Gray skies and rumbling, the precursors to the rain that falls persistently for much of the next day.

Louis left in the morning only to return some hours later to dry out by the fire. I am glad to see him. He is young and inexperienced and I was worried about his choice to leave alone. He is the peripheral one in the group, his age and his lack of experience set him apart. As the rest of the clan gels and grows closer, it seems that Louis has become more distant. Now, back from his aborted departure he expresses his sense of separation and acknowledges that he needs us. We hug him and tell him we need him, too. We need his compassionate spirit, his deep questions and empathy.

We tell stories from our childhoods. Our early experiences in nature for most of us were not very wild at all. Marcus traveled widely with his well-off parents, revisiting his mother's Japanese homeland. Falcon spent a large portion of her youth in Kenya where her parents worked for Doctors Without Borders, both highly conscious of their cultural and economic privilege. I tell them about my childhood joy in foraging for sweet chestnuts in an urban park, roasting them and eating them hot and buttery, lavishly dripping fat between my fingers. My mouth starts watering.

We decide that when a lull comes in this wet weather pattern we will make the move back to our first camp and the shelter that it provides.

The moon is new, the energy has shifted, we all turn our thoughts gradually and wistfully toward the return that is coming soon.

I'm surprised at how much farther south the sun has moved as it creeps above the ridge in these few short days. We are blessed again with good weather, now unmolested by the blood-sucking torment of insects.

We won't make it for the planned forty days, I know, even with a deer. I have seen it too many times before: when the food supplies diminish, a restlessness seeps in that together with the shortening days and cooling nights will send us in search of familiarity and comfort. I hope and believe, though, that every one of us will carry with us some Earth magic that has germinated within us during these weeks, untainted by blatant civilization. How could it not be so? For three weeks we have lain upon her breast, sheltered by the trees and fed by the clean, pure gifts of mountain spring, flesh, root, and fruit of the wild. It is in us, nurturing our cells. The world may beckon us but we shall be forever changed.

There is still one place I am compelled to visit before our journey winds us back to its origin.

The Hidden Lakes are calling me. I ask Falcon and Jenny if they wish to join me, and the horses bear us to the rocky base of the pass. It's not a long ride but it spares us energy and gives them fresh grazing. We thank them and turn them loose to graze the bunchgrass and continue on foot.

Leaving the trail, we enter—silence as our offering—the sacred place I call Hidden Lakes; it's like entering a fairyland. We are cleansed, body and spirit, in the cold, clear water. Sun obscured, I walk my naked body dry before clothing myself again, then I drift toward the rocky slopes as Falcon and Jenny make their own individual meanderings around the water's edge.

We fall asleep on opposite sides of the lake. When I awaken they are gone.

Here is that moment . . . Alone now. Touched for more days than I easily remember by constant contact with raw nature. Did I wake up to find that I have traveled back in time? That the life I thought I had led was merely a dream?

Somewhat disoriented and yet stunned by my surroundings I float in a surreal state of animal being that simply is.

I settle myself on a large flat slab of granite and I open my journal to write a love letter to limestone far away, not thinking it strange to be in love with the rocks or the trees or the waters.

Chére Mammut,
I write to you from perhaps my most holy place. I call it Hidden Lakes and they lay nestled in a mountain basin not far but still in some ways infinitely distant from my home. This is a sacred place.

I have brought your gift here. The gift I have carried since the spring, the little piece of limestone that I pried from your chalky body that has traveled with me daily and shared in my joy and wonder at this living Earth. I have bathed it in the waters; the boiling geyser at

Yellowstone, the streams and rivers of the West, and now here, baptized in the calm, silky water of the uppermost Hidden Lake. It has walked with me through sweat lodge ceremony and held the essence of my prayers. I have clutched it when fear and uncertainty have plagued me in my fragile moments.

I have felt your strength and it has carried me through, I have felt the essence of your endurance both in my dreams and between my fingers wrapped in the leather amulet around my neck.

Today my body is nourished and clothed entirely by the wild.

The elements are carving their marks upon me and I become their stone to sculpt.

I am in love also with the granite that I sit upon this moment. Sun, come warm me; I shiver in the breeze. The sun comes and I thank the sun. I lie in peaceful meditation, happy to know that this place exists.

I am in no hurry to return to camp so I wander the troughs and swells of the hidden valley before meeting up with Falcon and Jenny who are lying in the grass beside the horses waiting for me.

That night we eat a large, cooked meal: wild stew prepared in the big clay pots. We plan to move back to our first camp in the morning, where we can start the transition back to "there," the other world. The modern world. With full bellies we pass a pine cone to serve as our talking stick. Ali has quieted in these last days. Her eyes look very bright framed in her unwashed face. I know what she's thinking; she's wondering what it will feel like to go back home, back to the ghosts and demons. She has changed, slowed, settled, softened. She looks at each of us in turn, and those bright eyes water with tears, which brim and spill tracks down her cheeks, washing the grime away in two parallel lines. She is ready, she thinks, and adds a little laugh, to go back to the world with a new serenity. Ben has moved slightly away from her; he knows that their intimacy will soon be over. They both expect and accept it. He will continue his life with the serenity that has never left him.

Marcus is full of plans. He is finding it hard to keep the presence now that he will be going home to California. He's been gone a long time, almost a year, and he wants to work again; he says he will look for innovative engineering projects that will promote a sustainable future. Pragmatic as ever, he lays out an outline for our imminent departure and the days that will follow as we gradually adjust and re-integrate back into the modern world. Falcon cannot speak at all; she just gathers us all up in her arms and covers us with hugs and kisses.

Jenny considers aloud her concern that her partner will have no idea what she has been through. She is formulating how or if she will be able to maintain their relationship given her experience of clan that has so touched her. She knows she cannot return to a house without a supportive community nearby.

Louis wants to see his brother. He has missed him. He admits that it has been hard—from the solo night in the rain in the early weeks of our journey to his recent thwarted flight—but he says he feels a new and growing confidence, an understanding of what it means to live in and with nature and community. Recognizing his place and his strengths.

Rick is going to keep traveling, he wants to find his own land. He has been so inspired yet humbled by the hunting experience. He aims to keep shooting and making more bows along the way. He is unwavering in his conviction that he will shoot a deer someday with a wooden bow, and so am I.

Rick hands me the cone and I state simply, "If we had never known anything but this life, we would have no inclination to leave. We cannot yearn for something we have never known. It's like missing a child that was never conceived." I have nothing more to add and together we watch the sunset at the ceremonial firepit, beauty on the mountain and on the faces in the fading light. We speak again our thanks to the land and to the ancestral grandmothers from whose wombs we have come in unbroken lineage.

I do not sleep so well. I dream with horror of a forest of girdled trees. Trees killed with greed and ignorance by the culture from which I am spawned. I cry out loud and awaken.

Again, I hear the soothing voice, "Relax and enjoy your life," and so I write and speak these words in hope that someone or something bigger than me will listen and the great trees will be heard and spared.

Contrast is beautiful and balance is vital. No light without darkness, no comfort without pain, no joy without sorrow, no love without fear . . . It is the Way.

PART 4

Revelation

21

Smoky Mountain Exodus

My beloved lupines have everywhere turned to seed. Their sultry mauve and blue flowers now seem but a distant memory, their intoxicating fragrance recaptured for just a moment. I pluck a peapod and contemplate the changes we all encounter through the passage of the seasons. I feel the strength in my body: my lean, long muscles, my skin tanned and leathery, not unlike the lupine seed I hold in my hand. I think back on the time I left this valley after the sojourn down to the big lake just a couple of years ago, how depleted I had been back then despite the revitalizing elk steaks. We had come back to Ancestor Basin, to this very camp, and I had gotten sick. My throat was so sore it was hard to swallow. I dug and sucked on the healing osha root all day. Sleeping poorly on our last night here, I watched the big moon track between the branches of the spruces, throat hurting, head pounding, joints aching. I was bone tired.

I thought that if I had been old and really sick, my clan could have just left me here with a jug of water, a last morsel of food, wrapped in my buffalo robe to die in the serenity of this basin. But I was not ready to die.

This morning, cresting the ridge for a final hunt here, bow in hand and a quiver full of primitive arrows, I look down on Ancestor Basin. A fire is smoking in the meadow. The smoke is caught in shafts of sunlight. Buckskin clad, my family, for that is what they have now become, are cooking, and my heart is full of love for them. My hunt is half-hearted, more of a habit than a focused effort, and I trot back down to camp and sprawl upon a giant flat rock, bow still strung, yet open for the appearance of a fat marmot. Soon we shall pick up from here and leave this valley to their shrill piping. We have disturbed but we have fit, too, leaving tracks and scat and ashes and prayers to nourish the land.

Naked and bronzed, I soak up the energy of brief September sunshine. Perennial snowfields linger on the north-facing, bouldered slopes. I have been squirming into my buffalo robe sleeping bag the last few nights now, fully clothed against the freezing air.

Change, change is constant.

Jenny joins me and we sit together fiddling with little projects that need attention before our departure. I focus on sewing and mending a tear in my leggings; every little hole in our clothing releases precious heat. The sky has filled with clouds, and now a cool breeze ruffles the larch needles. Ali comes and sits down with us and our minds wander forward, out of the present. Where to go when we get back to the world below, what to eat, who to see? We laugh and joke about a trip into town, dressed in our worn and dirty buckskins. Jenny is sensibly cautious about how she will break this wild food fast. She is yearning for a bright, crisp, juicy apple. Ali exuberantly exclaims that she doesn't care if she gets a bellyache, she is going straight for the ice cream. I look at these radiant, shining young women and hope that I will know them in ten years' time, see their changes, share their joys and sorrows as we have done these last long months.

Tonight, I hesitantly sleep with my head to the west, choosing the warmth of close bodies over the comfort and familiarity of the east. For years I have noticed the differences in my sleep patterns when my body is oriented one way or another to the poles of the earth. I like the energy that my head pointing north or east brings me. I have often been uncomfortable and plagued by nightmares when my head points to the west, so I'm always conscious of which direction I choose to lie down for the night in a new place. But tonight, I need not have feared, and the next morning I feel so blessed as a clear blue sky and golden star greet my squinting, sleepy eyes. This is our last day in the Valley of the Ancestors. We speak of "presence," our only true moment of existence, and balance the preciousness of the "now" with the excitement and anticipation of the coming days of reintegration. Will we then yearn for the peace and sanctity of this day? Lost in perpetual longing for what we have right now? With senses fully alert, I recognize that I have dropped completely into an animal state of awareness:

Color, movement, shade and form, with these eyes I behold you Earth.
Texture, temperature, flow of air I feel your constant contact.
Bitter, sour, salty, sweet, I taste your flavors, gifts of nourishment.
Tone, vibration, soft and sharp, I hear you whisper, sing, and scream.
Fragrance sweet and rotting stench, I smell your scents all mingled.
With this heart, all open, broken, mended and confused,
I do feel the raging beauty, grace, and fury of this world.

We move. The journey back home could take only two days, but we want to go slowly, not rush things. We might spend another week if the food holds out or we kill a deer. Christy's packs are loaded. The little mare is old, but she has a huge heart. I ride Karma. She is young, but she's smart and learns quickly. I ride her all day up and over jagged passes. She impresses me. All the horses do. They carry us and our gear; they don't complain. I am glad when we stop for the night at good green pasture. They deserve it. Falcon and I unpack the gear and I tie Christy to a picket. The horses roll and shake themselves, then ravenously begin tearing at the thick sweet grass. We have arrived at the place we first slept on the arc of our journey. Our first night, how many days ago? I try to count them. It seems impossible but it is only about thirty. Time has warped and we are not the same people that we were. Those who walked are tired and flop down on the ground, resting against the boulders. Falcon and I rode, so we take up the slack and make two big pots full of dinner. We prepare the meal with few words; our actions are smooth, and we understand each other precisely. There is no need to ask or explain. I take the big pot down to a place on the little stream to fetch water while Falcon rummages for her fire kit. When I come back, a thin wisp of smoke is growing in her cupped hands; she expertly places the tinder bundle beneath a handful of tiny sticks that crackle and burst into flame as it ignites. She is energetic and strong despite the long day. Her long hair is sun bleached and braided loosely, her once pale complexion now ruddy behind a thin layer of grime. She adds more fuel to the fire as Ben brings in another armful, placing it carefully beside the precious clay vessels. His movements are concise, calculated, and fluid. His eyes are bright in his suntanned face.

One more day's hike will bring us there, one day's hike to the noise and chaos of cars, stores, lights, and bustle. Here in dusk light, I hear wind and horses munching. Sky above, Earth below. My being touching both. Gathered beside the fire, I look at my people. They move differently now; subtle changes have occurred: energy is spared, the frenzy and excitement of that first night here replaced by something poignant.

I lay out my sleeping gear in the open near the horses. I watch the stars appear. I watch as we spin through space throughout the night. I watch the stars disappear at dawn.

———————◄———

Marcus and I decide to ride to the lake, and we set off down the steeply sloped trail with fishing gear and gathering baskets. Close to the lake we see a figure with a small pack approaching us and with startled surprise realize it is James who had decided to stay behind in the last days before the embarkation of our trip. We hop off the horses and embrace him. He is also dressed in buckskins but has a modern fishing pole that looks alien to me. He feels like a stepping-stone back to civilization, giving us news from the world, our community, my home that feels close now. We have survived the fires. He is excited to find us and rattles off question after question. Marcus and I are happy to see him, too, but we are in a different, quieter, more contemplative space. He is out for a day trip only so has no sleeping gear and we tell him we will see him back down at my place on the river in a few days. He goes on past us up the trail to greet the others and we tie up the horses and continue toward the deep oval lake by foot.

I feel the rhythm. I am in it. I do not want to go home. Huckleberries are beginning to ripen. We gather them, blue-black and juicy. How can a bear live and grow fat on berries? I cannot imagine. I find some coral mushroom, orange pipes creeping out from their mysterious mycological origins. The fish are feeding on little brown flies and they laugh at my dried grasshoppers tied to the ludicrously large line. Marcus takes off his clothes and wades into the water, stirring up the silty bottom. He dives beneath the surface and emerges shaking out his mane of thick, wavy black hair that has grown and falls dripping on his brown muscled shoulders. He is utterly, breathtakingly beautiful, and for a brief moment I wish I was a dozen years younger.

Clouds build down at the lake. Will they bring more rain? Should we hurry back and pile our bedding into the rock crevices?

It does not rain, but the wind builds. I leave Marcus who has wandered off with his berry basket and return to camp taking the horses with me. Christy brings me back up without complaint, Karma and Chaco consenting, snatching mouthfuls of grass along the way. I am again full of admiration for these lovely willing beasts.

James has already left and I can feel the impact his visit has made on the clan. There is a buzz that is almost palpable. Marcus comes back with a bowl full of huckleberries that is added to a pot of wild rice and the final drizzle of bear fat. We pour hot water into the fat gourd to melt out every last calorie that it contains.

We talk after dinner. We plan now to leave very soon. The food will run out. Once that decision is made I feel the rapid shift happening that pulls me away from here and now. Projecting into the future, already thinking of my preparations for winter. There's a whole empty woodshed waiting to be filled. The anticipated whine of the chain saw fills me with trepidation.

That night, again I watch the stars. There is one who speaks to me. I ask out loud, "Who are you?"

"Alderbron," he answers. Have I heard of a star named this before? It feels like I made a new and special friend, someone I will always look for and recognize in the summer sky.

How have I changed?

Earth has changed me, molded me. First with gentleness . . . Rest, sleep, eat, come here to me, this is my rhythm, breathe, hear my heartbeat. Then with firmness . . . Act, move, plan. Reaffirmation of the magic, the faith, the love. It's all here; it has all been woven in and out of these last few weeks, together with the corresponding harsh reality, doubt and fear. The change is subtle. I cannot name it or even understand it fully. It will grow and blend into the new being that I am constantly becoming.

Disturbing dreams take shape, but like the clouds they form and disperse leaving their essence engraved somewhere deep within my being. The gusting winds add to the sense of movement and change. Still tired, I rise, string and stretch the yellow bow. Again I dance with the deer.

———————————————➤———

The horses are craving salt, licking on their own sweaty saddle packs and straps. The first doe is grazing by them, then three more does appear and I stalk close as they slant down the meadow, unaware of my presence. I want to be sure of my shot; I'm nearly close enough and I feel the excitement rising as I angle in toward them. Then the wind shifts, they catch my scent and bound away. I am almost relieved; it's a beautiful morning to hunt but with the decision to leave already made, a deer kill would somehow seem like an illogical delay.

Part of me is ready to go and part has so found its rhythm on this journey that I can't imagine anything else.

When I return to find the horses, they are gone. Christy has pulled loose her picket line and they've disappeared. With a sickening feeling I take off looking for horse tracks down the trail. Did they leave the camp? Are they also feeling the pull to return to the comfort of known pastures? There are no new tracks heading down valley since yesterday. I walk slowly back up, grazing on berries. There they stand upon a knoll, the wind gently blowing in their manes. I stake the picket back down firmly in a new spot and promise Christy a good long rest when we get home.

We circle for our last evening and give thanks. We shed some tears. The wind picks up, a gray sky rolls in. We delve into the boulder field to find shelter. Ali and Ben nest under a giant rock, and I see them pulling in green boughs like pack rats for a cozy bed. Mostly there is not much flat space under the rocks for people to snuggle up together, just enough for one here, two there, out of the wind and coming rain.

I place myself beneath a slanted rock overhang looking down the valley that we shall walk tomorrow. The rain spits down without passion.

I slept cold and alone for the first time in months. Violent dreams . . . preparation for societal reintegration? I can feel my subconscious struggling with the reality of our departure. It is up here in the high country away from civilization that I feel most completely myself. This particular journey has been the first Stone Age Project where the group has found perfect balance. We feel like an entity, a whole being, more than ourselves as individuals. Leaving this mountain means fracturing our clan, leaving a part of ourselves behind. I always dread reentry. I am always a little afraid. Who will I be back down there? Will I forget who I am on this windy ridge? Two-leggeds. Beings of fire. Praying for Earth from Smoky Mountain.

The morning sky is clear. Cloud remnants hurtle past from the west. I roll up my buffalo robe and gather my well-used but sparse belongings into my backpack. The rest of the clan are packing too. They are mostly silent, each of us trapped in our own feelings about what awaits us.

22

Caterpillars and Moths

Between the ages of seven and twelve, I lived in a block of council flats in Roehampton South London, with my mum, my big brother, and my little sister. After my parents' divorce, my mother wanted to move back to Sweden with us kids, but my dad refused to let us go permanently, so after several months in Sweden my mother managed to pull her life back together and we eventually found a flat in the London concrete housing estate.

Though I loved animals—they seemed kinder and less complicated than people—the council didn't permit residents to have pets. What I wished for most was to have a horse.

There were no trees or grass around our flat and we had to ride our bikes to get to the park, but nature has a way of creeping through the tiniest cracks and asserting herself even in a concrete jungle.

Behind the flat's barren "playground," I found a caterpillar on a spindly shrub that was defying all attempts at its suffocating destruction. I put him in a margarine tub and poked holes in the lid so he could breathe and snuck him into the sanctuary of the room I shared with my little sister. I called him Freddy and cherished him. In the mornings I'd run in my pajamas down the central stairway that smelled of old urine and get him dandelion leaves that grew in the cracks in the concrete. He'd munch along their edges, leaving little trails of poop behind him.

Then one day, I went to give him his breakfast and found he'd built himself a cocoon. I took the margarine tub into school where we learned more about caterpillars and their transformations. I loved the word *chrysalis*. Every day after that, when I would get to school, the first thing I would do was to go and check on Freddy. Nothing happened for ages but one morning when I opened the lid, he had changed. Metamorphosis! He was crawling out of his cocoon, wings wet and crumpled. The whole class came out with me into the green lot beside the schoolyard, and I carefully put him onto a stalk of grass. My Freddy had become a beautiful moth with a new furry body and painted black, red, and yellow design. The wind gently dried his wings, they opened out, and without a plan or intention he flew away.

While I wait in Nepal for my permit to continue my own unobjective trek, I have time to contemplate my circumstances. I miss Klara and wish she were here with me. My funds are dwindling. I had come to the Himalaya to feel closer to my mother. The grief caused by her death was slowly being replaced by something larger, something universal.

I am lonely but there is more waiting to happen, I just don't know what it is yet.

Finally the spell of inertia has broken. I receive the permit to Annapurna base camp.

A taxi driver hails me on the street. Before we set off his side-view mirror falls off and he wanders away for a while to try and fix it. I am a little impatient, but he comes back and sets it on the dashboard and

I am safely delivered to the bus station. Another local bus ride that steadily gets slower and bumpier as we head into the hills.

Walking finally. I fall in step with a Nepali dentist and her brothers for a while. She speaks perfect English. I move a little faster than them and become acquainted with a local woman who is heading back to her village in the mountains where she runs a hotel. Tekomarie is fifty years old and beautiful. She has a Swedish boyfriend. We hike all day together. We talk about plants and our lives. We climb about four thousand feet and she invites me to her hotel. We will reach it tomorrow. We stop and pitch camp for the night, lulled by the fluttering sounds of prayer flags.

Frosty dawn. My legs are tired. A waning crescent moon and the bright Venus greet my eyes in the clear dark sky. Orion disappears over the hill.

Tekomarie shares her Tibetan bread with me for breakfast and we prepare for the three-hour trek that she says will bring us to her village where she runs a hotel.

Stone staircases, endless miles of giant slabs placed by hundreds of thousands of sun-beaten Himalayan hands. The sun glitters through the moss-covered rhododendrons and I pause in awe. My own hands are sluggish in the frozen morning air. Men with sticks toss rocks, whistling, shouting, driving eighty or a hundred sheep past me down the mountain.

Nine thousand two hundred feet. I sit at the pass with the mountains before me. I search for words that are not clichéd to describe them. Machhapuchhre, can I reach out and touch you, still another ten thousand feet above me?

We arrive at Tekomarie's hotel, a sparse but clean two-room hut made of stone and mud. When the sun goes down, the temperature plummets. Overdressed on the last hike, I am underdressed this time.

After dinner I squat around the little illegal fire with my host and the four other women who live here. Burning precious wood was out-lawed six months ago with heavy fines for those who are caught.

Again and again the pressure of overpopulation reveals itself. Cut-ting down the forest for fuel and farming is evident everywhere. For these women, staying warm at ten thousand feet in December is a matter of survival. "It's hard," states a young woman from Mustang simply. Never before have I felt so privileged. I sleep on the floor of the "hotel" with the Nepali women.

I pay for my stay. It amounts to about $9.00 for a room and three meals. I feel like crying as I walk away. I leave them more money but it's not about money or having or not having . . . What can I truly give to ease the existence of not just these people who have touched me but all beings that make up the fabric of life? It is a vast and endless contemplation.

I am being molded and changed. I am being ripped open and re-arranged.

I bathe in a small waterfall amid icicles as an invitation to clarity as the mountains grow closer.

It's my forty-fifth birthday. I wake up on the sand among boulders after sleeping alone under the starry sky.

———————◀

My emotions undulate with the terrain. Uphill I struggle with home-sickness, loneliness. Part of me yearns for the dark cold nights of my home on the Twisp River and the steady swish, swish of touring skis sliding along the trail in the moonlight.

Downhill I am jubilant, exhilarated, fully in the moment. Mostly it's uphill . . . Gradually it becomes a meditation. This journey feels like a pilgrimage but to where exactly I'm still not sure. A place internal?

The Nepali guides and porters are continuously intrigued by the reindeer skin I use as a sleeping mat. They are shocked when I tell them I sleep outside.

"Are there no tigers in your country?" I admit we have no tigers but affirm that I do indeed live among lions.

"But up high, there is no need to fear tigers," I tell a young guide.

He stares at me and says, "But ghosts."

Then, climbing too fast, overly confident, I make an error in judgment, and I slip on some icy rocks at a stream crossing. It's a bad mistake. A Korean group is there that I have caught up with. They help me up. I have scraped my left shin and tweaked my right knee. I think I'm okay.

I go on, slowly, carefully, monitoring my injury, only too aware of how many days I am from the road should my knee swell up. How suddenly things can change. I reach the next teahouse not far away where I sit and eat fried potatoes with my legs up and wait.

The sun creeps down the mountainside as I limp onward and upward, climbing in a daze into the thinning air.

Thirteen thousand feet. Could I have climbed six thousand feet today? It seems impossible, but here I am at Annapurna base camp in a very basic dormitory room, in all my clothes, in my sleeping bag. There are no beds, just a dozen grubby mattresses on the floor. It's cold. My legs hurt, but they seem to be okay. I am grateful for the not-too-harsh lesson that I learned on the ice. I feel the altitude. I have a pounding headache and the last seven hundred to eight hundred feet were brutal.

I get up for dinner and eat the best dal bhat of the whole trip; it's the Nepali staple of lentils and rice with mixed vegetables and a curried sauce.

Happy excited tourists are all chatting together in the large, cold common room with huge windows that look out onto the high

Himalaya. I miss the depth of interaction that good friends and family enjoy. I wonder what Klara is doing? I wonder if she will ever experience this land. I wish she could feel the enormity of these mountains. I wish we could stand here side by side without words. Perhaps the spirit of my mother would join us.

The mountains soar miles above my head. To be entombed by them on every side is to feel the insignificance of mortality. My headache worsens and I am ready to rest even though it's only 5:00 p.m. I retire to my mattress on the floor. I am exhausted but I cannot sleep. The window looks onto the jumbled glacier. The snow glows pink on the peaks in the sunset. Why am I here? Just to be a witness to earthly glory?

I spend an uncomfortable night with altitude sickness and rise early, ready to begin the descent. I walk for about eight hours . . . down, down, down, stopping to bathe in an icy pool. The headache and malaise subside quickly and I hike all day. The last hour brings me up a stone staircase to Chomrong where I sit and eat chocolate cake in the company of a young French Canadian. Finally, birthday cake!

I am in a charming village where the roofs are mostly made of stone. I walk after lunch and fall in with a Korean woman about my age. Her name is Jane. Unsatisfied with this as a Korean name I have her coach me on her real name, Jai Eun. After several minutes of hopeless mispronunciation, we settle again for Jane.

She is a Buddhist convert after being raised Christian. Her family is not happy with her. We spend the afternoon hiking together and it is good to have company. She tells me the story of how she changed her faith. It is a moving story as we watch the sun paint the mountains red before us. It is a story of loss, grief, and searching much like my own. I am reminded of how we are thrown together for reasons.

I spread my sleeping gear on the grass that night with concerned Nepali villagers surrounding me. They are worried about tigers. Should I be worried about tigers?

If my obituary should read, "Lynx was eaten by a tiger high in the Himalayan mountains of Nepal while looking for Truth . . ." I will be content. So I test my fate.

I watch stars crawl across the sky. Besides the scar-faced dog waking me up barking, perhaps saving me from prowling tigers, the night has passed with no incident.

The signs seem to point me back to Kathmandu and some days later I am there having returned in the comfort of the tourist bus, but with no memorable stories or impressions to share of the ride this time. I take up residence in a guesthouse within the walls of Boudhanath and fall immediately into an exhausted sleep.

By a remarkable act of providence, I have arrived back at the shrine at Boudhanath just as an enormous world peace prayer has begun. I've come back to the city to get visa information and wait for more money to be wired and the relatively peaceful environment of the stupa was the only place I could stomach.

Hundreds of thousands of marigold flowers have been strung and draped around the enormous shrine and together with the fluttering prayer flags create a quietly festive atmosphere within the enclosed square contrasting strongly with the sounds that permeate from without where traffic noise, honking horns and business as usual clamor, is dampened by the shielding buildings that face inward toward the stupa. The all-seeing eyes of the Buddha gaze in each direction within his golden face, mounted on a great white dome.

Throngs of Buddhists have been making their way here over the last days and weeks to converge for this magnificent event. Beside the robed nuns and monks there are mountain people who have made the long trek down from their remote Himalayan villages. They contrast conspicuously with the city folk that inhabit Kathmandu. In a loose sense I feel I can relate to them.

I am awoken by a gong at three or four in the morning. It is struck in long, slow intervals, gradually increasing. I rise. Drums and horns and voices chanting fill the air. I dress and leave my room, compelled by the sound, only to find that the gate is locked and I cannot follow. I peer through the fence into a dark street. A lone masked, robed figure is out there.

"What's happening?" I call to him in a whisper. He comes close and says something I don't understand.

I walk all around the perimeter of the guesthouse compound; all gates are locked, so eventually I find a place where I can climb up on the garbage cans and scramble over the wall. I drop down to the dark street below. Like a moth irresistibly drawn to the light, I am led toward the sound.

As I leave the back alleyways I am suddenly among people all moving in the same direction.

Maroon-robed monks and nuns, Tibetans and Sherpas. Buddhists all drawn by their faith toward the great stupa.

Thousands of butter lamps are glittering, as the throng moves around the stupa, clockwise, prayers sung with melodious monotony or spoken softly under the breath. I take my place in the crowd with my own prayers and make the circumambulation of the stupa, moved, with tears in my eyes . . . Once, twice, three times as dawn light pales the sky.

A million prayers drifting on the air. I am in the presence of the sacred.

It is palpable. My desire to belong is as strong as my knowing that I do not.

I spend the whole day observing the growing crowds at the stupa. I sit for a while on the steps of the monastery; people pass before me spinning prayer wheels or prostrating themselves endlessly as they perform their slow acts of devotion. An incense carrier waves a smoky can of exotic scented herbs while uttering monotonous incantations, a blind man into whose hands I press my daily budget of rupees, a small sibling pair who take my hands as we go and buy them a loaf of bread, a scrawny yellow dog that lies there seemingly lifeless until a fly makes his ear twitch. I am approached by a Nepali woman who asks me if I have found Jesus? I mutter something about there being many paths to truth. She asks if she can pray for me after telling me her story of being raised Buddhist and converting to Christianity, the exact opposite of my Korean hiking companion Jane last week. This time, however, I am subjected to a rather intense lecture on the dire consequences of refusing Christ as my Savior and the subsequent promise of an eternity in hell. I finally excuse myself.

A little later, staring up at the golden Buddha I quietly utter to no one in particular, "So beautiful!" A voice behind me answers "Yes," and I turn to see a tall, robed monk. He asks me if I would like to accompany him to pray on a turn around the stupa since he would like to practice his English.

We walk, spinning the prayer wheels. We talk; he tells me his name is Konchog. He is Tibetan and fled his homeland years ago, crossing the Himalaya on foot together with other monks from his monastery that had been destroyed by the Chinese regime. Growing their hair and donning civilian clothes, they escaped penniless but with their lives and made a monthslong trek to Dharamsala, where they were received by the Dalai Lama, who relocates his refugees to an Indian monastery of their choice. Konchog has arrived here today to pray for peace in the world.

We enjoy our conversation and take butter tea at one of the teahouses then ramble through the stores that sell "thangkas," pictorial representations of the many Buddhist deities. I ask Konchog for assistance to find an appropriate one to take home with me. I think it will be a comforting piece of memorabilia to have an image of a serene Buddha gazing benevolently down at me on my wall. Konchog's idea of what I most need is quite different from my own, though, and he insists on an angry-looking deity with multiple heads, arms and legs performing all manner of hideous tortures to terror-stricken beings crushed beneath his malevolent feet. Not exactly the peaceful image I had in mind, but my new friend is very emphatic that Vajrakilaya, the wrathful one, is what most Westerners need and the deity was in fact crushing the obstacles to my own enlightenment, so it's for my own good. I'm in no position to argue, make my purchase, and with the blue demon rolled under my arm we make a plan to meet again the next day at the stupa when the peace prayer will begin.

The following morning I find Konchog again leaning against a wall gazing at the golden head at the top of the stupa. The square is teeming with people, a few Western faces visible in the crowds, but in my black yak wool lungi wrapped around my waist and my well-worn, handmade felt and buckskin coat I both blend in and stand out among the other pilgrims. People steadily move up the steps into the central area beneath the stupa where they sit with children, bags, and piles of woolen clothing. Konchog motions for me to follow him and we ascend in the crowd. As we near the prayer grounds I start to peel away to the left where the civilians sit—women, men, kids, and babies all together in a rabble of chattering—but Konchog pulls me with him to the right and places me beside him, motioning me to sit within the sea of black-haired, maroon-robed monks—all male. I feel highly conspicuous—

a Westerner, a woman, a misfit—but gradually I relax, settle myself, and fall into the trance that infects the crowd as the chanting prayers begin, accompanied by the gongs, crashing cymbals, and discordant horns that Tibetan Buddhism is so colorfully inclusive of.

After about four hours of prayers, monks come through the lines distributing food bags for lunch. I decline the offering, but Konchog takes the proffered bag and presses it into my hands. The prayers go on and on, the boy monks wriggling and throwing things, not at all holy. I'm in my own world, saying goodbye to my mother and at the same time considering the belief that her reincarnation could already be embodied on Earth, could even be swaddled in the arms of one of the women on the other side of the stupa—who can say?

After many hours, we rise as one and start slowly filing out toward the steps and back down into the square. I lose Konchog in the crowd. An older monk approaches and stops me along the way. With gestures he asks if I need money or something to eat. Here are people, not born into the wealth and opportunities that I had been, offering me sustenance, recognizing my pilgrimage, seeing my heart. I am humbled. This simple act strikes me like a lightning bolt. I find Konchog again at the stupa; we walk, we talk, we pray, we drink tea, we walk some more. He tells me a thousand things about Buddhism in English and Tibetan and I absorb less than 1 percent. He tells me Westerners have very busy minds and I remember this. His hands are the smooth hands of a monk who reads and writes but does not labor. He asks me if I want to reach Buddhahood in this lifetime and I have to admit that I kinda like it here on Earth. I ask him the same question and he laughs and says he likes it too. That evening I meet Tenzi, my guide, and his friend Ninim. We drink tongba, a fermented wine brewed from millet, and for the first time since arriving in Nepal nearly two months ago I realize I have spent the day with friends. How strange the offerings of the Universe.

I am going home. I am going because I want to and I can. I walk the stupa as I have done all week.

What shifted those many hours on the stupa? A cleansing, a surrender, a letting go. I can be whoever and whatever I want to be. Freedom is attainable. I have been given the grace to accept with equanimity the manifestation of each moment as it arises.

23

REENTRY

I ride Karma, my gear tied behind me on the skin saddle pad. Falcon is astride Chaco, her legs dangling over the rawhide pack containers and her nearly empty basket wobbling precariously behind her. Rick gives Jenny a boost up onto the back of Christy. The horses are infected with the change; they know we are going down, back to the familiar pasture without the toil of steep, uneven, rocky ground. It's hard to keep them from trotting and stumbling in their haste to head home. The rest of the clan follow behind us on foot at their own pace.

Halfway down the trail we find a good huckleberry patch and dismount. Tying the horses, we pluck the black berries deftly, enjoying the fruity sweetness. A murmuring noise reaches our ears and four hikers turn the switchback below us, heavily laden with bright modern backpacks. We pause just briefly from our feasting to greet them, fingers, lips, and mouths stained a deep, rich purple. They stop for a moment, speechless, stammer a returned hello as they pass and then walk slowly past the horses. I lick my sticky fingers and notice the dirt beneath the nails. I peer up the trail in the direction of the hikers like a preoccupied bear. They are standing looking back at us, and I hear one of them with a bemused look utter, "Unbelievable, simply unbelievable." Falcon grins at me, her teeth blackish; I poke out my purple tongue and we start to giggle. I wonder what the hikers will think when they meet the rest of our clan. A couple of years ago one of my students, an older man in his fifties, barefoot and dirty in his buckskins met hikers on his way out and for a bit of fun asked them with seriousness, "Is the Vietnam War over yet?"

Riding again, I notice the sharp geometric patterns that the hiking boots have left in the mud and dust. It hurts my eyes; the softness of wild human tracks, barefoot or moccasined, are all that we have seen for weeks now, and just this small reminder of the artificial world we will find down there gives me a faint shudder of uneasiness.

At the trailhead, I am shocked to see so many cars parked there and it slowly dawns on me that it must be Labor Day weekend. Reentry. My thoughts scatter like beasts fleeing into unknown territory. I try to round them back into single-minded focus but I fail. Only when the vessel has been full and overflowing can it also know emptiness and depletion. I slide off Karma and stash all our gear in the bushes, then I remount and we continue along the gravel road. There is still another nine miles back to my cabin, part of it on another trail so we can avoid the road. In the dreamy transition between my dual realities I shift back into linear thought processes governed by time and space concepts. The plan is that the others will wait at the trailhead and Falcon, Jenny, and I will trot home and pick up the truck then drive back for the clan and all the gear.

It's probably midafternoon when we turn into the driveway; dry, yellowing plants flank it, and there are still piles of branches and debris from the aftermath of the storm. We hear the sound of wood chopping and as we come down the trail toward my cabin Gareth looks up from the splitting stump. He's wearing a sweaty T-shirt and buckskin shorts. We pile off the horses, who dive for the unkempt lawn. Polly comes up from the river, sees us, drops what she is carrying and we are soon a bundle of laughing, hugging, kissing beings all talking at once. It's a bit surreal, and some part of me stands aloof beside the throng watching. James had told them we were coming so they were expecting us. Gareth offers to take the truck and go pick up the others and I gladly accept. Jenny and Falcon go up to the camp firepit, offering to help Polly who is making us all dinner. I am hesitant to enter my cabin and instead collapse on the grass and close my eyes. The truck engine roars and gravel crunches under the tires. It's loud and jarring, but as soon as it is gone I am enveloped again in peaceful tranquility. I drift into a half-dream, half-memory state.

I'm about five years old, at my grandparents' home in the countryside in Sweden. Their house on the edge of the forest seems big compared to our London flat. I love going there every summer when we get out of school. There's so much space to play in their yard. It's full of flowers and vegetables and berries. There's even a pond that has frogs and tadpoles in it.

Behind the barn is a big nettle patch and we play nettle wars with the neighbor boys. We tie nettles on the ends of long sticks then flail them around, thrashing at each other. I am the littlest so I usually get stung the most; it hurts but I don't mind because I like playing with the big boys. An ant bites me, pulling me back to the present and I flick it away, roll over and am gone again, climbing the staircase at my grandparents' house where a stuffed owl is always watching me when I go up to the bathroom. It always seems to be looking at me whichever step I am on. I run past the owl to my grandparents' bedroom where a secret door leads to the attic. It looks like an ordinary cupboard door but when you open it there are steep steps that go up to the ceiling. Pulling on a beanbag attached to a string that opens a trapdoor, I climb up into the dark, musty attic. There are old things up there, cobwebs on everything, spooky and exciting, like finding treasure. I hear Jenny's howl of laughter from the outdoor kitchen, try to open my eyes, but they slam shut and I drift away again.

In the basement, my grandfather has his woodworking shop. I love being down there with him and helping him make things. The smell of the basement is good, like the forest. Grandpa says there are trolls that live among the mossy rocks as we search for yellow chanterelles, my favorite. They taste of the earth. Like my home here in my dream reminiscence.

My grandparents have two small, bad-tempered yapping dogs that try to bite me if I touch them. I don't like them, either. There's a horse in the field nearby and I visit him, fantasizing that he's my own. I hear a horse sigh and am vaguely aware of my half slumber on the lawn, then I am walking down the lane to the horse near my grandparents again. The horse comes to the fence and I stroke his nose, soft like velvet. I smell the rich, musty horse scent and am comforted. Pippi Longstocking is the strongest girl in the world. I wish I was Pippi. She doesn't have to go to school. I don't want to go back to London. I roll over and stretch, my eyes adjust to the light, Karma sighs again nibbling grass just yards away.

I get up a little confused from my sleep and walk into the cabin. I look around at everything; it's like it belongs to someone else yet is soothing and comfortable. I take a cup, open the tap, and pour myself a drink of water. The little mirror above the kitchen sink has the image of a very suntanned woman's lined face in it, with startling blue eyes, and an unruly mop of bleached blond hair; we move closer, studying each other intensely. It's not the same face that I left with. It never is, the one that comes back in the first clear reflection. She is older, wiser, a bit wary, stiller, whole and unhurried. My gaze breaks and I go back outside again and sit with the others by the fire and sing.

Half an hour later the truck comes back in and Marcus, Rick, Ali, Ben, and Louis pile out of the pickup bed and we all tumble into one another's arms again. James arrives back from town but the camp still seems quiet now, with the other students gone home long ago: Marie to Germany, the Canadian family to Quebec. The kittens, Thunder and Dragon, have grown and sit purring in our laps while we eat the dinner that Polly has prepared for us. It's been carefully cooked with love. A big fresh garden salad with a vinaigrette dressing . . . wow, so amazing, such a delightful tangy sensation. There's canned buffalo meat, succulent and soft compared to the reconstituted dry jerky that we have been mostly eating. Squash, onions, and butter. Imagine butter! Molten gold seeping into the rich orange flesh of the squash. We eat voraciously; there is dessert, apples and huckleberries with a nutty crumble on top. It feels like heaven.

I ask Rick if they saw the hikers on the trail. He has the rest of us in stitches impersonating them bemusedly asking him if there were any more of "us" coming. He says he thought they might actually be frightened when Ali, Marcus, and Ben descended behind them. They just about leapt out of their polypropylene socks. We talk excitedly into the evening as Polly, Gareth, and James ply us with questions, finally retiring to our robes under the pines in the familiar spots we had slept for the preparation.

When I arrive late beside the hearth the next morning, the sun glinting through the needles, I feel the balminess of the lower elevation. No frost here last night. Ali is up and eager for the town trip that we have planned. Falcon and Rick seem distant from each other and I wonder what has happened. She comes to me, puts her head on my shoulder, and whispers, "I want to go back up there." "We can, anytime." I try to soothe her but I feel it too; the great change has occurred and we are already slipping away from those serene meadows and hazy peaks. We decide to go into town dressed as we are, still in our buckskins, mottled by the time and dust of the mountains. I am not afraid of being seen thus by the townspeople; they had plenty of time to watch the metamorphosis as the spring progressed to summer. We jump into the trucks with our wallets that we have not opened in a month and drive the ten miles down valley to the wonder of my greater community. Town is bustling with not only locals, for it is indeed Labor Day weekend, but also a horde of visitors, all perusing the busy farmers' market. It's overwhelming for Falcon, Jenny, and me, so we head to the natural food store for a fresh-pressed juice. I know many people here and they stop, hug me, and ask me how it was out there this summer. What can I say? *Great, fine, fun?* My wholeness is fractured, this is not home. I can't say anything so I just smile mysteriously and embellish my carrot juice mustache. I notice the difference, the need for focused attention here compared to the broad, peripheral vision that the wild places nurture. Ali and Ben come in. Ali looks a bit queasy; she says she has eaten a whole tub of ice cream. We are all thrilled by the variety of food choices. I order a big greasy burger on a gluten-free bun with sweet potato fries and sit with my clan at the deli counter. We gorge, gluttonous, hungry for carbs and fat. Louis has a cloth bag that is bulging with snacks and I shake my head. I had warned them but sometimes they just can't help themselves; the temptation is enormous. I hope they don't suffer too much. It has been the same for me. I have tempered my desires today but I have been there, belly churning, nausea mounting.

An hour later we go back to the homestead. I drive my truck and it feels strange to be moving so fast. The stimulation of town has exhausted us and I retire quietly to my shadowy bed, listening to the sound of someone puking. For the first time when coming back into civilization from these episodes in the Stone Age, I embrace the diversity that entertains my life. I can choose either way and know peace.

During the first few Stone Age Projects we just tried to fling ourselves back into our old lives and rhythms with sometimes disastrous consequences. The stimulation and speed of modern society after extended wilderness sojourns can trigger all kinds of detachment issues. It can be traumatic to be torn from the only people who can fully understand one's recent experiences.

We have been rewilded. We are wild, liberated from societal etiquette, and we feel judged upon our reentry. We smell of woodsmoke well beyond the first shampooing of our hair, and the black grime under our fingernails resists days of scrubbing. Mostly, we don't even want to replace the honest dirt of the wild for the sterile and chemical norms of the artificial world that have become repugnant to us.

I talked to one friend from the early years, a pharmacist from Chicago who had joined us for an immersion. I didn't think she would make it to the Stone Age journey at first—she seemed so conventional compared to most of my students—but she surprised us all and the change in her was exceptionally penetrating. She went back to Chicago afterward, spent the first couple of months trying to convince her friends and family to process roadkill with her, roamed the city streets in her handmade buckskin clothes, and moved into a tent in her parents' backyard but no one understood her. She didn't have anyone to relate to anymore, anyone who shared her interests or her experiences. When I spoke to her about a year later, she told me with much sadness that she had become very depressed and finally packed all her Stone Age gear up in the attic in an attempt to fit back into her "tribe." Since then I've realized how important it is for us to stay connected with one another. The friendships and liaisons formed are strong and lasting. Reaching out to our clan, even if only with an occasional phone call or email, keeps the bonds and support close to our hearts.

I started to incorporate a reintegration period after we return to civilization. A little time to stay together and process before we head back into the maelstrom. We make our first trips into town, organize, email, make calls, then come together after these adjustments to share how we feel, eat another meal of buffalo and berries, and speak out our dreams and fears. Even if it's just for a few days, the inevitable reintegration of travel, cities, and noise is softened.

———————◄———————

It's been a long time since I came down from the Smoky Mountain together with my clan. Ben lives in California with his partner and two little girls on their farm. They live just a short distance from a hip little town and only a stone's throw away from James who bought land near them. Rick has been staying there for a couple of years now, making music and helping with the crop. He and his girlfriend are also ready to look for a place to settle, maybe start a family. Our contact is sporadic but sweet, a few emails here and there, once in a while a phone call.

Marcus has strands of gray in his long mane now. He tells me about the engineering company he works for, designing and research-ing new cutting-edge methods of energy production. It's a bit mys-terious sounding but he seems content. And I am convinced that he must be onto something brilliant. On the weekends he works with troubled youths, taking them out into nature and turning them on to the secrets of semiurban wildlife.

Louis does not answer my messages, but I'm not worried about him. I am sure that he will someday just show up out of the blue.

Ali went back to Canada, reconnected with an old friend, and fell in love with him. They put a down payment on a rural property and are busy rewilding it, planting trees and planning to build their house there.

Falcon and I stay in contact regularly. When she and Jenny returned to their homes in England, they sought to explain to their community what they had experienced with the clan at Smoky Mountain. It was not easy but as their friends, families, and acquaintances begged them for more details they found themselves offering to share what they had learned. The sharing grew into teaching, and, like a proud parent, I watched them blossom into a force of indisputable knowledge. We started to collaborate, and our friendship grew and deepened.

Now they have a thriving business teaching hide-tanning classes. It has not been without times of deep self-questioning when Falcon finds herself wondering how it is that she lives in a house, bought a car, and spends more time than she would like on the computer.

Jenny recently visited me, staying at my place for a month. In the mornings we often shared our dream stories and I am touched and a little awed by her profound introspection and the work she is doing on herself, slowly revealing layer upon layer of long-hidden responses to our less-than-perfect world. As she lets go of the ideal scenario she wants to create, I watch her relax into what is curiosity and caring for all who surround her.

24

TWO WORLDS

Four years after our Smoky Mountain Project, I asked Falcon, my forest daughter, to come with me to Jokkmokk in January. Meanwhile, on my way north to meet up with her I visit my actual daughter, Klara, who is living in Europe now and following her own path for creating a sustainable future working for an NGO. We spend a few days together in her urban apartment where I try to sleep as far away from the humming refrigerator as possible. She assists me with technical problem-solving regarding the more challenging and mundane aspects of my life like my website, media engagements, and outreach to potential students. These activities are often frustrating for me and without her I would probably still be teaching only five students a year who had somehow managed to find me hidden under a rock. Knowing me so well, Klara has the ability to dole out technology in small enough doses so that I don't splinter and break. It's a fine line and I am grateful. Two days in these kinds of environments is usually plenty and we find the greenest parks and hidden corners, share some stories, laughs, and good meals then I'm off, pointed in the right direction and breathing a deep sigh of relief when the hustle and noise of the city recedes. In Stockholm, despite my renewed agitation, I eagerly await the arrival of Falcon in the train station, sprawled in the quietest nook I can find by the left luggage lockers, and we proceed on the night train to Jokkmokk where I will share with her a visit to the Sami market. The market is an added bonus; the true reason for this journey is the revelation of the drum maker and the sacred drum.

Sometimes it's hard to determine the beginning of a story, so I have to go back to the Cave of Angels in southern Italy, where I'd spent my last night deep in the long tunnel and had been suddenly struck by an uncompromising feeling that I must make a sacred drum.

I had slithered back out of the tunnel into the light, birthing breech in the damp, dark, vaginal mud. It was time . . .

I hadn't been sure where I should go to find a drum maker to help me. I knew I could make a drum without help, but it seemed important to find someone. It wasn't just a drum I needed; it was the journey the drum would take me on, and I needed a new mentor. I asked my friend the Gypsy Warrior if I should go to Mongolia or northern Sweden. He told me to go to the place of my Nordic ancestors.

The drum beats louder, the drumbeat strong.

Now, barely a year later, Falcon and I are on a sleeper train, heading north into the darkness, into frigid Arctic night, toward the empty spaces both on the map and the bare snow-enveloped land, toward the slow beating of the beckoning drum.

Within hours of arriving in Jokkmokk on the Swedish Arctic Circle, the drum maker is made manifest in the being of Tommy.

We will build a drum. It will echo through the dark, it will thrum and pulse and pound the ancient memories of your heart.

It will stalk resounding damp cave walls and fill the empty space, it will seep between the cracks of loss while tears stream down your face.

Where do I even start? Tommy needs a whole book to himself for me to describe him and what he has given me. His stories, his laughter, his crinkled dancing blue eyes.

Blacksmith, dog-musher, reindeer herder, ex–heroin addict, father of five, the first of whom died in his arms. His first Love and how she tried to teach him to count but, he tells me, he could never do numbers. To him when you add one plus one together they are still one. Everything put together becomes One. He tells me about how, after a rough start, he was raised by his Sami grandmother, of his one-man revolution that put him in prison, of his mentor in Egypt whom he called "The man with the green eyes," and how he spent the night alone in the Great Pyramid in Giza, some years after my own experiences in the Middle East.

On and on go the stories, the twinkling eyes, his long white beard stained with pipe tobacco juice.

He roars with laughter—it is Buddha laughter—and he admits that he is free.

———————◄—

Falcon and I spend those first few days marveling at the intricate Sami craftwork and stuffing ourselves with reindeer meat delicacies while I tell her stories of my own youthful trips and the remarkable people whom I had met. We pass the long evenings dancing in the barn, the light of Thorsten's eyes still shining brilliantly, recaptured in my memory, and the cold nights bundled in a snow shelter that we have built. We keep our boots in our sleeping bags to prevent them from freezing. The market is only a three-day event and by the time Tommy is ready to start the drum-building process with me, it's time for Falcon to head back south again.

We will be friends for life, Tommy tells me just hours after we first met. Now ten days later I know it is true.

We will build a drum and it will walk us to the door, accompany us to the end and sink us through the floor.
With beat so loud, so firm, so strong, so infinitely clear, let it take you boldly by the hand and strip away your fear.

The drum will be ready for its skin tomorrow. The hoop is made of layers of ash wood glued and overlapping. The skin of a reindeer has been soaked in coffee and its own blood giving it a deep, rich color. I have also made a drumstick of curved juniper, the head stuffed tightly with reindeer hair.

It is full of prayer, song, music, story, and laughter already. We have tucked a few bear hairs between a crack in the rim. We have anointed it with resinous oil. Am I ready for it? Yes, tomorrow the skin and the symbolic blood.

The heartbeat of the reindeer will be heard again whenever it is struck. I hear them in the morning, as I emerge from my snow cave, their feet padding across icy snow, ragged velvet dangling from pale emerging antlers.

I feel like I have been absorbed during these last two weeks into a mystical bubble that has tumbled me into a paradox of confused understanding.

Tommy tells me to stop asking "Why?" and just let things be for now.

On the eve of the drum's initiation, the skin has spent the day drying tightly around the hoop. Tommy and I walk down to the lake around midnight and I take it in my hands. Its first utterances, deep and slow, gradually gain momentum, and I am lost in its tone and resonance; how it changes depending on where it is struck. I turn my face skyward as I play and there, a faint glow emerges, green. The drum plays me and the aurora plays the drum, soaring, rippling, colors changing, dancing across the infinite starry background.

I have the extraordinary impression that I have been offered some kind of mentorship into shamanism, although this word that carries so much expectation in today's cultural yearning for spirituality has not been uttered.

Tommy calls himself a Helper.

We may journey through this timeless place forever it may seem, while together as we bind and heal the world in which we dream.

We will build a drum and it will find the other drummers of those whom we call kin, Earth will hear our singing as the light ignites within.

That autumn, I am back in my northern ancestral lands of Sweden. Tommy has invited me to walk with him for a few weeks in the mountains and implore the Spirits. We will follow closely the footsteps of Thorsten when he made his last trek.

A heavy coastal fog obscures the forest beyond the railway tracks, making the home I left in Washington raging in wildfire a strange double image. The fires have become habitual in the last few years in

the western United States, and this Swedish fog, though visually reminiscent of the lung-scorching smoke that filled my parched valley, is
moist and soft. Arriving on the coast of Sweden, I finally take a deep
breath that doesn't hurt.

Tommy greets me with his toothless smile; he does indeed feel like
an old friend. We make a few necessary purchases before we mount
the bus that delivers us to the last ferry and the beginning of our
trail.

How does one start to say something when all the words one can
muster express only the merest shadow of the reality they hope to
evoke? The same with the visuals; the stunning beauty of these ancient, eroded mountains is reduced to mediocrity through the lens of
my camera in my unskilled hands.

Ahkka. The Mother. The Grandmother. The first Mother. The
Sami holy mountain.

All morning her head is hidden in a flat veil of gray clouds that an
icy north wind keeps hovering above us.

We hike slowly, Tommy time, Jokkmokk time. I am cold and bundled in all my clothes. I have not fully arrived yet in my body after my
long journey and I am both irritated by Tommy's childish gaiety and
humbled by his happy presence. Is he a silly old man who won't stop
talking or is he the magical, enlightened being that I sought and found
last winter when I came in search of a drum maker and teacher and
found both? My judgments rattle noisily, guiltily, through my stormy
mind like a dirty train despoiling the fragile and pristine environment
of pure spirit.

It spits rain while we walk and then a hole opens in the clouds and
warm sun spills through. I curl up for a brief nap in its loveliness on
a soft nest of moss.

A gentle shake at my shoulder. Tommy says, "Come." I follow
him, he points without speaking. Ahkka wears a rainbow draped

across her shoulder. "Ahkka, Old Mother." I say your name out loud and start to cry.

I have arrived.

A thousand small dreams scatter and take flight, leaving me clasping just one . . . I hold my father, hugging him around the waist; he says it will be the last time I will see him.

I feel like I could lie here on Ahkka's mossy lap forever.

We walk on slowly savoring every small treasure of sight and smell and sound. We had taken the last boat to the trailhead and the other hikers quickly left us far behind. It feels like we are the only people left in this immense wilderness.

Tommy hates to rush into the land—he wants our entrance to be especially slow—so we skirt the hips of Ahkka and make a new camp only a couple of kilometers from the last one.

He says we are "cleaning," that the sound of the river helps.

Without the burden of our packs we climb onto flat, bare plateaus to search for reindeer antlers, most half eaten away by voles or lemmings and gray-green with moss. We separate in our wandering and I am glad for the solitude but I find myself wanting to hear stories, the old reindeer myths.

I discover new treasure in the form of the golden cloudberries. Here below the sky that showers us gently, the clouds open; and with a burst of sunlight another rainbow emerges, carried on the hip of Ahkka.

Damp birchwood fast falls to rotting. It's as if the gods had pity on us that they wrapped this wood in its highly flammable resinous white bark that lights as if it were soaked in gasoline. Without it we would have no fire in this wet weather.

Tommy gathers a big pile of green juniper bows to "smoke" me when we drum. "That's the way we do it here," he says. "You need it, it's part of the process, the cleaning, for the connection."

We take out the drums we have carried and warm them by the fire.

I sit in the swirling enveloping smoke and just when I think I cannot take any more, it veers away, granting me a window of fresh air.

We drum and I sing to Ahkka, asking her for something but not really sure what. The smoke dances wildly around us. *Suddenly I am high up on Ahkka on the edge of the glacier in the dim light of dusk. I walk out onto the ice in the thin fog* . . . I am drumming at the fire in the smoke . . . *I am walking on the glacier toward a dark hole at its edge* . . . I am drumming at the fire in the smoke. I flit back and forth, I open my eyes, is it smoke or fog? *I am at the entrance to the hole and Tommy tells me I can go in. The tunnel is dark and seems to go down into the mountain, I follow damp stone steps and now the walls are lit with flaming torches. I wonder where I am going.* I am drumming in the smoke. *I am walking the tunnel inside Ahkka. The downward tunnel spits me out incongruously on top of Ahkka's head where I see myself hooded, arms outstretched, and then I leap and fly down over the river in the windy dusk back down to the fire and the drums where I sing again.* Tommy reaches over and beats my drum once and it is over. I am back and my head aches.

As I slither into my bed inside a simple bivvy bag that will protect me from a downpour, an owl glides over me in a circle, once, twice in the silence of the Arctic night.

A new day dawns. The pollution that we bring in our minds starts to fall away. We bid farewell to Ahkka as we prepare to pierce deeper. Reindeer splash noisily through the bogs when they catch sight or scent of us and meander casually when we see them first and stop still. I walk ahead of Tommy and wait for him periodically. I am happy and at peace.

The nomadic reindeer herders of times past, in their cyclic migrations with the herds, would raise and dismantle their conical tents during their wanderings, laying the stone hearth, a significant element of their homemaking and all that remains to be seen today. I sing and play my mouth harp and leave offerings at the ancient stone fireplaces for the old ones who lived and walked these time-eroded mountains long before us.

We camp at the confluence of two rivers that Tommy says is teeming with the spirits of the ancestors. Beside a bright birch fire I carve a wooden spoon and we warm the drums.

We drum, I sing. I thank the ancestors, the old ones for their presence.

I am running in a sea of tawny fur and velvet amid the moving backs of a throng of reindeer.

I am astride one, his dark and gentle eye beneath his spreading antler. Then we are swimming the river, the herd packed tightly around us and I am spinning back to the fire and the drumming, with an aching arm.

I ask for dreams all day and awaken in the night with a pounding, fearful heart. Running and hiding from the many people who will kill me, I try not to recall the details and fall again into an uneasy sleep, begging, no more nightmares.

——————◄————

A misty rain keeps me bundled in my bed. Tommy is up beside the rekindled fire. He says we will stay here for another night. I tell him I don't want to. I don't want more bad dreams. I think this place is too powerful for me. He gives me one of his looks with his glittering eyes the color of glacial melt and says, "Isn't that what you came here for?"

I acquiesce. We have a lovely day, anyway, mostly close to the fire. We walk around a little and Tommy shows me the old campsites of the Sami, then I spend an hour or so sawing off a birch burl to make a cup and occupy myself with it until dinnertime. Tommy chooses a new place for me to sleep and this time I dream of pizza and a new sweetheart!

The next morning I study the map, count the miles, check out my food supplies and the distance we have traveled so far: nine miles in five days. We still have about ninety to go and I wonder if there is any chance that I will make it back to Stockholm in time to catch my flight home.

It's hard to talk about this to Tommy, who already thinks everyone is in too much of a hurry. He says my biggest weakness is not letting go of control. He's probably right but I still prickle at the judgment.

We walk. Today the sun shines on our grateful bodies and the gray bank of clouds recedes to the east.

I look back at Ahkka, unveiled and capped with fresh snow.

Sometimes I walk in front, sometimes behind and we wait for each other. In a cold, clear youthful creek, we take a well-needed bath and walk some more.

When we finally stop, I am surprised to see that we have covered nine miles (as much as in the first five days), but Tommy is beat and his blood sugar plummets. He's diabetic. While I search for a camping spot he gets dizzy and takes a few glucose tablets. I carry tablets for him as well.

I throw out a fishing line from the bridge, then having no luck I explore and find more cloudberries. We retire early with the gnats and late-hatched mosquitoes buzzing.

I wake in the night, open my eyes, and am greeted by a shimmering, writhing ribbon of aurora borealis. I try to hold my heavy eyelids open but I'm soon back in dreamtime. When Tommy taps on my bivvy bag, I look out onto a hard frost.

We walk separately on the well-defined trail, the cool air and undulating terrain gradually heaving us upward. We meet up regularly for tea breaks. Sometimes I ask him a question. He tells me where I can go look for more reindeer antler and I go ahead and look but don't find any. When he catches up with me he asks if I found any, I tell him no and he says I went to the wrong place. I say that I guess I didn't understand properly and he says I didn't listen and walks on in his meditation.

Did I not listen or did I not understand? I feel judged. We speak mostly in Swedish and my Swedish is far from perfect. I have two languages crawling around in my brain.

Certainly my mind is busy but I don't want to judge myself for that. I am loving it here, this experience, and in the many moments that I am fully present it is lovely but I'm also enjoying my rambling "wordy" reverie. I'm not going to beat myself up for not being in a constant state of wordless meditation.

I feel the wind on my cheek, the sun on my back, the chill on my bare fingers, and the hard stone that I am sitting on. I am happy!

When I catch back up with Tommy, he says, "Okay, go and sit on that knoll for ten minutes." I'm not sure if this is a kind of test or if, like a naughty child sent to stand in the corner, I am being scolded.

But the knoll stands out starkly amid the marshes. I feel attracted to it, so I walk the undulating half mile or so willingly.

Along the way I do in fact find some weathered antlers. After zigzagging my way to the top, I pause and wonder which way to face, to the lake or to the mountain? I sit down facing the lake. After a minute I close my eyes.

I am walking on the fjalls, I see a little hut on stilts with a turf roof like the ones the Sami kept their food cached in. I start to walk toward it but Tommy's voice tells me to turn around. I turn and there is a "goahti," a turf-covered hut. He tells me to go inside. I can't see him but his voice is clear. I am flitting back and forth between me on the knoll and me at the door of the turf house. *I pull the door open. It's dark inside but a small fire is burning and there are people inside. Tommy tells me not to look around but to sit down and look at the fire. I sit on a reindeer skin and do as I'm told. Someone starts to drum and chant a word that*

I can't comprehend over and over; I have no idea what it means. I shut my eyes there in front of the fire and imagine another self in another age sitting on top of a knoll. I'm flitting back and forth but which one am I? Who's imagining who? There is a brief moment of this duality and then it passes and I am again just me, sitting on the knoll. I turn and breathe in the sunshine then get up, pick some downy white feathers, and poke at owl "balls."

I walk slowly back to Tommy and he gestures for me to sit down in front of him. "What happened?" he asks, looking at me intently.

When I am finished recounting, he tells me things about the knoll that he forbids me to disclose, but he is pleased. He says that he could only follow me partway and if I had felt nothing we would have to go to that circle (he points out an indistinct circular area not far away). "Then I would have to leave you, but," he adds, "we don't have to, we can move on."

Having evidently passed my test, I feel relieved and Tommy's mood has lifted. We hike slowly upward. The gnats and mosquitoes have made a miraculous comeback after the frosty night. They love Tommy's hyperglycemic blood, and his arms and face are covered with little bloody welts. I feel fortunate for my buckskin armor but a little too hot. I choose excess heat over biting insects and am glad when we find our breezy camp spot alongside a creek adorned with carved plunge pools where we can bathe and eat in relative peace.

We drum the sun down and I get up and dance on the great flat boulder here in this land that I am starting to remember.

I watch the stars appear. Polaris seems so close now, nearly overhead on this Arctic tundra. Each time I awaken the sky is moving with either a gently pulsating luminous ribbon or a full-on show of wild green ecstatic dancing.

My dream door has been unlocked and the dreams flow.

The sparse birch forest has all but disappeared as we travel higher and higher. Most of the reindeer have moved down on their fall migration and it seems that we are alone in the company of the voles and lemmings who scurry before us.

Above the tree line we can no longer build a fire to cook on and we're dependent on the liquid fuel that we brought with us. Tommy tells me of the last two bottles of this vile stuff he drank before his final departure from his years of alcoholism.

He paints the stories of flying through this country on a sled with fourteen dogs running ahead of him in -40 degrees and a biting wind. The near escapes from covered leads in the ice, the storms where everything had to be tied to the lines so they could be unburied, eating dog food when his own food ran out. It's a miracle that he is alive and I am glad to be walking this miracle journey with him.

We walk down, down, down then up, up, up. Straggler reindeer are spotted high on the mountainside. Tommy says he has some people he wants me to meet.

I recognize a Seite when I get there. It is one of the holy stones of the Sami. It's about ten feet tall and juts out at its bulbous head while balancing on a significantly narrower foot like a giant fossilized mushroom. Tommy tells me to make an offering and say prayers. I poke an owl feather down into a hole and add tobacco, then I sit and sing for a while.

I give thanks for the old ways, the holy ways, and ask that they not be forgotten.

I close my eyes. *Figures approach in the windswept snow. They stop at the Seite and ask for protection.*

I point out a little coin tucked into one of the holes and Tommy says, "Oh, is that still there?" He'd put it there himself years before.

I ask if anyone else makes offerings here and he says "no" then adds "Don't worry, there are still some of us left with the power and connection." I feel a little sad as we walk on.

When we start our descent, Tommy leaves the trail. "Walk behind me," he says, agitated. He seems to be looking for something.

Finally he tells me to step into a circle through a "doorway" that appears as a narrow dip in the moss. He tells me to sit down and then he walks away into the sunlight and I watch him for a moment with the sun's bright halo around him.

I close my eyes and drop my head. *I feel very small and round and old, and then an old, old woman is standing there. She wears a scarf tied around her head. She is so wrinkled and small and stooped. She goes to Tommy in the sunlight and they point across the valley and exchange words, then she goes to the spring and fills a cup of water that she gives to him. Refilling it she brings it over to me. I drink and she settles back into my body then sinks into the ground.*

When I tell Tommy all this, he says, "Oh, she has finally come home." He tells me I am sitting on the site of a very old camp. When we leave, he says I must never come back to this place but he won't tell me why.

We are both tired and hungry when we reach the river, but, before we make camp and eat, we pick flowers for the marked grave of an unknown soldier, probably a Pole or Russian fleeing from Norway in 1944. I find one lone harebell and place it at the base of a metal cross. Tommy says in older times, sometimes the aged would wander off into the fjalls to die.

The river roars noisily over the rocks, and the wind is cold and blustery. I find a little nook to set up my bivvy and gratefully crawl inside.

Dreams come thick and furious. In the morning, Tommy says he did not sleep well, many dreams for him, too.

I am a little concerned at how quickly our food and fuel is consumed. Tommy thinks we can make it to Kvikkjokk in six days, but it's eight or nine by my reckoning.

Clouds, big and high, have drifted in. It could mean more rain that will slow us down, but there are fjall cottages along the way. Even though the hiking season is over, there is always one left open for hikers in need of shelter.

A black bank of cloud blows toward us in the brisk wind. I arrive at Arasluokta before Tommy and explore the empty summer village beside the lake. The human boot prints on the trails are gradually being replaced by tracks of reindeer, wolverine, moose, and the many small rodents that inhabit this land.

There is a hut open, and when Tommy arrives we shelter there from the wind and make coffee. This is Sweden. I love how "Allemansrätten," a historic custom law, gives public right of access, freedom to walk anywhere, public or private, with the responsibility to treat land and property with respect. The hut is spotless. We leave our shoes outside and enjoy the refuge from the howling wind. The storm passes by to the east, and we sweep the floor and continue on to the next village.

We look at the map together. I prefer not to think of the dwindling food supplies. I will stuff myself more on the abundant crowberries so juicy and tasty, spitting out the hard little seeds.

Each day the colors on the landscape become more vibrant and vivid; green, yellow, orange, and a dark, rich red. Tommy says to breathe in the color for that is what will take us through the long, dark winter. I am swimming in it.

We talk of good and evil. I say I can't believe that any baby could be born evil. Tommy says it all depends on where one puts one's power . . . into the light or dark. Those born with natural power have to choose each day where to put it. He talks of Hitler and Jesus.

"Do you know that guy Jesus?" he says. "He was the biggest shaman of all, but the church couldn't have that." He holds up his fingers in a cross. "But there are many shamans now, we are blended."

We have about two miles to get to our planned destination for the day. I walk ahead. Tommy has instructed me to look at the rocks.

I don't know what rocks he means. There are rocks in the lake, rocks on the knoll, rocks everywhere. Then I see black sand and stone. I pick up a handful, it's heavy, it's iron. *This is it*, I think and put a piece into my pocket.

Later, when I show him, he is satisfied. "There, now you have found your Seite," he says. "The best of the best."

I reach the hut long before him in the deserted summer village of Staluluokta that sits beside a large lake. I quickly make dinner then go looking for him, throwing a headlamp and dried meat into my pocket. Fortunately I don't go far before I see him coming, slightly bent under his heavy pack. He looks up at me beside the lake and says, "Say Virijavrre." He rolls the "r's" softly like an idling motor. "What does it mean?" I ask. "The big lake." He laughs.

I am captivated, I feel like I could spend a long, long time in this place on the lake. It feels strangely familiar.

Back in the hut we find to our great delight that one cupboard is full of food left by hikers. We decide to stay another day here so we can rest and eat and rejuvenate tomorrow.

After a night in the hut that was a little too warm, too soft, and too quiet, I wake up not feeling rested.

I walk up to the church building and enter. It's made in the Sami style of vertically stacked poles against a bent pole frame, the whole structure covered in birchbark and sod. I'm reminded that the Christian church took many of the traditions of the Indigenous and made them their own, to be more palatable to the heathen natives. Perhaps I will sleep here tonight, out of wind and rain but next to earth and fire.

In a fit of impulsive heresy I suggest to Tommy that we drum in the church tonight. He thinks it a splendid idea so just before dusk I take up candles and light a fire in the chapel hearth.

We start to drum and sing. A beautiful song. I feel like someone else's hands are beating out a light rhythm. Sometimes the tone changes so significantly I'm surprised and open my eyes to see what has happened. *Then I am gone, flying out of the roof and over the lake. Fire. There is a fire and a woman burning in it, burning for her wisdom and knowledge and love for the earth. I can hear her cries but not feel her pain.*

My prayer comes from my lips out loud, "I come here to drum not against a God filled with love and compassion or against his son Jesus but against the torture and terror inflicted upon the old ones who did not follow this patriarchal religion. I come here to drum for the wise ones who spoke with the wild things. We have not forgotten you. We come here to drum and sing and remember. Thank you for your sacrifices."

I sleep and wake yet still in a dream, the drum still lying beside me. The priest and his two sons enter, followed by a magnificent untethered white horse. The priest says, "What are you doing here?" I tell him I've come to light a fire and candles, to sing and pray. I try to hide the drum under my bedding but it will not be hidden and works its way back into view. "What's that you have there?"

"A hand drum." I answer simply.

The priest isn't angry as I had feared; he is accepting and a wave of relief sweeps through me.

Perhaps now is the time for tolerance and acceptance of cultural and religious beliefs.

———✦———

If the wind had ushered us firmly down to Staluluokta two days ago, today it seems intent to keep us there as we struggle the thirteen miles to Tuoddar with a relentless headwind.

After a chain of equally stunning lakes and grand vistas, I take off my boots and ford a shallow, ice-cold river. Ahead of me appears the hut at Tuoddar. Entering the immaculate room, I flop down on the bunk that I claim for myself. I left Tommy a few miles back and hope he shows up in the next hour so I won't have to wade back over the river to look for him. Luckily he arrives soon afterward and we investigate the cupboards for leftover food from previous hikers and make ourselves a bland dinner before succumbing to an exhausted sleep.

The following two days blend under a low steel sky and driving wind. I am cold on this high, windy plateau. We follow the trail down alongside the growing river until suddenly the forest appears, the birches all golden and glowing.

A huge smile sweeps across my face as we descend, breathing, swooning, soaking up the colors. It makes me half delirious and I sing and sway and float upon a golden, pink carpet in a sea of orange and yellow. A dark reindeer calf sprouts out of the bushes and grunts at me. I grunt back and it circles me warily, sniffing the air.

Sometimes my pack feels so light, I turn to check that I didn't leave something behind, sometimes it gets so heavy I stop and find some fuel to keep me going.

Back in the forest the mosquitoes and gnats have been waiting. Lower, lower, losing elevation, the leaves have lost their radiance, the season flipped irrevocably toward winter.

There is that first twinge of melancholy as I drift closer, in both body and mind, back down to the rush and hurry that represents our civilization.

My life, though, is full of grace.

It has been raining steadily and the little streams have swollen to fair-size creeks. Much of the trail is underwater and I manage to hop between the rocks and tussocks for a couple of miles but give up as the trail becomes just another course for the overflowing streams.

The mist hangs low and heavy on the hills. Tommy is behind me. I hope he doesn't slip. I told him I would wait if we came to a difficult stream crossing.

After several hours of hiking in the persistent drizzle, I catch sight of the lake ahead that the river flows into. I know the next hut is there and the possibility of getting dry and warm. I know we are close to the end of our journey and our final destination. I am ready for it.

However, soon I hear a loud roar of rushing water and, coming through the next cluster of trees, I find a raging torrent blocking the trail. Cold and dripping wet, I investigate both up and down stream searching for a place to ford but everywhere looks way too dangerous to cross. Tired and desperate, I open out my bivvy, wring out my socks, and crawl inside to wait for Tommy.

The options are to wait and see if it stops raining and the water subsides, look for an alternate route, or as a last resort go back to the previous hut and use the emergency phone to say we are cut off.

When Tommy arrives, he assesses the situation and comes to the same conclusion. We decide to stop and camp right there in the hope that the rain quits and the river subsides. We make a hurried dinner among the hordes of nibbling gnats. I retire to my bag that is damp but keeps the insects at bay.

I sleep warm but awaken in the morning in a damp pool. It's still raining. I scour up and down again looking for a place to cross, but the water is even higher after another night of continuous rain. I pointlessly put on dry socks.

Tommy and I confer. He decides to wait here while I hike the six or seven miles back up to the last hut and call for a helicopter.

"But I hate going back," I say. Tommy beams at me even though I know the pain is burning in his legs and has been getting worse over the last few days.

He laughs and says, "But at least we are alive . . . and happy!" I leave my pack and make quick progress back up the soaking wet valley to the hut.

Using the emergency phone that directly connects to the police I explain our dilemma and fifteen minutes later I hear a whir of propellers and there is the helicopter. It stops and picks me up and then stops again for Tommy and all our gear and whisks us away.

It's all a bit of a blur with such a fast transition. The harsh abruptness of the change sets me off kilter. After many reentries from my Stone Age journeys I am not a stranger to the knowledge that we need to transition ourselves gently and with care.

Sitting on this bus back to Jokkmokk with Tommy after our wandering, I have to remind myself over and over that this is the dream, the real world is just behind me, the earth is there, holding us unseen but not forgotten. We must not forget.

In the years since my time with Tommy, I have returned to the land of my ancestors. I am home. As I once willed my spotted horse, Karma, to materialize, I call for the moment when I will have no need to brace myself for adjustment back into the industrialized world. No reentry, only return. I call forth the notion that I am living whole and in peace, held in the secure web of my clanspeople. I place my feet on this ground where rest the bones of my forefathers and mothers. I promise the earth my own bones, my blood, my last breath. I envision the concept of Lithica, people of the stone, rewilding ourselves, rewilding the lost and crippled souls that yearn, as I have, for something they can sense but cannot name. A place where we can heal together. As I have sculpted and cocreated my life with the invisible forces in the Universe, I see how one day it will become our reality.

EPILOGUE

When I Am an Old Woman

When I am an old woman my hair shall turn white
At a hundred and thirteen my steps remain light
And the next world will beckon me, Shuwa Awah
And I'll dance from this Earth in my power.

Lithica 2037

. . . I glance up and look out the window that is framed into the wall facing south, sealing my home that has been designed and built to creatively incorporate the shallow cave behind me. I sit at a table that has been split and crafted by hand from a large old tree that fell nearby in a winter storm. There is no electricity in here, the handmade candles have stood unlit for the last week, unnecessary now with the lengthening days that race toward midsummer. Behind me on the wall above a simple altar hangs a drum, a guitar, and a violin. A partition separates a second room that serves as kitchen where shelves of home-canned goods and wooden bowls and plates are lined up neatly, comforting both aesthetically and practically. The berries will last until the coming summer's ripen. There is a large comfortable couch-bed draped with a luscious buffalo robe, but like the candles it has been unused since I moved back outside to my bed in the treehouse when the days ceased to be continuously frozen. I appreciate the simplicity, comfort, and beauty of my home as I take another sip of tea from the large clay mug that Klara made last time she visited.

My horses, Baldur and Idunn, are standing quietly nose to tail under their favorite tree. They turn their heads, pricking their ears toward something that I cannot see or hear, and a few moments later a little boy runs past them clutching something. He runs up the stone steps and bursts through the door calling me. "Awah, Awah!" He speaks three languages fluently but now addresses me excitedly in English as I open my arms to him and draw him in close. "Awah, look what I caught down at the lake." His grubby little hands open and a bright green frog blinks at us then attempts to clamber over his thumbs. I take the soft-bodied amphibian from him gently and examine it while it sits, in my palm. Ivar Thorsten looks at me questioningly. He's seven years old now and the time we spend together is precious beyond all measure. I suggest we take the frog back outside. The boy takes him from me carefully and I follow him out the still open door. "Over there, by the stream is a good place." He puts the creature down in the damp earth beside the water.

"Come, Thorsten." I often call him by his second name. Reaching out my hand to him, he takes it. "Let's go for a ride and see what's happening down at the Lithica camp, shall we?" He nods approvingly, and the horses, still under their tree, turn to face us as we approach. I pat Baldur, faithful Baldur who has been with me for sixteen years now and think back to the beginning of our journey together, the pushy young Norwegian Fjord stallion who arrived, tore the lead rope from my hands, and charged through the fence to meet Karma for the first time. His name comes from Norse mythology: Baldur was the beloved son of Odin and Frigg, the primary godly couple. After experiencing disturbing dreams of his own death, Baldur confided in his mother, who, fearful for her son's well-being, bade all beings throughout the cosmos to swear they would never harm him. By a cast of fate she forgot Mistletoe, and the jealous trickster god Loki went and harvested some with which Baldur was finally killed.

Idunn, named for the goddess of eternal youth, was born the following year as I sat beside Karma lying in the straw of the barn and encouraged her. The wet body slid out, front hooves and nose first, and there she lay wriggling while Karma nuzzled and I stroked her. The foal was a dun gray at birth with a blanket of brown spots intersected by her Fjord sire's dorsal stripe. She was absolutely adorable.

I pick up Ivar Thorsten and set him on Baldur's broad back where he laces his fingers into the thick, coarse mane as I have taught him. The child is a natural horseman, intuitive and observant with the sparkle and drive of his mother. He waits patiently while I vault up onto Idunn. I give a silent prayer of thanks that she is not as tall as Karma had been and that I am still able to mount in this manner. Idunn walks unhurriedly down the path then I veer her with a slight pressure at her flank toward the lake trail; we weave between the trees for a while, Baldur and young Thorsten right behind us. We have no saddle or bridles, and I enjoy the sensation of my horse's soft summer coat and warm back against my bare legs. We meander lazily for the ride down to the camp where the sounds of stone hitting stone and singing greet us. Lithica, the land of the Stone. I smile when I see a few youths sitting in the flint knapping pit. A teenage girl in a beautifully tailored buckskin dress is instructing a boy about her own age where to strike the stone he holds in his hands. Two other boys gaze at her in admiration, mesmerized as much by her grace as the skill and knowledge she exudes as she takes and turns the flint cobble, pointing to a potential striking surface. She is a Lithican, daughter of one of my dearest friends, and has been raised here her whole life. Making stone tools, tanning skins, and tending fire is as natural to her as swimming in the broad river beside which she was conceived. There are about thirty of us long-term Lithicans here, founding members such as myself who shaped the vision when we moved onto the land. A group of eager students is staying in the longhouse for the summer and now, halfway through their stay, I observe the changes in them as their bare feet toughen, their steps become both surer and gentler, and a confidence starts to gleam in their eyes. The song ends with a peal of laughter. Two children, also Lithicans and dressed in skins, erupt through the longhouse doorway. Ivar Thorsten slithers from Baldur's back and scampers after them.

At the open-air kitchen hearth, Lithica residents are cooking, aided by new volunteers who stand out in their modern clothes. The volunteers chop vegetables that are poured into a large clay pot already boiling above the glowing coals.

I dismount Idunn and lead her by the mane through a simple pole gate into the meadow. Baldur follows and I give them both a pat behind their front legs, the signal that they are at liberty to make their own choices. Idunn tosses her head and snorts, then races off with Baldur in pursuit.

Three men and another buckskin-clad woman arrive with armfuls of sticks that they add to the woodpile. They greet me and come over.

"We are having a council tonight with Otter Clan to discuss building the new sauna, do you want to join us?" I will enjoy the new sauna no doubt, but the clan will work it out just fine without me. I shake my head. "No, but I will be here for dinner," I say, as the smell of roasting meat and garlic wafts in the air. I continue to walk down toward the lake where a row of dugout canoes usually line the sandy beach area. There is just one there now, and I see the others out on the water, checking the nets. The smokehouse tipi is unlit, but the scent of smoke and fish hangs close as I pass by that, too.

I enter the community garden and pick up a netted bag from the utility shed. I will harvest onions and carrots on my way back, but first I want to get some wild food: the mineral rich nettles that are growing in profusion down by the old boathouse and whatever other fresh greens I might find along the way. My steps are light as

I enter the forest trail again and I have the urge to run for the sheer joy of it. Folding the bag under my belt, I take off with short quick strides, landing on the balls of my calloused bare feet. The well-worn trail is covered in pine needles and I leap over the scattered boulders with ease. The trail divides and I peel off to the right and head uphill slightly toward the Offering Rock. When I reach the big, moss-covered granite boulder, I stop for a minute to catch my breath. Looking out through the gap in the trees, I can see the lake again, glistening with the early summer sunshine. I clamber up the backside of the Offering Rock and crouch at the top amid the stones and bones that have been brought here with the prayers of my clanspeople. Closing my eyes, I take a deep breath and then release it with a tone that hums and vibrates in the back of my throat. I breathe in again, slowly, deliberately, the fresh, clean mountain air and release another tone that shifts and rises. The song is for the moment only, for the rocks, the trees, the forest, my people, the earth that I love so dearly, and then it is gone, set free into the world rippling with my gratitude.

I climb back down and, walking now, continue back on my original trajectory to the boathouse where I pull the bag from my belt and carefully pinch off the upper few inches of the young, fresh nettles with my thumb and forefinger; the stinging is a small price for the reward and settles into a tingling sensation that is not unpleasant. When my net bag is almost full, I hear heavy steps coming up from behind the boathouse, sticks cracking under feet whose cadence brings a little smile to my lips. She already knows I'm there from my scent no doubt that is wafting waterward in her direction and I watch her round the edge of the old building looking straight toward me. I croon at the young moose cow that approaches and stops just a yard in front of me. I lean toward her, blowing gently at her nose like I would to a horse, and she steps one step closer. I reach up and scratch her behind her long soft ears and she leans into the touch with pleasure. It was two years ago now since Falcon, who was visiting Lithica at the time, found her nearly dead beside her mother who had evidently been hit by a car and managed to take her young calf deep into the forest before lying down to die. The calf was just weeks old. Falcon had bundled her in her arms and carried her, weak and wasted as she was, all the way back to Lithica where we had nursed her back to health, feeding her fresh goat milk. The children of Lithica named her Tiny, and when Falcon left, I had continued the raising and turned her out with the horses as she became strong enough. Tiny grew out of her name in the months that followed, and she had stuck close to the village all winter that first year. I was afraid when she disappeared the next spring that she may have been shot by hunters, but she returned in the late summer and stuck close again through the following winter, browsing on the willows along the lakeshore and bedding down at night in the forest near my home. She was very tame and unafraid and I've made a modified packsaddle for her, and I'm starting to add a little weight to it and leaning on her back as I scratch her tall withers while standing on my porch. This year we will ride her and I am curious how she will respond to the training. Now, as I jog back toward the village, she follows me, sometimes stopping to browse but then gamboling to catch up with me again.

When we reach the garden, some of the students are harvesting greens, and they run out to fuss over Tiny while I pull a few early carrots and onions from the beds. I whistle for Idunn in the meadow and she and Baldur race to the gate where I climb on her back and one of the students hands me my bag of nettles and the fresh vegetables in a small basket. Ivar Thorsten is down at the hide-tanning area; he has a bone scraper in his hands and his two friends stand beside him at the beam taking turns scraping while a couple of adults do the same. A tall, dark-haired Lithican man is wringing a hide out at the wringing beam. I call Thorsten and ask him if he wants to come back up with me for lunch. He looks up grinning, his hair hanging in his eyes in an untidy mop. He tells me he will come when he gets hungry and continues in the engrossing activity. Joseph, the Lithican man, says they can walk up together in a while. He was coming up, anyway, to pick up the dried herbs I had prepared for his partner who will soon give birth to their second child.

I turn Idunn and head back up the forest trail. Tiny has decided to join us and we would have made a startling sight to anyone but a Lithican: a wrinkled little old woman in a buckskin tunic fastened with a hanging knife at her belted side, bareback astride a peculiarly patterned mare with a short draft pony trotting behind and a gangly moose in tow. Nobody in the tanning zone pays much attention, though.

When I reach their tree I dismount and carry the bag back inside my house. I light a small fire in the fireplace and hang an iron pot above it that is half filled with water. I hear a faint whinny coming from the lower trail and the close, shrill answering calls of Baldur and Idunn. I toss the nettles into the pot and stir them briefly. As I stand up I see him dismount and remove the halter from his big dun horse. I notice how he moves a little slower these days but his body is still straight and strong. His short graying hair is receding at the temples but his beard is full and flecked with gray. He wears the dark jacket of reindeer skin that I made him and some half-length breeches, also of leather. He carries a backpack made from birchbark that he takes off as he climbs the steps to the porch. My third husband enters the room with a cheerful smile as his eyes alight on me. "Caught us a fish for lunch," he says. Rummaging in the pack he pulls out a bundle wrapped in burdock leaves and delivers a twelve-inch trout to the cutting board beside the sink. He rinses his hands in the bowl of water that stands there, wipes them on the hand towel, and comes over to me where I again sit at the table. He leans down and gives me a kiss on the top of my head then drops into the chair beside me. We look out the window together at the horses who have resumed their rhythmic tail swishing. My hand creeps toward his and our gnarled fingers interlace on the tabletop. Silently we gaze out into the world that we have cocreated, each lost in our own thoughts.

I am transported back in time to a distant reentry from the Stone Age as my clan and I walked back down into the civilization I have always resisted. Walking last, both whole and broken, I repeated the mantra that fell in time with my steps.

> *Give me the power to keep walking*
> *Give me the power to know the Truth*
> *Give me the power to offer Love*
> *Give me the power to keep Peace*
> *Give me the power to open hearts*
> *Give me the power to see beauty*
> *Give me the power to know grace*
> *Give me the power to keep walking*

I have asked the Spirits for power and they have constantly obliged me. My heart, tender beyond belief for the Emerald Planet.

ACKNOWLEDGMENTS

It has been more than twenty years since I first had the notion of writing a book. With volumes of journals from my travels and experiences with my students on our wilderness immersion trips there was plenty of written material but I had little idea how to tie it together into a fluid, cohesive narrative. Deep gratitude to my brilliant daughter, Klara-Liv, who kept me on track throughout, shared my vision, gave me her old computers, and taught me the most rudimentary of technological skills, typing out lots of handwritten notes besides. My literary agents, Laura Nolan and Jennifer Gates, who reached out and asked me if I had ever thought about writing a book and were always available with their encouragement. Lilly Golden, who spent months as my Zoom-buddy editor, making it a fun instead of daunting prospect. Anna Paustenbach, HarperOne senior editor, who supported my unorthodox style and brought up questions that needed addressing. My friends Molly Bigknife Antonio for reviewing material from a Native American perspective and Caspar Brown for reading the sections about the San people of Namibia, each of whom shared valuable insights. My mentors and teachers throughout my life who set me on my path, including Tom Brown Jr., Peter Bigfoot, Jim Riggs, David Wescott, David Holladay, Steve Watts, Tommy Blomfeldt, and Herbert Backhaus. I trod for years in a very male-dominated world; thankfully this has changed now, and you men are some of my heroes. My soul sister, Bernice Ende, who introduced me to working with horses and shared many adventures.

To all my students who have taught me so much themselves, especially Jane, Jessie, Mat, Emma, Austin, Neil, Max, Kiliii, Shanti, Jesse, Epona, Alex, Stefan, Helena, Merrick, and Klara-Marie. I've drawn characteristics from many of my students over the years to create composite characters in the Smoky Mountain chapters. These characters' names and life events have been fictionalized.

Lastly, I thank my family; parents and siblings in all our complex constellations of blood and heart.

And Niila, whose devoted love and attention kept me smiling even when he was stepping on the keyboard while I was trying to write.

ABOUT THE AUTHOR

Lynx Vilden has traveled, explored, and researched the nature and traditional cultures of arctic, mountain, and desert regions from Hudson Bay to the Kalahari Desert. Lynx is the founder and head instructor of the Living Wild School, which is dedicated to learning and sharing the ancient skills of primitive living. She currently lives on an old homestead in Norway with her horses and cats. She can be found at www.lynxvilden.com.